THE
COMING BOND MARKET
COLLAPSE

THE
COMING BOND MARKET
COLLAPSE

How to Survive the Demise
of the U.S. Debt Market

MICHAEL G. PENTO

WILEY

Library of Congress Cataloging-in-Publication Data

Pento, Michael, 1963-
 The coming bond market collapse : how to survive the demise of the U.S. debt market /
Michael Pento.
  pages   cm
 Includes bibliographical references and index.
 ISBN 978-1-118-45708-5 (cloth) — ISBN 978-1-118-45717-7 (ePDF)
 ISBN 978-1-118-45716-0 (Mobi) — ISBN 978-1-118-45715-3 (ePub)
  1. Bond market–United States.   2. Bonds–United States.   I. Title.
 HG4910.P426 2013
 332.63'23—dc23

                                                                              2012049828

Printed in the United States of America.
10 9 8 7 6 5 4 3 2 1

To my wife, Jenifer, and my two children, Michael and Giamarie. It is my hope and prayer that my kids will grow up in a land that offers them the freedom to bring their dreams to fruition, rather than a government-provided guarantee of mediocrity. To my parents, Frank and Mary, who ignited my passion for freedom. And to God for allowing us all the autonomy to choose.

Contents

Introduction

n November 2011, I founded a money management firm, Pento Portfolio Strategies, for the primary purpose of preparing clients' investments for what I saw as the next financial crisis. Back in 2005, I correctly predicted the bubble in real estate. However, the new catastrophe I see emerging makes the housing bubble pale in comparison. America now sits in the latter stages of the biggest asset bubble in the history of the planet. The bursting of this bubble will send shock waves throughout the global economy and will have a gravely negative impact on the American standard of living. This bubble will have a profound effect on all Americans—especially those who fail, or refuse, to see it coming. It will affect your job, the value of your house, your savings, and your way of life. The bubble is U.S. Treasury debt.

But don't think of this author as some Cassandra that is calling for the end of the United States. Cartographers will not have to expunge America from their maps. This great country will survive and thrive after the collapse of the U.S. debt market occurs. The point of this work is to guide our leaders down a path that leads toward a direction that mollifies the damage already done. It will also offer investors the best chance to preserve their current standard of living.

Investors, seeking refuge in what they perceive as the safest of all havens (U.S. Treasuries), have been procuring government debt at unprecedented rates despite the record low interest rates they offer. The Federal Reserve, under the stewardship of Ben Bernanke, has rendered our continued solvency as a nation dependent on the perpetual continuation of artificially produced low interest rates. However, it is clear that Bernanke cannot keep rates low forever. The Federal Reserve's misguided effort to counterfeit our way to prosperity, coupled with the flawed Keynesian deficit spending model that our government embraces with alacrity, has led to record debts that will never be able to be repaid.

The bursting of the bubble in Treasuries will cause a massive interest rate shock that will drive the U.S. consumer and the government into bankruptcy and send many people throughout the globe into poverty. In order for you to survive the coming debt crisis, you need to be informed and prepared.

In this current economic environment, our government seeks a condition of perpetual inflation in order to maintain the illusion of prosperity and solvency. The problem with this addiction to money printing is that once a central bank starts, it can't stop without dire, albeit in the long-term healthy, economic consequences. And the longer an economy stays addicted to inflation and borrowing, the more severe the eventual debt deflation will become. As a result, our central bank is now walking the economy on a very thin tightrope between inflation and deflation. The prevalent idea among our government and central bank is that we can borrow and print even more money in order to eliminate the problems caused by too much debt and inflation. But more inflation can never be the cure for rising prices, and piling on more debt can't solve a condition of insolvency.

Since its inception in 1913, the Federal Reserve has been the perpetuator of asset bubbles. From the Fed-induced bubble of the 1920s that led to the Great Depression, to modern-day bubbles in Nasdaq and real estate, the Federal Reserve's manipulation of the cost of money has created a bubble economy. And today, the Federal Reserve is perpetuating its largest bubble since its inception—the bubble in the U.S. debt. This book will give you the tools to understand how the Fed created these bubbles and what we as a nation can do to return this economy to a more stable footing. In addition, investors will learn the best way to protect their wealth before and after the bubble bursts.

After World War II the world moved away from hard metal currencies in favor of fiat currencies. Fiat currencies are created by government decree, backed by nothing, and have their worth based on the faith placed in autocrats. Governments can incur tremendous amounts of debt and can always make good on their principal and interest payments because they can print money. Therefore, default initially comes through inflation. Default via inflation is worse than actual default. Inflation is a hidden tax that disproportionately affects those least able to pay it: the middle class and the poor. Default via inflation is always the last step before an actual default.

The fiscally irresponsible administrations of both Democrats and Republicans have placed this great nation on the brink of bankruptcy. And in this book you will learn that throughout history, government spending and money printing has always led nations down the wrong path—the path that leads to a currency and debt crisis.

Currently, the Federal Reserve is pumping scores of billions of dollars each month into the economy in an attempt to reflate the housing bubble. Of course, rising prices occur every time the central bank prints money in excess of what is necessary to address population and productivity increases—the Fed knows this. Inflation is often defined as too much money chasing too few goods. The Fed wants the "too much money" they are pumping into the economy to start chasing real estate in order to reflate the real estate bubble and rescue the banking sector. But the Fed's fake money isn't only going back into real estate; sure, it's driving mortgage rates to the lowest they have been in history, but it's also driving up the costs of food and energy, while— most importantly—allowing the federal government to, for now, painlessly take on an enormous amount of debt.

Bernanke and Company are operating under the assumption that they can turn off the easy money spigot anytime they want. Instead of providing a strong and stable dollar that would encourage saving and investment, they have opted for cycles of counterfeiting and monetizing that will lead this economy into a depression never before seen. But the truth is, in the long term, the free market controls the cost of money and when our creditors demand an interest rate closer to historic norms, the

United States will experience a debt crisis the likes of which the world has never seen.

But you still have time to protect all that you have worked hard for. And we as a nation still have a small window to turn this all around.

In this book we will explore how the bubble was created and delve into the failed fiscal and monetary policies that have gotten us to the dire situation we are in today. We will look back through history and explore how currency debasement and debt monetization has always led to hyperinflation and chaos. We will compare the current condition of the United States to that of Europe and Japan and question how long a worldwide economy can continue on the fiat currency model.

We will explore some historic debt debacles and speculate what a bond market crisis would look like here. We will also suggest how following the path our founders set out in the Constitution, coupled with free-market principles, will get us back to prosperity—and what we can do now as a country to ameliorate the crisis.

Finally, you will be given some great ideas about how you should manage your portfolio to navigate through the tough times that lie ahead.

The United States is now facing an entirely new paradigm. Onerous debt levels have reached the point to which the central bank will soon be forced into a difficult decision—either to massively monetize the trillions of dollars' worth of our nation's debt or allow a deflationary depression to wipe out the economy. History clearly shows that the path of least resistance is to seek inflation as a panacea. But you don't have to let the whims of government wipe out all that you have worked hard for.

The 30-year bull market in bonds started when the U.S. Fed, under Paul Volcker, vanquished inflation. In sharp contrast, we now have global central banks in a coordinated effort to fight deflation—with Banana Ben Bernanke in the vanguard. Once they succeed in generating the inflation they so greatly desire, it will commence the ugliest bear market in bonds that has ever existed. But this coordinated Fed-induced disaster doesn't have to be your ugly bear. This book will arm you with the knowledge to not only understand and prepare for the inevitable economic cataclysm but to capitalize on it as well.

Acknowledgments

I want to provide a special thank you to Justine Coleman for her efforts in creating this work. Her knowledge, skills, and talent were indispensible toward its creation.

Chapter 1

As Good as Gold?

Nature's first green is gold,
Her hardest hue to hold.
Her early leaf's a flower;
But only so an hour.
Then leaf subsides to leaf.
So Eden sank to grief,
So dawn goes down to day.
Nothing gold can stay.
              —*Robert Frost*

On a hot summer night, August 15, 1971, the Who played to a sold-out crowd in Bloomington, Minnesota. Their music spoke to a generation that sought a journey down a different path from their parents . . . a generation that had grown hostile with rules and authority . . . a generation eager to put aside the old ways and forge a new path . . . create a new world, a better world. They promised themselves they wouldn't get trapped in the sins of the past; they vowed that this time things would be different.

On that same night, a president addressed the nation in a similar vein. It is unclear if Richard Milhous Nixon knew who "the Who" was, but his message for the country was much the same. He, too, wanted a new direction. Toss out old rules that were holding back an economy, in favor of building a *New Prosperity*—one that would move America forward while "protecting the position of the American dollar as the pillar of monetary stability around the world." He addressed the nation . . .

> I have directed Secretary Connally to suspend temporarily the convertibility of the American dollar except in amounts and conditions determined to be in the interest of monetary stability and in the best interests of the United States.
>
> Now, what is this action—which is very technical—what does it mean to you?
>
> Let me lay to rest the bugaboo of what is called devaluation.
>
> If you want to buy a foreign car or take a trip abroad, market conditions may cause your dollar to buy slightly less. But if you are among the overwhelming majority of Americans who buy American-made products in America, your dollar will be worth just as much tomorrow as it is today.
>
> The effect of this action, in other words, will be to stabilize the dollar.[1]

If you needed any more proof that Dick was not only a horrible president but that he also knew next to nothing about economics, that should close the case. According to Mr. Nixon, Americans need only to worry about a crumbling currency while on vacation—if they could still afford to take one. He either was lying or simply just unaware that when a central bank can print money by decree and is not fettered by the strictures of a gold standard, not only does it lower the exchange rate of the dollar against foreign currencies, but it also lowers its exchange rate against everything you need to purchase within the United States. But even more damaging, the ability to increase the money supply at will has also been the progenitor of every bubble that was ever created.

Nixon's plan for "New Prosperity" was decided in haste over a weekend summit at Camp David. With this speech, Nixon ended the agreement of Bretton Woods that placed a value internationally on the U.S. dollar's ability to be exchanged for gold at a fixed amount—in this case, $35 an ounce. It is clear from tapes later obtained from that weekend that Nixon wished to remove any impediment that would keep the Federal Reserve from "printing like crazy." Nixon was up for reelection. The recent influx of soldiers returning home from Vietnam was creating a spike in the unemployment rate, a spike that he wasn't sure the market could work out in enough time. Paranoia was setting in. . . .

With this speech, the U.S. dollar was no longer collateralized by gold; it no longer had a precious metal backing. The U.S. dollar was now a fiat currency—a currency established by government decree. Although Nixon loathed economics and monetary policy, it wasn't lost on him that a fiat currency gives a government carte blanche to spend without taxing. Governments can incur tremendous amounts of debt and can always make good on their principal and interest payments because they can print money. Default comes through inflation instead. Default via inflation is worse than actual default.

Inflation is a hidden tax that disproportionately affects those least able to pay it: the middle class and the poor. Inflation provides a disincentive to savers; it favors borrowers, as borrowers get to borrow in today's dollars and pay back in tomorrow's cheaper dollars. Inflation destroys the standard of living of the elderly and those who rely on a fixed income. Inflation breeds resentment among economic classes and contributes to political unrest and disunity. A nation that resorts to the use of fiat money has doomed itself to economic hardship and political disunity.[2]

On that fateful night, Nixon eliminated the final link the dollar had to gold. It was Franklin Delano Roosevelt (FDR) in 1933, in a move that accelerated bank failures during the depression, who originally took the dollar off the gold standard. We will address the Great Depression in more detail in the next chapter; however, it is clear from centuries of history that when a nation moves off of specie (metal), its population loses confidence. As Ronald Reagan once said, "A great nation that moves off gold doesn't stay a great nation for long."[3]

It is no surprise that the 1970s were a tumultuous period in American history. Much like today, it was a period of stagflation—rising prices and zero economic growth. Your income went down and the cost of everything you purchased went up. Since 1973 the American paycheck has been decreasing in real dollars. Between 1971 and 1982, the cost of living increased from 3 percent to 15 percent, yet the unemployment rate soared from below 6 percent to just under 11 percent. Taking into account Nixon's decision to go off gold in

1971, it's no coincidence that the cost of living started to increase from the 3 percent level to the double digits later that decade.

Let's put in it terms even "Tricky Dick" could understand. Take Pat Nixon's "Republican cloth coat." If that coat cost $18 in 1971, it would cost $100 today—good thing Pat didn't want the mink! In 1971 the Nixons could buy a can of dog food for their dog Checkers for $0.22; that same can costs $1.25 today. How about the cost of bugging the White House or a Watergate break-in in today's dollars—yikes! Nixon would have a hard time making his famous claim "I am not a crook" because on that day in August 1971, Richard Nixon robbed from every American alive and from future generations—he stole a precious-metal-backed currency from a nation and robbed its people of their purchasing power.

One has to wonder if a young Tim Geithner was watching on the night Nixon addressed the nation. Sitting in front of his Philips color TV, with his Little Joe cowboy hat and holster on, geared up to watch *Bonanza*, his favorite show. Ah, the disappointment that little Timmy must have felt knowing it would take another week for him to enjoy the exploits and adventures of the Cartwright family on Ponderosa ranch. I can't imagine that little Timmy realized then what a favor was bestowed on him that night. His future job just got a whole lot easier. He would never have to ponder the question of "who is going to buy all this debt I'm selling at these lousy rates?"[4]

Thanks to Nixon, Tim just has to tell Ben to keep the printing press going.

The Great American Money Machine

Today our counterfeiter–in–chief, Ben Bernanke, holds the lofty position as the veritable "Master of the Universe." He sits at the helm of the ultimate printing press and controls the reins of the Great American Money Machine—also known as the Federal Reserve. Ben holds the ultimate power of the known universe: the power to create the world's reserve currency, the U.S. dollar, out of thin air. I often wonder how many people in the country even know who Ben is or what the Federal Reserve does. One could conjure a "man on the street"–style inquiry affirming who has more name recognition: Ben Bernanke or Kim Kardashian? Unfortunately, while some were busy "keeping up with the Kardashians," the "geniuses" at the Federal Reserve have been wreaking havoc with our economy, destroying the purchasing power of the dollar and savaging the middle class. Now you could counter that Kim seduced her audience into watching an entire season consumed by her sham marriage to Kris Humphries. But since I have just told you everything I know about Kim Kardashian, for the purposes of this book, let's focus on Bernanke, the Federal Reserve, and how they have helped create the biggest and most deadly bubble in the history of the planet.

To do this, our story takes us back to the year 1907, and like all great government power grabs—this one begins with panic. . . .

The panic of 1907 was a financial crisis that almost crippled the American economy. Major New York banks were on the verge of bankruptcy; at the time, there was no mechanism to provide timely liquidity. J. P. Morgan, a prominent banker of his day, stepped in personally and took charge, resolving the crisis. Similar to banks today, the banks in 1907 operated on the assumption that people don't move in unison in demand of their deposits on the same day. The "run on the bank" that ensued after the 1907 crisis gave the public anxiety and led the politicians to create a mechanism for a "lender of last resort."

The United States had forayed in central banking over its, at that time, more than 100-year history. Past attempts at central banking had failed miserably; they proved the central bank corrupt and left a population disillusioned and disgusted. But those who embraced an illusory concept of a "new paradigm" certainly saw a "new time" in America. One can speculate that some in the political establishment of the day thought that this time things were different—that different times called for this kind of authority and that these "new times" would result in a different outcome.

It's important to explore the political climate in place in 1907 and the years leading up to the creation of the Federal Reserve. Teddy Roosevelt ran as a Republican, but he was really a Progressive. I love the term *Progressive* because it is so unapologetically misleading. The term *Progressive* makes you think "progress," and who doesn't want progress? Progress is great. If you look the word *progress* up in the dictionary, it's defined as moving toward a goal, to advance. I love progress and advancement! Progressives must have been great . . . WRONG! These Progressives aren't interested in my progress or your progress; they aren't interested in the advancement of the individual. Progressives want the government to progress; they want the government to advance. They see progress when the government takes power from the individual and transfers it to government. So when I eat right and exercise, I think, "I'm making progress toward my goal of staying healthy and getting in shape—great!" But it's only progress to a Progressive when Michelle Obama tells me what to eat and how much to exercise. I think you get my point.

The Federal Reserve was created during a time when all kinds of "progress" was being made, so you would have to assume a major government power grab was in play, and believe me . . . this power grab didn't disappoint!

There are hundreds of books written about the creation of the Federal Reserve, and this book doesn't pretend to be one of them. I do not plan at this time to labor through the political posturing and the various iterations that went into the creation of the Federal Reserve. It is noteworthy that unlike Nixon's ending the gold standard, the architects of the Federal Reserve took a lot longer than a weekend. Like Rome, the Federal Reserve wasn't built in a day. In retrospect, maybe too long—by the time the Federal Reserve opened its doors on December 23, 1913, it was clear that its original purpose, to prevent a run on the bank, was obfuscated.

In his book *The Creature from Jekyll Island*, author G. Edward Griffin points out that the Federal Reserve is neither federal nor is it a reserve—in fact, it is not even a bank.[5] But the deception just starts there. It is, in fact, a private company whose directors, or governors, are made by public appointment. It was deceptively designed to appear separate from the federal government, to delude the *masses* into believing that it was making sound monetary decisions independent of political pressures. It is a centrally planned organization that directly influences every aspect of the American economy. It holds a monopoly on dollar printing and runs a cartel on short-term interest rates. It is an organization like no other. It is the money machine of the federal government that enables the state to borrow far in excess of the private sector's savings.

Just think, as recently as a decade ago Ben Bernanke was pontificating economic theory with a bunch of college students at Princeton

University. Then, we can imagine, one day while Ben was debating the Keynesian theory of money demand in the faculty lounge with Paul Krugman, the "red phone" rang. Ben was selected to join the group of "superheroes" tasked with managing the economies of the world at the Halls of Justice, also known as the Federal Reserve. A mere three years later, Ben ducked into a phone booth with Alan Greenspan. When Ben later emerged, he donned the cape and held the title of "Master of the Universe."

Now if you are a fan of comic strips, and even if you're not, you know that all superheroes have superpowers—Ben's powers at the Fed are no exception. The Federal Reserve has three powers at its disposal to manipulate the supply of money.

The first is the reserve requirement, or the amount of money depository institutions must hold on hand against specified liabilities. And by liabilities I mean your money on deposit at the bank. The Fed dictates how much of a depositor's money needs to sit on hand with them for safe-keeping. We will go just a bit more into this when we consider how money is created and discuss fractional reserve banking later in this chapter. For now, just consider that an easing of the reserve requirement theoretically gives banks the leeway to increase their lending; in turn, increasing the requirement would have the opposite effect.

Next is their cartel on the discount rate. The discount rate is the interest rate charged to commercial banks and other depository institutions on loans they receive from their regional Federal Reserve Bank's lending facility, also known as the discount window. This gives the Fed complete control over the short end of the yield curve. When the discount rate is lower than the prevailing market rate and the yield curve is high, it provides a huge incentive for banks to borrow from the Federal Reserve and loan out at higher rates. Today's rate stands at zero percent, and Ben has promised it will stand for a very long time.

Finally, we have Bernanke's favorite superpower—drum roll please—open market operations (OMOs). Through OMOs the Fed usually purchases government securities from banks. However, as the credit crisis has clearly illustrated, if the Fed desires, it can also buy an entire array of toxic assets that are worthless.

Now, like Superman had kryptonite, Ben also has something that he believes weaken his powers—congressional oversight. One would assume that in giving a small group of unelected pseudo-bureaucrats so much power, the people who appointed them would need to know exactly what they were doing. Well, you would assume wrong. Remember, the Federal Reserve is a private company. So you don't expect that Pepsi is going to open up meetings to the public where they discuss changes to their secret formula. The difference is that if Pepsi were ever to water down their product, the consumer would have the right to switch to Coke. When the Fed waters down its product (money), few people are afforded the discretion to make other monetary choices.

Therefore, the Fed enjoys not only a monopoly on money but also the latitude to hold many of its meetings in the "cone of silence." In other words, nobody really knows what exactly these clowns are up to. Now, we can give Ben a little bit of credit—his predecessor, Alan Greenspan, seemed to speak in tongues. The media coined the term *Fed Speak* to describe Greenspan's cryptic communique. It would take a panel of economists and financial types to decipher what Greenspan was saying. So, in this way, Ben is a veritable man of the people—even going as far as an appearance on *60 Minutes*. Mr. Bernanke believes it should be Glasnost at the Fed. However, when your stock-in-trade is counterfeiting money, it isn't really a good idea to promulgate what you're up to.

Putting aside Bernanke's plain-spoken and more accessible posture, he still is obstinate about keeping most meetings and dealings with other central banks secret. There is currently a movement in Congress to audit the Fed, which Bernanke is vehemently opposed to. Apparently, if we knew what he was doing, this would weaken his superpowers and jeopardize the power he holds to control the economy. Maybe Ben should realize that's the point.

"Dad, Where Does Money Come From?"

As a father of two young children, I grow anxious for the day my son will ask the question every parent anticipates: "Dad, how is money created?" My answer will go something like this: "Son, when the U.S. Treasury and the Federal Reserve really love each other, they create money." . . . Judging by the amount of money being created today, it is clear that Ben and Tim have a Brangelina kind of love.

The Federal Reserve doesn't actually need the Treasury; it can create money all on its own—but money is usually created at an administration's prompting. Tim and Ben, like so many high-profile couples these days, make use of a surrogate to create money. The Federal Reserve introduces new money into the system by increasing its balance sheet through the purchase of financial assets and by lending money to banks. Then, something amazing happens—the money multiplies. This money magic is brought to you by the fractional reserve banking system and this is how it works:

Let's assume a very simple banking system: we have one bank (Bank A) and a central bank (the Federal Reserve).

You make a deposit of $100 in a checking account, and the Federal Reserve requires Bank A to deposit a fraction of it, let's say $10 of the $100, with it for safe-keeping. This is the Fed's Reserve Requirement, and they reserve the right to increase or decrease the percentage held in reserve.

Bank A now has $90 burning a hole in its pocket, ready to loan. Now, technically, this is your money, on loan with Bank A, and you have the right to demand this deposit at any time, but Bank A isn't going to spend a lot of time worrying about that. After all, it just deposited $10 with the Fed, so it's good—right?

Well, not much time has to pass before another person comes along and borrows the $90 from Bank A. Now, Bank A pays you interest on your deposit at today's rate (which is likely next to nothing) but charges this new person, let's call him Bob, 5 percent for your $90. This may not seem fair, but remember, with the deposit at Bank A, your money is "safe"; it's not just tucked under your mattress—it's now safely deposited in a vault at the bank. Well, actually a fraction of it is deposited, the rest just walked out the door with Bob, but I'm sure he's a great guy.

Now, Bob has all sorts of plans for your $90, but while these plans coalesce he decides to deposit the $90 in Bank A, so it stays "safe." Bank A considers this as an additional $90 deposit and it deposits $9 with the Fed and has $81 to lend out. It then loans that $81 to Mary, and this continues. Of course, you can forget most of what you just read because: *U.S. regulatory changes implemented during the early 1990s effectively removed the requirement for banks to hold reserves. They must hold reserves for demand deposits, but through the process known as "sweeping" they are able to get around this requirement by moving that money into time deposits. Therefore, in effect, banks can expand the money supply far beyond the reserve requirement as long as they have the required regulatory capital to do so.*

As I said before, this is called *fractional reserve banking*, and it allows money to multiply; this calculation is conveniently called the *money multiplier*. Now, all this is great until Bob and Mary buy houses that they really can't afford and default on their loans, and you get antsy and want your $100 back. This is where the Federal Deposit Insurance Corporation (FDIC) and the Federal Reserve come in; they stand ready to bail out the bad decisions that Bank A made with your money.

Over the past few years, the Federal Reserve has been utilizing its OMOs to push money into the economy in a system called *quantitative easing* (QE). QE is a "last resort" for central banks when interest rates are already at zero percent. Simply put, the Fed buys Treasury notes and bonds from banks, giving banks money. The hope is that the banks will use the proceeds to lend more money—often to the government—and increase the amount of money in circulation.

We suffered through multiple rounds of it, and the only thing it did was boost inflation to 3.9 percent (as the government miscalculates it) and boost the money supply of M2—a measure that includes outstanding currency and money in checking and savings accounts—to a 29 percent annualized rate.

That is, while the U.S. economy is still in the doldrums, the amount of money in the system ballooned. If you don't feel the effect of that money, that's because it hasn't made it to your pocket; you'll see where it ended up in a minute.

So what went wrong? Why didn't QE fix everything?

Well, the Fed was right—if you give banks money, they will lend it out. The problem is, instead of lending it to you or me, they happily lent most of it to Uncle Sam. Yep, the banks sold Treasury notes to the Fed and then used the proceeds to buy more Treasury notes. This obviously hasn't helped the economy, but it has enabled the government to sell debt at low rates and run an annual budget deficit in the trillions.

As I write, the Fed through its OMOs will be moving toward a run rate of funding about 75 percent of our annual deficit. We have indeed become a banana republic that now monetizes most of its new debt. While most global central banks have adopted the specious idea that prosperity comes from a depreciating currency, the Bernanke Fed is leading the way toward ensuring that the U.S. dollar loses its status as the reserve currency of the world. The United States has left interest at near zero percent for almost four years and has the central bank on record saying that inflation is far below their comfort zone. Therefore, because Bernanke is doing everything in his power to step up the dilution of the dollar, the rest of the world may soon reconsider their decision to continue to park their savings in dollar-denominated assets.

Since the endless QEs have failed to get this economy moving, Ben has created a new dance move he calls *Operation Twist*. This is Ben's attempt to manipulate the long end and flatten the yield curve. With long-term interest rates at an all-time low, this new move seems a little like kissing your sister—in other words, pointless. Apparently, the individuals at the Fed aren't satisfied with all the destruction they have already caused by printing money, keeping reserves low and keeping the discount rate at zero. Ben and his "Merry Men" of manipulators seem not to be content with their cartel on the short end of the curve; these legalized counterfeiters are determined to do the maximum intervention possible in order to not allow this economy to liquidate and experience a real recovery. Imagine that! I realize it's terribly out of fashion, but the only way this economy will achieve a viable recovery is if we allow markets to work.

There is no doubt that Bernanke has been remarkably successful in destroying the purchasing power of the dollar and in his quest to increase the rate of inflation. However, the truth is that there is no credible exit strategy for the Fed. There is only the prospect of suffering through either a deflationary depression or hyperinflation. Such will be the consequences of not appropriately dealing with our problems of debt, asset bubbles, and inflation in recent history.

The Implications of a Fiat Currency

Let's review. First, the U.S. dollar is no longer in any way, shape, or form linked to gold. Now, you might say, "Pento, enough with your obsession with gold—who cares?"

My response is: First, I don't have an obsession with gold. But I do want to make a few points about why it matters—please bear with me.

Take out a dollar from your pocket and think to yourself—what is this worth? The answer is that it's worth what it will buy you. So if I take this dollar and go to the store and buy a cup of coffee—which, by the way, if you know of a store that sells a cup of coffee for a dollar, I would like to know where that is; I pay a lot more than that. But I digress; if you buy a cup of coffee for a dollar, then that's the value of the dollar—a cup of coffee. Now, let's imagine that next week that same cup of coffee costs $10—now what is the value of the dollar? You are less certain because you are starting to lose confidence in your dollar's value. The next week the coffee is $100—wow! Now you use all the dollars you have to stockpile coffee—you cling to a hard asset, and it dawns on you what a fiat currency really is. That dollar was worth something only because you believed it to be worth something.

The dollar is a fiat currency—it has no real value beyond your confidence in it. No one worked to produce that dollar; no one put their hands in the dirt and got sweat on their brow to deliver that dollar to you. That dollar was created by the Federal Reserve and the fractional reserve private banking system out of thin air. And your confidence in it is your confidence in them.

To paraphrase Milton Friedman, there are no angels in government and there are no angels at the Federal Reserve. They are men and women who have intellectual limitations and are subject to the same pressures as all humans. Earlier, I spoke in jest of Ben Bernanke as a superhero—in case this point needs clarification . . . he's not. As far as I know, and maybe Donald Trump could verify this, Ben Bernanke was born on planet Earth—he is a human being. Prior to joining the Fed, he was a professor at Princeton University; I mention this only to inform you that he wasn't beamed down to Earth by some great deity who bequeathed him with all the answers to the world's monetary questions. Yet he gives the pretense that he was. But ask yourself: is Ben Bernanke smarter than the institution that brought prosperity and stability to the Byzantine Empire for over a thousand years? Can he outintellectualize the standard that engendered the Industrial Revolution—the most prosperous time in this nation's history? Is Ben Bernanke as good as gold? He's not. He is just one man who has been erroneously granted too much power.

The chairman of the Federal Reserve is not superhuman and, as such, should not be bestowed with such supremacy over money. You see, even though Superman is a fictional character, his creators had the foresight to have him originate from another planet. Why? Because they know that any human who has x-ray vision would spend his days undressing Lois Lane, and any human that could leap tall buildings would be a starter with the New York Knicks, not making minimum wage as a beat reporter at a second-rate newspaper. Superman is from Krypton because his creators knew that if humans here on Earth were given such power they would find it impossible to exercise such restraint; humans are vulnerable to their own mortal imperfections. Federal Reserve chairmen are vulnerable to facilitating reckless government spending and temerariously using their power in a misguided attempt to save the world.

Why a gold standard? The gold standard is the world's natural God-given money supply regulator; it has held the test of time. Gold is mined at about a 1 percent increase per annum in supply, so that would mean that gold would flow into the system and the money supply would grow at 1 percent—which is about consistent with U.S. population growth. Take into account a mild deflation resulting from productivity growth, and there you have it: stable money, limited government debt, and no bubbles. A gold standard saves political types from themselves; it forces nations to make choices. No currency should be held hostage by the inherent weakness of man.

During the Johnson administration, the political debate revolved around the need for guns or butter. Up until recently, we haven't required those choices from our politicians; it's been guns, butter, health care, bridges to nowhere . . . the list goes on. And there is an illusion that we haven't been paying for it, but we have—through the devaluation of the dollar and the accumulation of future government liabilities. After all, government debt is simply a tax on future private-sector production with interest. And unless our government wants to admit that U.S. debt is a Ponzi scheme that can be financed only through rollovers, the buyers of our debt must be convinced at all times that we can pay back every dollar borrowed.

But lately they haven't been fooling as many as they used to; people out there are starting to realize it—people feel what is happening. You can delude the masses for only so long. From tea party rallies to Occupy Wall Street, their lives embody the effects of a fiat currency. Their voice is born from the erosion of the middle class.

Remember—with a fiat currency, governments can incur tremendous amounts of debt and can always (ostensibly) make good on their principal and interest payments because they can print money. Default comes through inflation instead. Default via inflation is worse than actual default. The political types will always implicitly default via inflation before they explicitly default. An inflationary default is surreptitious in nature and so much more palatable at the start.

So go ahead—call me a dinosaur, claim that I am archaic and a barbarous relic . . . I admit it, I believe in the virtues of the gold standard. In the following chapter, we will see that throughout history a deliberate increase in the supply of money has disastrous consequences—and provides a foundation for my argument that the current increase in the money supply courtesy of the Fed has led to what I believe to be the biggest bubble ever.

So fasten your seatbelts—it's going to be a bumpy ride. In the next chapter, we travel all the way back to the 1600s.

Notes

1. Office of the Federal Register, "Richard Nixon," containing the public messages, speeches, and statements of the president—1971 (Washington, DC: U.S. Government Printing Office, 1972), 886–890.
2. G. Edward Griffin, *The Creature from Jekyll Island: A Second Look at the Federal Reserve* (New York: American Media, 2010).
3. Ron Paul, *End the Fed* (New York: Grand Central Publishers, 2010).
4. Although it is unclear if Tim Geithner actually watched Nixon deliver his speech, we do know from Watergate tapes later obtained that Nixon's staff struggled with preempting *Bonanza*.
5. Griffin, *The Creature from Jekyll Island*.

Chapter 2

The Anatomy of a Bubble

History doesn't repeat itself, but it does rhyme.
— *Mark Twain*

In the middle of the seventeenth century, the Dutch Golden Age bestowed many marvels on the world—the artist Rembrandt; the scientist Huygens; the first stock exchange, multinational corporation, and, unfortunately, central bank. It shouldn't then be a surprise that the creation of the first legalized counterfeiting institution brought about the first speculative bubble revolving around a frenzy over tulip bulbs.

The Netherlands became a major political, economic, and scientific power in Europe during its 80-year fight for independence, spanning the years 1568 to 1648. A large influx of money and intelligence helped the rise of the Dutch republic. These factors are recognized as the main driving force of establishing the Dutch Colonial Empire and mark the beginning of an era in Dutch history now known as the Dutch Golden Age.

At the height of the Dutch "Golden Age," 1634 to 1637, it is surmised that the price of some rare tulip bulbs garnered as much as 5,000 guilders, or as much as 10 times the annual income of a skilled craftsman. At its peak in 1636–1637, it has been said that an average tulip bulb changed ownership as many as 10 times a day. At times, the price of a tulip bulb was deemed to be worth more than the ground they could be grown on. It may have been the bubonic plague talking, but the Dutch seemed in an absolute frenzy over their newly imported tulips. In February 1637, the number of tulip bulb sellers greatly outnumbered the tulip bulb buyers, and the tulip bulb price fell dramatically, ending what was referred to as *tulip mania*—the first speculative bubble in modern history.

A cursory review of tulip mania may lead one to conclude that the Dutch during this time period were caught up in a phenomenon Alan Greenspan, centuries later, would refer to as *irrational exuberance*. John Maynard Keynes hypothesized this as "animal spirits." Both Greenspan and Keynes propose that people working spontaneously in their own self-interest in search of profits are apt to make reckless decisions. These initial investments yield a sizeable profit, leading additional "speculators" to enter the market; the cycle continues until some poor fool is left holding the proverbial tulip bulb with no seller to be found. Anyone who lived through the 1980s and bore witness to the parachute pants and mullet frenzy would conclude that people do synchronously make questionable decisions. However, as we shall see, a speculative bubble takes more to galvanize than just some enigmatic fashion choices or a fascination with tulips bulbs.

Let's follow the money in search of some other explanations for tulip mania. In his book *Early Speculative Bubbles and the Increase in the Money Supply*,[1] Doug French explains that an enormous increase in the money supply at the Bank of Amsterdam from 1630 to 1638 coincided with tulip mania. During the 1600s, the Netherlands was the banking and trading capital of the world. Everyone wanted to partake in the strong Dutch currency, and courtesy of the Dutch Central Bank they were able achieve that. Now, I want to make one thing clear: the Dutch Central Bank wasn't run by the counterfeiters that run the central banks of the world today. To the contrary, the Dutch had a hard metal currency. While other governments were debasing their currency, the Dutch model provided a sound monetary system.

The Bank of Netherlands partook in a monetary practice called free coinage. With free coinage you could exchange gold or silver bullion at the Bank of Netherlands for guilders and ducats. This allowed foreigners to deposit their worn-out gold and silver foreign currency and receive a beautiful, shiny guilder. Dutch currency was in demand, as the Dutch were sought-after trading partners. In some respects, the Dutch fell victim to their own success. The free coinage system in conjunction with the stability of the Dutch banking system led to an inflow of precious metal toward Amsterdam. It was this that led to the increase in metal or specie into the Bank of Amsterdam and thus an increase in coinage and the notes issued (i.e., the money supply).

As in all speculative bubbles, the inflation that the increase in the money supply created led to an increase in speculation and malinvestments. Those malinvestments manifested themselves in tulip bulbs. Similar to today's speculative bubbles, we see evidence of financial pain in the Netherlands subsequent to the bust—an enormous increase in the number of bankruptcies indicates that the consequence to the economy may not have been limited to tulips.[2]

A little less than a century later, Scottish economist John Law would distort the Dutch banking paradigm and mold it into his inauspicious model of a central bank that would lead to another speculative bubble. John Law was an eighteenth-century Ben Bernanke–meets–Bernie Madoff. Born in Scotland in 1671, son to a wealthy Scottish goldsmith, Law gambled away his inheritance and killed a man in a dueling match over a common love interest. Law managed to bribe his way out of jail and began writing his piece of monetary fiction called *Money and Trade Considered, with a Proposal for Supplying the Nation with Money* (1705). Disseminating his fairy tale economic theories that only the likes of Paul Krugman would appreciate, Law laid out his "Real Bills doctrine." Ironically, this unequivocally refuted doctrine was used as a cornerstone of the Federal Reserve Act of 1913. Shocking!

Law proposed the blueprint for a central bank that would be able to increase the money supply at whim. According to Law, money didn't need to be backed by gold or silver; money could be backed by land or by nothing at all. The increase in money would subsequently be at the discretion of government. Increasing money would create all sorts of great things—a kingdom could enjoy low interest rates and full employment, all the while keeping prices completely stable. WOW— sounds great! Why doesn't anybody think of doing that today? Oh, that's right—that's what our Federal Reserve does. At the beginning of the eighteenth century, Law's ideas were novel and heretical; today, unfortunately, these misconceptions are commonplace.

Law peddled his piece of propaganda fiction to various kingdoms with no success. Finally, the French government, struggling with an enormous amount of war debt and the untimely death of their king, wasn't in the position to let the truth get in the way of what was obviously a very good story. In 1716, John Law created the Banque Generale that later became the Banque Royale, France's first central bank. The Banque Royale was a private company that had a monopoly on money and financed the French debt; 75 percent of its capital was the debt of the French government. Hmm . . . this is sounding familiar.

Law initially enticed the French people with hard currency in order to gain their trust, and then he peddled his bank note paper currency. Law eventually outlawed the hoarding of precious metal—even jewelry—forcing the French to use his newly created currency.

The French government was straddled with debt from all their various wars. Law and a friend came up with a clever plan to assist France in unburdening itself of debt. Law, through the government, bought and consolidated a trading company called the Mississippi Company, which held France's rights to trade internationally and more specifically in Louisiana. Law developed elaborate schemes to drive up the price of these shares. Later decreeing Mississippi stock a de-facto currency, as the stock went up in value the King would get 75 percent of the profits, Law would get 25 percent, and the French people would get . . . well, they wouldn't make out that well on this deal!

Greed quickly set in. Looking to increase his profits, Law created a marketing campaign that greatly exaggerated the wealth of the Mississippi Company, driving speculators in. In 1720, people started to wise up, shares of the Mississippi Company fell, and Law was run out of town.

One can only muse that Law, if he were around today, would have secured a reappointment or perhaps even a promotion to Treasury secretary. After all, as the current logic goes, who better to "fix" all the problems than the person who created them in the first place? Unfortunately for Law, the government of France was not that naïve; Law was extradited to Naples, where he lived out the remainder of his life trying to convince the Italian government to partake in a similar scheme.

Over the past few centuries, enormous innovations have transpired; however, the basic principles of economics still hold true. Like tulip mania in the 1600s, an increase in the supply of money fuels all bubbles and can create a euphoric feeling, giving way to irrational exuberance. Greenspan conveniently fails to mention that this exuberance is actually a symptom of easy money and not a phenomenon unto itself.

Counterfeiters like John Law have existed throughout time and are in abundance in central banks all over the world today. Over the past thousands of years, nations have promulgated devaluation in their currency as a means to mitigate their economic problems. Today, central banks in Europe and the United States are counterfeiting money as a means of alleviating malaise brought about by insolvent nations saturated in debt. Sadly, as history will attest, this never ends well.

Every generation likes to think of itself as living in unique times; many are deluded to believe that their encounters are unique and perpetuate the myth of a new paradigm. Empires that hold the world's reserve currency eventually succumb to their own hubris and delude themselves into thinking they are above the laws of economics and mathematics. Pundits often argue this new paradigm as a way to dispel universal truths concerning monetary policy and economics. There is no new paradigm; throughout history, nations have never printed their way to prosperity. This time is no exception.

The Great Depression—A Historical Comparison

Today's counterfeiter-in-chief, Ben Bernanke, touts his bona fides as a student of the Great Depression; he credits his easy monetary stance on a belief that the 1930s' Fed provided policy that was excessively restrictive and these policies prolonged the length of the Great Depression. Let's take a look at the Great Depression and see what really happened.

Immediately after its inception in 1913, the Fed got right to work funding World War I—"Wilson's War." The newly created Fed set the interest rate on what was then called a Liberty bond. The low-yielding Liberty bond enabled the United States to painlessly enter World War I, a war one could argue the United States may not have entered had a tax on its people been levied.

When the United States exited World War I, there was a retraction in the money supply as the Fed was no longer funding a war, and a corresponding deflation in commodity prices ensued. The depression of 1920–1921 was characterized by extreme deflation—some prices dropped as much as 36 percent, worse than any year during the Great Depression. The deflation was a natural occurrence of the market in response to unwinding the deliberate inflation created by the Fed to fund the war. If you have never heard of this depression, it is because it was short. Why? Because the deflationary process was allowed to occur, malinvestments were allowed to be liquidated, and the economy quickly healed.

The political climate had changed; it seems that America had enough "progress" and elected Warren Harding, who promised a "return to normalcy." Warren Harding died in office, and Calvin Coolidge became president in 1923. Calvin Coolidge was the last bastion of true conservatism in this country. Coolidge was a leader who believed in minimalism in governing, or laissez-faire—he had faith in what Adam Smith described as the *invisible hand*.

The newly created Federal Reserve, in a move that would eerily mirror events that occurred in the mid-2000s, decided to take an activist role in the 1920s' economy. In an attempt to raise prices, help farmers, help the British, and help bankers (most particularly Paul Warburg, one of the creators of the Fed), the Federal Reserve engaged in reckless monetary behavior—what a surprise!

At its inception, the discount window was viewed as the Fed's "lender of last resort" refuge—a place where banks could come in an emergency, borrowing at a penalty, set to reflect a slight increase to the market. This was designed so the Fed knew that the new money created would retreat from the economy when the emergency subsided. However, during most of the 1920s, that rate sat well below market rates and provided a constant source of liquidity to the economy. Many economists and market strategists, including myself, have studied the Fed in the 1920s and have concluded that the Fed was excessively accommodative during this time. The Fed's easy-money policies perpetuated an overextension of credit that led to the 1920s' bubble.

The 1920s boasts a robust economy, and some if it was real: houses were getting electricity, families were buying cars—the real economy was growing. However, the easy-money policies courtesy of the Fed created a bubble in the real estate and equity markets. It is clear that the real economy slowed down in 1927. Between 1927 and early 1929, a preponderance of bank loans were created for purposes of speculation. In the 1920s, an average household often engaged in buying stocks "on the margin." In other words, they borrowed money from the bank to make a bet in the stock market. Bets on stocks coupled with real estate speculation and all the excess spending generated from the fictitious "wealth effect" associated with any bubble put household debt in a precarious position. Wow, that sounds just like today![3]

Let's take a moment to review inflation and deflation. Inflation is always a deliberate act of a central bank to devalue the currency. One can make a valid argument for an increase in the money supply that would complement an increase in the growth of the labor force and productivity. Any money in addition to growth based on this formula should be viewed as inflation. After all, there is simply a limit to how fast a population can grow and how much more productive it can become. Population growth is limited by biology, and productivity is limited by our capacity to innovate. Historical trends dictate that the increase in both labor force growth and productivity growth equals about 3 percent. Therefore, any increase in the money supply over 3 percent will usually lead to a misallocation of capital, bubbles, and rising aggregate prices in the economy. When superfluous money is pushed into an economy, the value of the money will decrease in respect to an item or a basket of goods in the marketplace. Therefore, in general, prices on most goods and services will increase as a result of an increase in money. Newly created money is never distributed evenly and, hence, it often pools in certain asset classes. Deflation is the market's solution to rectify the imbalance caused by inflation. Falling asset prices is a naturally occurring process that helps to normalize an economy. Deflation gets a bad rap, but it's a healthy process. Deflation and the recession that can often follow are part of the healing process to return the economy back to normal. Deflation won't garner many votes for (re)election, but it is the salve that heals the damage caused by asset, debt, and money supply bubbles.

The Fed-induced inflation witnessed in the 1920s was dissimilar to the inflation experienced in the 1970s. The inflation existed in certain commodities, the stock market, and credit. The price associated with a basket of consumer goods in the 1920s remained relatively stable.

In the 1920s, the Federal Reserve was a little like Thelma and Louise. They had their foot on the gas, the top down, wind in their hair; they were cruising down the highway at record speed, creating all kinds of chaos, but by all accounts it was a fun ride—that is, until they crashed into the Grand Canyon. On October 29, 1929, the 1920s' joy ride came to an end. The inflation that was created by the Federal Reserve had ended months before, and the country suffered deflation and entered into a depression. Many of the speculative loans that the banks extended were worthless. The Fed, whose original purpose was to prevent bank failures, allowed banks to fail. In just 16 years since its inception, the Fed managed to wreak havoc on the economy and failed to achieve its original mandate. This is a great example of the unintended consequences associated with government intervention. The people most surprised by this are the perpetrators themselves!

In March 1929, Herbert Hoover became president of the United Sates. In the 1930s, it is likely that when mothers put their children to bed they told them a story of President Hoover, who did nothing when the stock market crashed and the economy fell into depression. Well, this tale should be placed on the shelf between *The Three Little Pigs* and *Little Red Riding Hood*—because it is a fairy tale! Hoover was, in fact, the architect of what FDR would later refer to as the New Deal.

History has mischaracterized Hoover's political posture to be similar to Coolidge—laissez-faire. In fact, nothing could be further from the truth. These historians are either ignorant of the facts or purposely confuse Hoover's tariff on imported goods (Smoot-Hawley), raising income taxes from a top rate of 25 percent to 63 percent, and government-sponsored projects to create jobs in public works, with free market principles; they argue that Hoover retreated during the downturn in favor of allowing the market to liquidate. The truth is that Hoover refused to allow the free market to liquidate; he used his authority to coerce businesses to retain employees and not lower compensation!

Hoover was an engineer—a "doer," a "fixer." Politically, he was a self-proclaimed progressive, and economically, although the term was not yet in vogue, he was a Keynesian. He believed that the government should play a deliberate role in revitalizing the economy; he viewed the business cycle as something that needed to be controlled. Hoover held the belief that high wages create a robust economy instead of a robust economy leading to high wages. Most ideas for the New Deal started under Hoover—Roosevelt came in four years later and doubled down on that specious reasoning. The Hoover administration marks the end to laissez-faire government in this country. We were all Keynesians now!

John Maynard Keynes was a British economist who challenged the prevailing free-market economic preference of the time. Keynes sought an economic utopia and advised governments to use countercyclical policies in hard times, running deficits in recessions and depressions. His theory that government should spend during financial downturns has given political cover to administrations up until today.

Let's take a minute to compare the Great Depression to today's Great Recession.

During the Great Depression, real gross domestic product (GDP) plummeted 32 percent. GDP refers to the market value of all officially recognized final goods and services produced within a country in a given period. The contraction in GDP during the Great Depression was the direct result of a reduction in the money supply caused by consumers' selling off assets and paying down debt—a painful but necessary step toward a healthy consumer and economy. Household debt as a percentage of GDP reached nearly 100 percent in 1929, before falling back to 20 percent of GDP in 1945. To put that number in perspective, household debt did not go back above 50 percent of GDP until 1985. It was not until the first quarter of 2009 that household debt once again approached the Great Depression level of 100 percent of GDP. When household debt reaches these levels, it reflects a household's inability to continue to spend. The household spent yesterday and needs to pay off debt today, so the accompanying reduction in GDP is a natural process—it reflects the household's diligence at cleaning up its balance sheet.

Between the start of the Great Depression and the end of World War II, household debt fell from 100 percent to just above 20 percent of GDP. Getting there was a painful process, but such deleveraging was the only real cure for an economy swimming in debt. In 2012, thanks to government efforts to carry on our debt-fueled consumption binge, today's Great Recession household debt has barely contracted at all. To make matters even worse, during this current crisis, our government's response has been to dramatically increase its own borrowing. At the start of the Great Depression, gross federal debt was 16 percent of GDP. It peaked just below 44 percent when the depression ended. While the national debt did increase significantly during that period, it was still relatively benign when viewed from a historical perspective.

The United States entered the current Great Recession with gross national debt equal to 65 percent of GDP. It has since exploded to over 100 percent of GDP! Comparing the relatively innocuous level of the 1930s with today's pile of government debt clearly illustrates the perilous state of the economy.

National debt did rise dramatically during World War II, topping out at 120 percent of GDP in 1946. But consumer debt plunged concurrently. So while the nation was adding debt to fight and win a global war, households were taking the necessary steps to ensure their balance sheets were well prepared for the aftermath of the battle.

Today, gross national debt and household debt are both near record highs as a percentage of the economy for the first time in our history (household debt 85 percent, national debt 104 percent). Such are the consequences of truncating the Great Recession of 2008 (GDP fell by only 3.6 percent from peak to trough) by massively counterfeiting money in an effort to prop up home prices and the economy.

Many observers—unfortunately, including most of those in power—have concluded that the government must spend more while consumers rein in their debts. Their strategy is based on the belief that once the economy perks up they can unwind that debt.

There are two problems with this Keynesian theory. One is that government spending doesn't increase GDP; it only chokes off private-sector growth. The other is that politicians never regard the present as a good time for the government to pay off its debts.

Mr. Bernanke likes to give tutelage to his expertise and study of the Great Depression, but one has to ruminate on what specific part of the Great Depression Mr. Bernanke was a student of. Mr. Bernanke appears to be a politician first and an economist or student of the market second—if at all. In his study of the Great Depression, it is clear he failed to ascertain that the depression of the 1930s, similar to the Great Recession of today, was a result of an overleveraged economy. In both cases, this overleveraged economy was brought about by artificially provided low interest rates from the central bank, and this spurred on superfluous lending on the part of commercial banks. The easy money provided by banks eventually brought debt levels in the economy to unsustainable levels. It was, in fact, the flawed Keynesian economic policies and growth-killing tax hikes that rendered the 1930s' depression great in length. Bernanke has limited his focus of study to what he believes to be restrictive monetary policies in place at the Fed in the 1930s. He is working off a flawed hypothesis, and thus the easy-money direction he is exhausting in navigating us out of our current Great Recession is fallacious.

We can speculate that if the 1930s' Fed partook in Banana Ben's easy-money policies, just like today, the money would have further fueled the Keynesian-bent government to engage in additional deficit spending in a fruitless attempt to boost growth. In fact, the only viable solution then, just like today, is for the private and public sector to go through a protracted period of deleveraging. If Hoover had listened to his Treasury Secretary Andrew Mellon's advice to liquidate, instead of trying to manage the economy and stop the natural process of deflation, the depression would have been abbreviated. Instead, like Bernanke, these men didn't see the ensuing depression for what it was: a healing, which is marked by deflation.

Common wisdom states that if you are caught in an avalanche, you leverage the laws of gravity and spit in order to ascertain what position you are in to prevent you from digging yourself further into a hole as you try to dig yourself out. If you do not know the real cause of a problem, you should also be unable to provide a genuine solution. It is obvious that the Fed under Bernanke's direction is taking its cue from a flawed playbook, and instead of allowing the economy to heal, he is digging us further into a hole—a hole that is leading us into a bubble even larger than the one we have just encountered. In fact, it is the biggest bubble in the history of planet Earth, and its demise will dramatically affect your standard of living if you are not prepared.

Two Decades of a Bubble Economy

There is a phrase that is used in describing unfortunate things that happen in war that fall outside the scope of the engagement: *collateral damage.* As we will see, a managed global economy also reaps collateral damage, sometimes with just as harmful consequences.

The 1980s were a prosperous time for America. Ronald Reagan was president, and his administration sought to wring out the inflation brought about by the easy-money policies of Nixon, Ford, and Carter. This brought about what my friend Larry Kudlow refers to as "King Dollar." King Dollar was great and America was back on top; unfortunately, you can't make everyone happy. The manufacturing sector actually prefers a weak dollar because they believe it helps them sell goods overseas. They sought to slay "King Dollar" and replace him with "weak dollar." This went against the policy of the Reagan White House; however, they were willing to compromise. In 1985, the G5 met at the Plaza Hotel to discuss how currency could be manipulated to favor the U.S. manufacturer.

I have to stop here for one brief moment to state that currency exchange rates should be determined by the free market, not the bureaucrats from five countries pontificating at the Plaza Hotel. So right now alarm bells should be going off: *"Go back—this isn't going to turn out well!"* And, in fact, it doesn't. Indeed, a stronger currency doesn't hurt exports because deflation allows domestic producers to import commodities at lower prices and lowers the cost of production. Thus, they can reduce prices, which serve to offset currency changes. But let's continue with our story.

The Plaza Accord, as it was called, devalued the U.S. dollar against the yen, the pound, and the deustche mark, allowing U.S. manufacturers to hopefully better compete overseas. It is amusing to learn that the unintended consequences of trying to boost exports by destroying your currency actually led manufacturing as a percentage of GDP to *drop* from 18 percent in 1985, to 12 percent today.

The Bank of Japan, in an attempt to offset the rising yen, drastically reduced its discount rate, creating one of the biggest asset bubbles in history—oops. Now the Japanese economy, following a strict Keynesian diet of easy money and reckless deficit spending, never liquidated that asset bubble, and the Japanese economy is still suffering from this event. It seems that instead of one or two years of pain, the Japanese chose what has been several lost decades and counting.

After the G5 succeeded in effectively blowing up the Japanese economy, they met again in 1995 to do the Reverse Plaza accord—don't these imbeciles ever learn? Apparently not; the Reverse Plaza accord was an attempt to prop up the Japanese economy. This devalued the yen and propped up the dollar—enticing foreign investment in U.S. assets, especially the U.S. stock market.

The world was becoming controlled by Kamikaze Kenyesian Couterfeiters. In the 1990s, central planning bureaucrats weren't content blowing up their own economies; they took their show on the road and proceeded to blow up economies all around the world. As you can imagine, the late 1990s provided us with all sorts of crises: the Mexican crisis, the eastern Asia crisis, the Russian debt crisis, and, of course, the Monica Lewinsky crisis. Alan Greenspan, reacting to all the crises, lowered the discount rate in the late 1990s even though economic data in the U.S. economy didn't support his doing so. In response to the Long Term Capital Management hedge fund blowup, he even lowered the discount rate midsession—sending a clear message to Wall Street that he had their backs.

The Fed's easy-money policy increased the money supply in the late 1990s. Furthermore, the Fed's lowering of interest rates encouraged venture capitalists to pour their money into Internet start-ups. In the late 1990s, the increase in money didn't end up in tulip bulbs; it made its way to Internet stocks. Just like the Netherlands in the late 1600s, an increase in money had the United States in a frenzy, which Greenspan coined as *irrational exuberance*, for anything with a dot-com at the end of it.

The Fed's easy money left investors in the late 1990s giddy; analysts argued that the Nasdaq bubble ushered in a new economic paradigm. Earnings were replaced by eyeballs—a new Internet site needn't make money; it just needed to attract visitors stopping over. Eventually, Greenspan, whom Bob Woodward ceremoniously dubbed *The Maestro*, sought to curtail this in his latest masterpiece, the "Nasdaq Concerto," and after six rate hikes, the exuberance waned; the Nasdaq bubble played its last note. When the curtain fell, investors were left unexuberant and with irrational valuations on stocks of companies that had no earnings.

So, sadly, in the fall of 2000, we learned that the new paradigm was no different than the old paradigm, and that eyeballs don't pass for earnings. Speculative bubbles remind me of parties I went to in high school; they can be a lot of fun if you get there early and leave before the cops come. When the inflation in the Nasdaq bubble popped, many of the dot-com companies went under and the country fell into a recession.

By now we have concluded that speculative bubbles are fueled by easy money, so next we need to contemplate what asset class the money has inflated. To conclude that an asset class is a bubble, you need to understand that all bubbles share the same basic genesis and structure. Of course, Fed-heads are notorious for admitting that they are completely clueless in the knowledge of the very bubbles they create. Remember, Alan Greenspan is on record saying, "Bubbles generally are perceptible only after the fact."[4] So allow me to assist them in identifying one. The asset in question must be significantly overowned, overpriced, and oversupplied as compared to historical measures. So let's review Nasdaq stocks in the late 1990s using this simple model.

First, Nasdaq stocks were extremely overowned; in fact, in 1998, I would have defied you to get into a taxicab in Manhattan and go more than three blocks without getting a stock tip from the driver. The volumes on the major exchanges were breaking records nearly every day and were far above its historical levels.

Next, Nasdaq stocks, and especially their dot-com inhabitants, were extremely overpriced. The late 1990s saw price-to-earnings (PE) ratios in the stratosphere, while Yahoo! traded at 108, AOL at 100, Pets.com at . . . hey, what happened to that cute little sock puppet that made such a splash at the Super Bowl? Sadly, it's not a happy ending; that poor sock ended up bankrupt and now lives in the bottom of the sock drawer. He can be found at the bar with William Shatner, cursing his decision to take the stock and not the cash.

Finally, Nasdaq stocks were oversupplied. We recently bore witness to the Facebook fiasco that financial media companies billed as the new age of the American economy. During the dot-com boom, we had a dot-com public spectacle at least once a week. The initial public offering calendar in the late 1990s was unprecedented in American history.

The deflation resulting from the Nasdaq crash gave way to a mild recession. Easy-money Keynesian economists such as Paul Krugman put massive pressure on Alan Greenspan to ease and he acquiesced. Unfortunately, after the unforeseen and tragic events of September 11, 2001, Alan Greenspan further succumbed to the pressure and reduced the Fed funds and discount rate, and thus made money easier than it needed to be and failed to tighten soon enough. Please do not confuse my remarks about Fed policy with my sincere sorrow about the human tragedy that stole the lives of innocent men and women on September 11. Putting the obvious human tragedy aside, it is clear that from late 2000 to mid-2004 the Fed had its foot firmly pressed on the gas pedal of the economy, and the maestro started composing his final and most tragic symphony: the housing bubble.

Does CDO Rhyme with Tulip Bulb?

There are countless books available today on the causes of the housing bubble, so I am going to make my summary brief.

The bubble that led to today's current Great Recession was twofold; the most obvious was a bubble in the real estate market, and what may have been less apparent to the average person before 2008 was the bubble in the collateralized debt obligation (CDO). A CDO is a financial instrument most Americans were introduced to for the first time after the banking industry blew up. It is an instrument that banks and financial institutions use to theoretically reduce risk and to provide liquidity. This is how it works.

Let's say that you take a mortgage from the bank. Your mortgage would have a duration of either 15 or 30 years. Now, banks are unwilling to sit on this loan just collecting monthly payments, so they sell it. When they sell it, they make a fee and are freed up to make another loan, and the cycle continues. After all, why expose your bank to interest rate risk if you can easily offload the loan to the government?

Banks and the institutions that buy and sell mortgages saw more risk in your individual mortgage than if it were packaged with others as a group. These mortgages get pooled, and a CDO is born, then it gets rated. The people who create CDOs and the agencies that rate them utilized computer models that showed a history when housing prices only advanced, so their models told them that your group of mortgages would never default, and if you did, they would have your ever appreciating house as collateral. These CDOs therefore were stamped AAA, the highest rating you can have, and off they went into the hands of unsuspecting foreign and domestic investors seeking a higher-return, low-risk vehicle.

In order to further protect risk, financial institutions took out insurance on the CDO called a *credit default swap* (CDS). The CDS gets a little complicated because you can buy or short a CDS even when you don't own the underlying asset. A lot of institutions treated the CDS as a hedge against their portfolio or as an option to be traded. Up until 2005, AIG was a primary player in the CDS market. Now, all this was fantastic for a while, and CDOs were very successful. With interest rates low, investors hungry for yield flocked to CDOs in droves and, in turn, Wall Street demanded more mortgages to feed the CDO market.

Starting in the 1960s with fair housing initiatives, Washington politicians began to think that the American dream of home ownership was something that could be given instead of something that needed to be earned. Washington pinheads working under the guise of "helping people" passed legislation allowing the public to buy houses they really couldn't afford. Legislation that initially sought to create fair lending practices, low interest rates, and incentives for neighborhoods in need of renewal eventually manifested into regulation that allowed for no money down and no proof of income. These loans were called *liar loans*, and qualification relied on little more than an applicant's ability to make up a favorable fable about their financial condition.

The investor class's desire for those solid-yielding, low-risk CDOs coincided with the individual homeowner's desire to own a home or several homes and extract the appreciation from it. The easy mortgage regulations and teaser rates also attracted new home buyers to the market. So, in effect, the two bubbles fueled each other—the financial institutions' desire to underwrite mortgages, package them, and sell them off, and the public's desire to partake in the housing market both as an owner and a speculator—a win-win! Not so fast. Things started to get a little sloppy, and in 2007, with the distress in the subprime mortgage market, mortgage companies started to get "jingle mail." The jingle was the sound of house keys that were sent back instead of payment. It didn't take long before savvy investors started to question the soundness of their CDOs, and since the liability was pooled instead of specific, it made it difficult to determine what was performing and what was nonperforming, and the entire CDO became toxic.

Now, unless you have been living under a rock for the past four years, you know how this turned out. Here are some highlights: Freddie Mac and Fannie Mae went into conservatorship, Bear Sterns was sold in a fire sale to JPMorgan Chase, Lehman Brothers went bankrupt, Hank Paulson strong-armed Ken Lewis at Bank of America to purchase Merill Lynch, AIG called Banana Ben for an $85-billion-dollar loan, and Hank Paulson stopped dry heaving in his garbage can long enough to terrify mindless political leaders into supporting his bailout of the banks.[5] We will get into the bailout that occurred by both the Federal Reserve and the Treasury in detail in the next chapter. But the most important take-away here is that, once again, the government and private banks caused a rapid and extensive increase in money supply growth, which led to the formation of another pernicious bubble. This is a key factor in the creation of the current bubble in U.S. debt.

Today's Bubble in Bonds Rhymes with the Debt-Fueled Real Estate Crisis

Over the past dozen years, the investing public has been burned in the stock market. From the Nasdaq and real estate bubble to the fraud in Enron and WorldCom, to the Flash Crash and even the Ponzi scheme developed by Bernie Madoff, financial events have investors seeking security. The need for capital preservation has trumped the desire for capital appreciation. Investors have eschewed the ownership of stocks and have piled into bonds like never before.

The similarities between the subprime mortgage crisis and that of the coming collapse of the U.S. bond market are uncanny. In fact, Mark Twain may have had the U.S. debt market and the previous debt-fueled real estate crisis in mind when he said that "history doesn't repeat itself, but it does rhyme."

As we discussed, the housing and credit crisis first became evident to most in 2007 with the distress in the subprime mortgage market. As with all bubbles, the foundation for the housing bubble was easy money and low interest rates, which were provided by the Fed and passed along to consumers via commercial banks and the shadow banking system.

Similarly, today's rock-bottom interest rates provided by the Fed and from foreign central banks recycling our trade deficit are misleading the government into believing it can take on a tremendous amount of debt by spending significantly more money than it collects in revenue. Those low rates have also duped the Treasury into believing it can sell a virtually unlimited amount of debt without ever incurring a substantial increase in debt service expense. Of course, this is not unlike home-owners who took on onerous mortgage payments, believing home prices would always increase.

Another similarity between the housing and bond market bubbles is that the housing market of circa 2006 and the U.S. bond market of today contain all three elements of a classic asset bubble that we have discussed: massive oversupply, an unsustainably high price level, and overownership of the asset class in question.

In the early part of the last decade, home builders began to increase construction volume to twice the intrinsic demand for home ownership. Home price-to-income ratios eventually reached unsustainable levels. And levels of home ownership reached a record high percentage of the population. Likewise, the U.S. Treasury is dramatically increasing the supply of debt each year to fund our $1 trillion deficits. The public has plowed their savings into the U.S. debt market as commercial bank holdings of Treasuries have reached an all-time high. And bond prices have soared, pushing the yield on the 10-year note to all-time lows, which is far less than the 7 percent average yield on the 10-year going back to 1969.

One last similarity between to the two bubbles is that the prevailing consensus of not too long ago was that home prices could never decline on a national level. Today, we are being told that the U.S. dollar will always be the world's reserve currency and that Treasuries will always be viewed as a safe haven by global investors. Remember how those in Washington and on Wall St. also assured investors that the subprime mortgage problem was well contained and would not bring down the housing market—much less the entire global financial system. Well, regardless of what those same people are saying now, these record low yields on U.S. Treasuries are unsustainable and cannot last given our massive nearly $17 trillion national debt, $110 trillion in unfunded liabilities, and the record-high $2.9 trillion Fed balance sheet. Remember, that Fed balance sheet is the rocket fuel for rapidly growing the money supply and creating inflation. And inflation is the bane of bond prices.

Therefore, all the elements of a bubble in the bond market are in place, just as they were for the real estate market in the middle of the last decade and the dot-com bubble during the late 1990s. The housing and Nasdaq bubbles not only rhyme with tulip bulbs, but they both seem to rhyme perfectly with the current bubble in the bond market.

Notes

1. Douglas E. French, *Early Speculative Bubbles and the Increase in the Money Supply* (Auburn, AL: Ludwig von Mises Institute, 2009).
2. Ibid.
3. Murray N. Rothbard, *America's Great Depression* (Auburn, AL: Ludwig von Mises Institute, 2000).
4. This quote is taken from Greenspan's appearance before the Joint Economic Committee of Congress in June 1999.
5. Hank Paulson confesses to dry heaving in his garbage can throughout the financial crisis in his book *On the Brink* (New York: Business Plus, Hachette Book Group, 2010).

Chapter 3

Bernanke's Hair-of-the-Dog Economy

Insanity: doing the same thing over and over again and expecting different results.

—*Albert Einstein*

There is a common colloquial expression, "hair of the dog," that originated centuries ago and originally referred to treating a rabid dog bite by placing hair from the dog in the bite wound. Today, this phrase is predominantly used to refer to alcohol that is consumed with the aim of lessening the effects of a hangover; it is believed by some that you can cure a hangover by drinking from the same bottle that "bit you" the night before.

Now, say it is September 2008, and you wake up with an enormous hangover and you decide to follow this age-old advice. You drink the same alcohol that got you sick in the first place, and when the first drink is not met with much success, you polish off the entire bottle and start to feel pretty good and that maybe this is working. There is one problem—the next day you wake up hungover again and this cycle continues day in and day out for four more years!

Some days you feel good—but a lot of days you're dragging and feeling sluggish. Every time you think you should stop, you contemplate how severe the hangover that started four years ago would be now. So you continue, and now even the slightest feeling of a headache makes you itching for happy hour. Congratulations—you're the U.S. economy!

Our counterfeiter-in-chief, Ben Bernanke, has concocted an identical poison for the U.S. economy. Following the real-estate bubble debacle, he put the United States on the path of "hangover" avoidance. Instead of allowing the economy to deleverage, Ben chose to kick the can down the road—which is, by the way, the most insipid and trite saying we've got going today. It is much more accurate to use my own description of Bernanke's strategy, which is, "He's trying to avoid a hangover by attempting to stay drunk forever." How's this working for him? What a surprise . . . not so well. The economy is actually feeling just like you did in the scenario—sluggish and limping along. Yes, there are days when the economic data look slightly positive and we anticipate a recovery, but then very soon the data turn south and we realize that we are headed straight toward that hangover and seek comfort in monetary intoxication.

So addicted is this economy that at the first hint of deflation, the market, in Pavlovian fashion, clamors for the next round of QE (or quantitative easing)—that is, the continuation of massive counterfeiting, when you've already printed so much money that interest rates are at zero percent. It seems that Mr. Bernanke has lost faith in the free market's ability to rebuild itself; instead, he has resorted to placing the economy on what is tantamount to a vodka drip. Bernanke thinks he can wean the economy off the easy-money bottle at any time.

To hear Ben avow his plan for easing the economy off Fed-induced low interest rates one would conclude that Ben has delusions of a painless detox, where the economy sobers up at a cushy celebrity rehab clinic.

Unfortunately for Ben and the economy, there is no painless recovery.

Austrian Trade Cycle Theory versus Keynesian Toys and Candy

There is no painless detox for this easy-money hangover; the only way for the economy to heal is to go through the natural deleveraging process that comes with deflation. This is something I will emphasize throughout this book. A refusal to accept deleveraging is a crucial ingredient to the formation of bubbles that grow more intense with each lost opportunity to heal. Let's review the trade cycle theory to address the normal process an economy uses to heal after a Fed-induced inflationary bubble.

Famed Austrian economist Ludwig von Mises developed a theory to explain the boom–and-bust cycle that results from the extension of credit brought about by central banks' manipulation of a fiat currency. Murray Rothbard, in his noted book *America's Great Depression,*[1] updated Mises's theory that I would like to elucidate.

The entrepreneur is a business forecaster, he is trained to stay in tune with messages that the market sends in determining the capital investment that should be expended. Business cycles vary, and it is common for individual businesses and even industries to make errors in judgment and over build. However, when you get a cluster of businesses and industries making erroneous capital expenditures at the same time, it is always a result of monetary intervention. Here's why . . .

When banks print new money and lend it to businesses, they receive a false signal that there is an increase in saved funds available for investment. This newly created money masquerades as savings and leads to the eventual misallocation of capital. Businesses invest these funds and bid up prices of capital and other producer's goods and overbuild. The overbuilding percolates downward and affects the consumer market in the prices of wages, rents, and interest. If this were a result of a genuine increase in savings, all would be fine, but since this is due only to bank credit expansion, demand eventually returns to old proportions and we experience the bust cycle. The business investments made during the illusory boom were wasteful and need to be liquidated.

Rothbard goes on to explain that "a favorite explanation of the crisis is that it stems from 'underconsumption'—from a failure of consumer demand,"[2] but this is not the case. In essence, the market receives false price signals and inflation becomes concentrated in just one, or a few, asset classes. Capital is then siphoned from other, more viable uses and into that sector of the economy where specious demand is most evident. Bubbles form and eventually burst under their own weight. This occurs when nearly everybody seems to own the asset, the asset has become too expensive to purchase, and there is a massive overhang in supply.

During the boom, business was misled to invest too much; "as soon as the inflation permeates to the mass of the people, the old consumption-investment proportion is reestablished, and business investments are seen to have been wasteful." Rothbard continues:

> The "boom," then, is actually a period of wasteful misinvestment. It is a time when errors are made. The "crisis" arrives when the consumers come to reestablish their desired proportions. The "depression" is actually the process by which the economy *adjusts* to the wastes and errors of the boom, and reestablishes efficient service of consumer desires.[3]

It is only through the rapid *liquidation* of the wasteful investments that the economy can purge its misinvestments. Some of these investments may have to be abandoned altogether; others will be shifted for other uses. "Always the principle will not be to mourn past errors, but make the most efficient use of the existing stock of capital."[4]

Let's put this theory to the test. As we discussed in the previous chapter, the Fed's easy-money policies in the late 1990s created an enormous amount of money that funded speculation in Internet start-up companies. Venture capitalists leveraged the Fed-induced credit to make new investments in Internet companies. With money flowing and profits to be made, they often made imprudent business decisions. Caught up in the frenzy to bring dot-coms to market, eager venture capitalists often failed to think through the business model. A good example of this is the now defunct Internet start-up company Pets.com.

We can imagine that the premise for Pets.com may have sounded promising when it was presented at the venture capital (VC) pitch meeting in San Francisco sometime in the mid-1990s. After all, the United States is home to 78.2 million dogs and 86.4 million cats,[5] and all of these dogs and cats need to eat. And in case you didn't know this already—pets don't drive. I can imagine the light bulbs illuminating over the heads of the venture capitalists in the conference room as they marveled in the revelation that in fact "pets do not drive"—so how are they going to get their pet food? Why of course, they'll have to buy it online. Sold—we'll go public next week!

This was obviously the easy money talking, because once the dust settled they soon realized that although pets can't drive, the people who own them do, and pet food is fairly expensive to ship. Pets.com went public in August 1998 to the typical fanfare that dot-com stocks were reveling in at the time. Sadly, 268 days and $300 million in VC dollars later, Pets.com went out of business, forcing pet owners everywhere to get back into their cars to buy pet food.

Pets.com and other Internet companies in the late 1990s were flush with cash. New-economy businesses utilized old-economy businesses for services such as advertising, media, technology, and recruiting, just to name a few. Both were given a false signal of savings and were led to misinvest.

When Pets.com and other Internet start-ups went out of business, they not only exposed their flawed business model but also exposed the malinvestments made throughout the economy. Pets.com and other now defunct Internet start-ups needed to be liquidated and abandoned—and, thankfully, they were. Liquidation and abandonment is a painful process; the economy will lose jobs and money—however, it is the necessary process for the economy to rebuild. The advertising agencies, media companies, and recruiting firms will have to shift investments and downsize to accommodate the actual demand that is in the market now that the central bank credit has subsided. This is the natural cleansing process the economy uses to remove inefficient business models in favor of efficient models. Any attempt the government would make to stand in the way of this process and slow it down would divert funds from the functioning economy and slow down the recovery process. After all, how much of our money should the government spend on keeping businesses alive that don't expand the productive capacity of the economy and don't boost our standard of living?

Liquidation of malivestments and the recession that follows are capitalism's reset button, or what economist Joseph Schumpeter referred to as "the gales of creative destruction"—tearing down inefficient business models in order to rebuild new and efficient ones.[6]

I mentioned before that I am the father of two young children, and anyone who has children has sat through their fair share of birthday parties. During these parties I can't help my mind from converging on the Trade Cycle Theory. And so, I have concluded through my observation that there is a reason that a party ends and not begins with cake—because sugar to a child is like money to an economy. Every child is more apt to make poor decisions when they are riding an easy-sugar high. Parents intuitively understand that a child needs a time-out—a natural process to work through bad decisions.

Recessions, depressions, and time-outs are difficult—ask any child and they will tell you a time-out is no fun. Politicians find economic time-outs just as intolerable. Instead of viewing a recession as a natural healing process, today's politician views recession as an economic obstacle to their reelection. Unlike children, politicians employ economic advisors whose job it is to try to avoid time-outs. John Maynard Keynes once said that policy makers "are often slaves of some defunct economist".[7] That's ironic because today's policy makers seem to enjoy the Keynesian candy of their advisers, then become slaves to the flailing economy their advice serves up. These Keynesian-bent advisers endorse deficit spending and easy money as the only remedy for an ailing economy.

Now, we can muse that perhaps children should garner their own "advisers" to jettison their time-outs. This team of "advisers" would mirror the economic teams today's leaders use, in other words, consist of people who have no hands-on knowledge of kids. The team doesn't have kids, doesn't know kids, and doesn't spend time around real kids, and when they were kids they didn't have any friends. But they went to an Ivy League school where they studied adolescents extensively. Their comprehensive study of adolescents at play leads them to the conclusion that play utopia can exist with no time-outs and lots of candy. They have extensive mathematical formulas that support their research and are recipients of the Nobel Prize in this area. According to the "team," if the child makes some bad choices, it's nothing a bowl of candy and a trip to Toys-R-Us with Daddy's credit card can't fix. Now this all sounds great—to a five-year-old!

Keynesians peddle the same kind of snake oil that John Law (from the previous chapter) pushed. They argue with lots of intervention and lots of "candy" an economy can move along smoothly with no time-outs. Like Law, they argue that an increase in money leads to lower interest rates and full employment. So, if they were right, one would imagine that with all the printing they are doing at the Fed, we'd be at

0 percent unemployment—wrong! As I write, we have been hovering around 8 percent for more than 30 months. So what went wrong? If you ask a Keynesian, it's because we need more deficit spending and money printing; apparently, those starched shirts at the Fed don't know how to party. We need more than three bowls of candy to give this economy its sugar high; we need an endless stream of candy and more reckless numbers of trips to Toys-R-Us with Daddy's credit card.

Even a Keynesian comprehends that money printing is inflationary, but they have us convinced that inflation is good. After all, who doesn't love rising prices? Nobody wants prices to fall—that may mean we are heading into a time-out, and Keynesians don't do time-outs; it's just candy, spending, and party all the time! It appears to be a formula that only a child would postulate; unfortunately, it's one that way too many politicians choose to advance. Time-outs are no fun. Every politician knows that, and if the recession coincides with their reelection, they are unbearable. Therefore, people in politics are willing to affirm the Keynesian fairy tale.

Unfortunately for the U.S. economy, the Keynesian-led spending spree that this country has been on for the past 80 years has left us over $16 trillion dollars in debt and counting. The easy money provided by the Fed is permitting the government to spend with little immediate consequence. Unfortunately, the Fed can't continue to keep interest rates low in perpetuity; the market is eventually going to supplant Banana Ben's authority and drive rates up, exposing their latest creation—the bubble in the bond market.

"End This Depression Now!"—The Game Show

Paul Krugman is the embodiment of Keynesian thought. He writes an op-ed for the *New York Times*, where he unabashedly espouses reckless government spending under the guise of fulfilling the centrally planned utopia of John Maynard Keynes. In his book *End This Depression Now!*, Krugman champions government spending as a means to bring down the debt-to–GDP (gross domestic product) ratio.[8] This is tantamount to a person who works on 100 percent commission deciding to purchase products from themselves in an attempt to secure a large paycheck.

He relentlessly endorses that any kind of deficit spending is beneficial during a recession—"even if you paid people to dig ditches and refill them." This statement encapsulates the Keynesian ideology and exposes how absolutely reckless and profligate they encourage government spending to be. I recently heard Paul Krugman on CNN not only support this ridiculous statement, but outdo it by indicating that *"If we discovered that space aliens were planning to attack, and we needed a massive buildup to counter the space alien threat, and really inflation and budget deficits took secondary place to that, this slump would be over in 18 months."*[9]

Apparently, Mr. Krugman has so little faith in the economy's ability to rebuild itself he has resorted to proposing a faux "Space Alien Attack" stimulus plan. Mr. Krugman is held in exalted esteem in Keynesian circles of thought, and the best way he sees to stimulate the economy is to partake in a fabricated attack of space aliens in order to garner completely reckless spending.

It is fairly clear that his "Space Alien Attack" stimulus plan is futile at best and dangerous at worst, in its attempt to "End This Depression Now!" However, I would like to challenge Mr. Krugman on his "Ditch Digging and Filling Recovery Package" versus my "Free Market—Let Deflation Take Its Course Recovery Package" (that I will abbreviate as *Pentonomics*) and see which plan can "End This Depression Now!" Think of this as an economic reality game show.

Here are the rules: We are going to apply both recovery plans to the real estate bubble crisis starting in September 2008, after the collapse of Lehman, and see who can "End This Depression Now!"

I am going to allow Mr. Krugman to retain all the government managing tools—or the "acronyms"—TARP (Troubled Asset Relief Program), TALF (Term Asset-Backed Securities Loan Facility), all the QEs, even Operation Twist (even though it's not an acronym—I'll let him have it—see what a nice guy I am). Since Krugman and his fellow Keynesians are perpetually whining that the reason the "American Recovery and Reinvestment Act" failed was that it was too small, I am going to give Paul what not even Nancy (food stamps are a great stimulus) Pelosi would give him—$2 trillion dollars in deficit spending to get his "Ditch Digging and Filling Recovery Package" up and running.

I am not going to take any kind of stimulus for my "Pentonomics: Free Market—Deflation Plan". No bailout, no acronyms, no "American Recovery and Reinvestment Act"—nothing. We are going to apply both our strategies on today's great recession and see who can "End This Depression Now!" Is everyone clear on the game rules? Good, let's start.

On your mark . . .

Get set . . .

GO!

This is me applying Pentonomics to the economy after the real estate bubble burst—fade in to me doing nothing . . . spinning my thumbs, looking around . . . *bring in some music*—the "Girl from Ipanema" is playing softly in the background. Time lapses . . . OK, six months has passed—how am I doing?

Right now, not so well—the economy, as you can imagine, is going through a free fall. Home prices have fallen 50 percent, unemployment is 30 percent, a lot of banks and businesses have gone out of business, and there are bankruptcies. I didn't promise this was going to be painless. I hope you didn't put any money on this. If you did—don't worry, I'm optimistic! Let's see how Paul is doing. . . .

Paul charges out of the starting gate; sweat streaming down his forehead, he races with his $2 trillion clenched firmly in his fists, and he barely goes a city block before—ouch! He runs right into every member of Congress charging right at him. Ouch . . . ouch . . . this is getting hard to watch.

Now he's back up on his feet and waiting for Congress to come out of committee. So while Congress decides how to allocate his $2 trillion, Paul is also sitting around twirling his thumbs; he just has a more pensive look on his face. Again, I will concede to him the advantage and allow for a two-year time lapse.

How is the "Ditch Digging and Filling Recovery Package" doing two years later?

After grueling deliberations, the "Ditch Digging and Filling Recovery Package" was rolled out just where we would assume it would be—in the swing states.

The first problem with government spending is that decisions are made based on politics and not best business practices. Entertaining this scenario, one would assume that if the private sector were to create a company to dig and fill, they would place this company in the farm belt, where you have open land, manageable soil, and a labor force that is skilled in digging and filling. However, government makes decisions for political purposes, so you have digging and filling facilities in the Rocky Mountains of Colorado or the suburbs of Ohio.

We travel with Paul for inspection of the ditch digging and filling facility located just outside of Cincinnati, Ohio. This facility has been employing 500 ditch diggers and fillers for almost 18 months, and even though it is a completely unproductive job, the employees enjoy a "living wage" of $80,000, plus full benefits. It is clear that the 500 employees at the Cincinnati Digging and Filling Facility are living well. In fact, houses are being built in the area as well as businesses to service the facility—grocery stores, barber shops, restaurants, and, of course, if you are going to spend your days digging a ditch today that you are going to fill up tomorrow, you are going to want to have a couple beers at night—so there are bars and liquor stores.

I am allowing Krugman an optimistic albeit improbable scenario. The reality is that businesspeople are acutely aware when short-term stimulus enters the market place. Instead of building new facilities, they most often opt to fill the temporary demand with overtime from existing employees.

Exiting his car and stepping on the ground of the Cincinnati Digging and Filling Facility, emotion overcomes Mr. Krugman, tears well up in his eyes, and as he hugs his picture of John Maynard Keynes with one hand, he raises the other in victory and proclaims—"Utopia—the Spending Multiplier at work—what a beautiful sight to behold—not only did I beat Pento in his stupid game, I saved the economy and I am bound to win the Nobel Prize once again! I wonder if there will be enough room on my mantel if I remove the hammer and sickle."

Uhh . . . Paul . . . Mr. Krugman—not so fast. Don't take that victory lap just yet. You see, you only had enough money to keep this facility operating for 18 months. Remember, you said after 18 months the "slump would be over." This facility is set to close down tomorrow, and your entire Keynesian ditch digging and filling coupled with the spending multiplier utopia is set to close down with it.

You spent $2 trillion and you built nothing; sure, you got some short-term consumption, but that's going to immediately dissipate when the plant closes down. You failed to create anything of value that the free market wants, so the demand you created is ephemeral.

Government spending must increase the economy's productivity and standard of living better than what the private sector is capable of doing. Since that is impossible to accomplish, government spending does not in the long term increase economic growth. Government spending steals money from the private sector that would have deployed that capital to better use. All you will have achieved is to create rising inflation, a weakening currency, and an intractable increase in the debt-to-GDP ratio.

Krugman has a stunned look on his face, and one can see the hamster spinning in the wheel of his brain. We are going to give him some time to ruminate on these revelations and see how I am faring.

When we last left the "Pentonomics: Free Market—Deflation Plan," the economy was in free fall, deflation had set in, unemployment was ranging around 30 percent, housing prices had dropped 50 percent. So how are we looking two years later?

Wow!—Remarkably well! You see, after the initial painful market free fall, something amazing happened—the market bottomed, and through the rubble the free market availed and capitalism rebuilt itself.

The 50 percent drop in housing prices was steep, but they bottomed eight months later. People who couldn't afford their houses in the first place were removed from the market; the steep drop in housing prices quickly drove out the weak players, and stronger players emerged. Once the homes transferred into stronger hands, the housing market started to accelerate, with stronger players rushing in before housing prices increased.

Since labor and capital was allowed to move freely, the job market also rebounded. The depression exposed weak business models, but the recovery gave way to new and more viable businesses.

You may concede that I have effectively laid out a faster recovery, but maybe you are thinking that this plan is too painful. It's too difficult to imagine the ruin that we will encounter—maybe Krugman has a more painless remedy.

A popular misconception about Keynesian philosophy is that it allows an economy to heal without experiencing pain. The truth is that additional people ultimately get hurt. Taking my example of the economy experiencing a massive deleveraging—the people who get hurt are the same people who are in the process of foreclosure now. They were most likely the same people who shouldn't have owned their homes in the first place. So while they are living in their houses stalling foreclosure procedures, their homes fall into disrepair, bringing down the market value of the homes on the block and inhibiting a market bottom. This harms the homeowners who haven't overextended themselves. Bailing out those who are the guiltiest creates a moral hazard by punishing success and rewarding failure.

Over the past 30 years, we have endured a political philosophy that has engendered the belief that the American dream of home ownership was something that could be given, and not something that has to be earned. Generations before us viewed home ownership as an achievement that came as a result of discipline and hard work. Sacrifices were made; things were given up in lieu of securing enough money to attain the 20 percent down payment that was traditionally needed to buy a home. That down payment represented the homeowner's hard work and solidified a commitment to the house that they were unlikely to walk away from.

My great grandfather, Francesco Locascio, left his family and all his meager possessions to find a better life in this country. He took a boat from Italy at the turn of the century in search of the American Dream. He labored tirelessly building the New York City subway system in hopes that his children would have a better life and own a home someday. He died at 45 years old from pneumonia and never saw any of his dreams come to fruition. However, he would be happy to know that his grandson (my father Frank Pento) graduated magna cum laude from college and built his dream house with the money earned from his electrical engineering degree. Life is seldom fair, and there is nothing for free. The American Dream isn't easily achieved, and the government shouldn't guarantee happiness—only the freedom of its pursuit.

Don't confuse my contempt for the imbeciles running the Federal Reserve and Washington with my confidence in the American people. I have tremendous confidence in the American worker, the entrepreneur, the businessman to stare into the abyss and prevail. I view Americans as the builders, the inventors, the creators, and the dreamers—not the guys who dig ditches and fill them back up. Americans are better than that. I had faith in my recovery plan because I have faith in Americans' ability to overcome obstacles and persevere. Paul Krugman's plan failed because he had no faith in the American people; he only has faith in governments' ability to drive consumption by creating menial jobs or staging fake alien attacks. What he doesn't understand is that government can be only as strong as its people because that's where the state derives all of its power.

Apparently, Mr. Krugman has not yet conceded defeat. He has gotten word from the White House that his "Ditch Digging and Filling Recovery Package" has obtained a six-month extension.

This is not surprising; once businesses start to rely on subsidies from government to stay afloat, politicians find it impossible to curtail this spending. The private sector spends its own money, but the government spends our money. Therefore, two distinctly different motivations exist. The private sector wants to create only jobs that are economically viable, and the government focuses on creating jobs that fulfill political agendas.

I am going to amuse Mr. Krugman and see how his dig-and-fill economy will work out. Since this new industry is incapable of sustaining itself, it is going to have to rely on 100 percent government subsidies. Mr. Krugman has no problem obtaining funding for his new industry by implementing taxes on the productive economy. He is actually unapologetic about it. Mr. Krugman perceives his workforce as contributors to the economy because they are consumers, they are receiving a paycheck and spending it—so to Mr. Krugman, they are being productive by driving demand. Mr. Krugman decides to implement a tax on the productive economy in order to redistribute money to his digging and filling and spending workforce. Initially, these taxes may be insignificant, but over time they are onerous—so onerous, in fact, that businesses start fleeing the United States in favor of more favorable tax treatment somewhere else. Or the tax rate becomes so high that it destroys the incentive to innovate and take risks. Hence, the entire economy is hurt . . . even the government sector.

Government should, in most cases, spend only what it has raised in taxes—although that is not what Krugman believes. However, he neglects to account for the fact that the redistribution, or theft, of the private sector's money would have been deployed in a more productive and economically viable manner.

Now in Krugman's ditch digging and filling economy we are importing everything, we have no viable businesses left to tax. But Krugman still won't concede, he has one more trick up his sleeve—he previously worked for Ben Bernanke at Princeton—he can have the government borrow money and have Ben counterfeit money to support his ditch diggers and fillers so they can consume us back to prosperity. After the Fed becomes the only buyer of the debt, the U.S. dollar and bond market are depreciating faster than a box of Linsanity T-shirts sitting at a Modell's warehouse.

Let me put Mr. Krugman out of his misery: There is no way out—an economy cannot rely on consumption, it has to produce something first; it has to make something that the market demands. Demand does not drive an economy, production does.

In the movie *Field of Dreams*, Kevin Costner heard a voice that led him to build a baseball field and realize his dream; the voice said, "If you build it, they will come." For the past two centuries, American entrepreneurs have been hearing that same voice. Thomas Edison, Henry Ford, Walt Disney, Bill Gates, and Steve Jobs, just to name a few—they aren't men who made products to meet consumer demand; they were men who created consumer demand with the products they made. They are the geniuses of American ingenuity that leveraged the free market system and made America the most prosperous nation on earth. That genius still exists—we just have to get the government to stop counterfeiting and spending and allow the free market to prevail.

Paying people to dig ditches and then refill them sounds ridiculous. So does starting a war with pretend aliens. But, sadly, this is commonplace with government spending. The solar company Solyndra was a recipient of government stimulus funds and built solar panels that they subsequently disposed of—that sounds a lot like digging a ditch and filling it to me. If you want further proof, take a look at our defense budget. The U.S. government is notorious for continuing to build obsolete weapons in order to forestall closing a plant. Take a trip on Amtrak, a business model that the free market rejected and exists on perpetual government subsidies.

Currently, Democrats in Washington are touting their recent success in saving the beleaguered automobile company General Motors. The 2009 bailout confirms when the U.S. government saddles their citizens with an additional $50 billion dollar debt and rescinds rules of bankruptcy; an inadequate business model such as GM can emerge successful, at least in the short run.

According to the Heritage Foundation, for each active worker at GM there were 3.8 retirees or dependents in 2006.[10] Oppressive legacy costs rendered GM unable to survive the severe 2008 downturn as a viable going concern. After much debate, they were compelled into a government-managed Chapter 11 bankruptcy. A government engineered bankruptcy proceeding driven by politics that placed the United Auto Workers (UAW), a Democrat apparatchik, ahead of suppliers, dealers, and investors that would have fared better under a more normalized bankruptcy process.

On November 24, 2008, Congressman Ron Paul (R-TX) wrote:

> In bailing out failing companies, they are confiscating money from productive members of the economy and giving it to failing ones. By sustaining companies with obsolete or unsustainable business models, the government prevents their resources from being liquidated and made available to other companies that can put them to better, more productive use. An essential element of a healthy free market is that both success and failure must be permitted to happen when they are earned. But, instead, with a bailout, the rewards are reversed—the proceeds from successful entities are given to failing ones. How this is supposed to be good for our economy is beyond me. . . . It won't work. It can't work. . . . It is obvious to most Americans that we need to reject corporate cronyism, and allow the natural regulations and incentives of the free market to pick the winners and losers in our economy, not the whims of bureaucrats and politicians.[11]

Fruitless government spending engendered to entice demand, and crony capitalism that seeks to subsidize obsolete or unsustainable business models, has allowed us to incur $16 trillion dollars in debt. This failed Keynesian demand model coupled with the Fed's easy-money policies are the driving force behind the bubble in the bond market.

The federal government is spending money at an unsustainable rate. In doing so, they are confiscating money from the free market and accumulating debt that will never be able to be paid. Government spending will not alleviate the problem of government spending. Furthermore, the Federal Reserve's reckless easy-money policies are propagating this spending and allowing the government to elude the true effects of their destructive behavior. But interest rates can't stay low forever, and when they start to rise, Ben Bernanke will see that he has no way out.

"I'm Not Addicted to Easy Money . . . and I Can Stop at Anytime"

The government, under the misguided stewardship of Keynesian philosophy, has saturated themselves in reckless deficits and debts under the illogical premise that they can consume their way to prosperity. So if Keynesian dogma has gotten us fat, and the Fed has gotten us drunk on easy money, it's easy to see why this economy is having a hard time moving.

Ironically, out of the Great Depression we got a treatment program called Alcoholics Anonymous (AA). I say ironically because Ben Bernanke is a self-professed student of the Great Depression. We saw in Chapter 2 that he failed to discover from his studies that it was the Fed's easy money that engendered the boom that created the depression in the first place. But one can wonder if he has given any erudition to AA and its 12 steps. Let's help him out.

Step 1 is *admitting you cannot control your addiction and compulsion*. In his famed *60 Minutes* interview, Bernanke said, "One myth that's out there is that what we're doing is printing money. We're not printing money. . . . What we're doing is lowering interest rates by buying Treasury securities."[12] With QE the Fed is buying Treasury securities by debiting bank reserves at the Federal Reserve with electronic funds. Bernanke is parsing his words; he isn't taking out the actual printing press to counterfeit money. He is electronically counterfeiting money by debiting banks accounts. This is like an alcoholic saying that he is not drinking, he has a vodka drip appendaged to his arm that allows for steady drips of alcohol to ruminate throughout his body, but his mouth is dry—he is in fact not taking a drink. . . . So he doesn't have a drinking problem. It is clear that Banana Ben is not willing to admit he has a problem—the prerequisite for overcoming your addiction. Ben has failed the test, but just for the fun, let's run through some of the other steps.

Step 2 is *recognizing a higher power can give you strength.* For Ben, that higher power would be the gold standard—the God-given natural central bank that has held the test of time. When the market anticipates that Ben will acquiesce to another round of counterfeiting, gold begins a steep climb up. Unfortunately, Ben fails to read this as the market's lack of confidence in the ephemeral nature of his easy-money dollar. Ben has been quoted as saying, "I don't fully understand movements in the gold price."[13]

The next two steps will have Ben *examining past errors* and *seeking redemption*—in Ben's case, this will be a laborious endeavor. We can muse that Ben Bernanke will be a little like Earl in the TV show *My Name Is Earl*, with all his past errors scribbled on a piece of paper. He has a lot of people to apologize to; for all his past blunders—he has more than a few. If Ben does take the economy on that trip to the Betty Ford Center, I have put together a highlight reel of his past digressions to help him in his effort to wean the economy off its easy-money addiction:

We've never had a decline in house prices on a nationwide basis. So, what I think is more likely is that house prices will slow, maybe stabilize, might slow consumption spending a bit. I don't think it's gonna drive the economy too far from its full employment path, though. (July 2005)[14]

House prices have risen by nearly 25 percent over the past two years. Although speculative activity has increased in some areas, at a national level these price increases largely reflect strong economic fundamentals. (October 2005)[15]

With respect to their safety, derivatives, for the most part, are traded among very sophisticated financial institutions and individuals who have considerable incentive to understand them and to use them properly. (November 2005)[16]

Housing markets are cooling a bit. Our expectation is that the decline in activity or the slowing in activity will be moderate, that house prices will probably continue to rise. (Feb 2006)[17]

All that said, given the fundamental factors in place that should support the demand for housing, we believe the effect of the troubles in the subprime sector on the broader housing market will likely be limited, and we do not expect significant spillovers from the subprime market to the rest of the economy or to the financial system. The vast majority of mortgages, including even subprime mortgages, continue to perform well. Past gains in house prices have left most homeowners with significant amounts of home equity, and growth in jobs and incomes should help keep the financial obligations of most households manageable. (May 2007)[18]

The Federal Reserve is not currently forecasting a recession. (Jan 2008)[19]

They will make it through the storm (Jan 2008—referring to Fannie Mae and Freddie Mac two months before they were nationalized).[20]

The risk that the economy has entered a substantial downturn appears to have diminished over the past month or so. (June 2008)[21]

The financial crisis appears to be mostly behind us, and the economy seems to have stabilized and is expanding again. (Aug 2010)[22]

Of course, nobody is perfect, and I've made some errors of my own in judging markets during my 20+ years in this business. Therefore, since no individual is perfect, neither I nor any one individual should have the power to set the most important price in an economy, which is the cost of money. What Machiavellian hubris! How can one person or even a small group of people claim to have the omniscience to deserve monopoly power over the level of interest rates?

But despite his lofty position as chairman of the Federal Reserve and his superpower to create the world's currency out of thin air, it seems that Ben isn't at all a very good economic prognosticator. He appears constantly blindsided by economic events that he himself created and that are right in front of him. In fact, he admitted to this when he said, "I wish I'd been omniscient and seen the crisis coming."[23] Yes, it is clear that Mr. Bernanke is not Nostradamus, but it's worse than that—he fails in not only being able to amply analyze data, but also to recognize his role in enabling these events. He is like the hapless cartoon character

Mr. Magoo, who has only enough sight to be completely dangerous. He meanders around town creating all sorts of chaos brought about by his lack of vision and clear misinterpretation of events, compounded by his stubborn refusal to admit the problem. It is clear that Bernanke is just as blind to the bubble he is facilitating in the bond market today, as he was to the bubble he helped perpetuate in the housing market.

Instead of acknowledging his complete inability to envisage economic events he has helped to engender, he speaks with foolish confidence of his ability to curtail the coming economic cataclysm. In his 2010 op-ed in the *Washington Post*, Bernanke boasts, "We have made all necessary preparations, and we are confident that we have the tools to unwind these policies at the appropriate time."[24] What gives Bernanke the hubris to believe that he can easily unwind his policies or that he knows when the appropriate time is? By his own admission, he is not all-knowing. It is clear that Ben is naive about where his policies are taking us.

The chairman of the Federal Reserve has deluded himself into thinking that when the time comes, he will be able to shrink the size of the Fed's balance sheet and reduce the monetary base with both ease and impunity. He also has deluded himself into thinking inflation will be easily contained.

The Fed believes low interest rates should not be the result of a high savings rate, but instead can exist by decree, a conviction that has directly led consumers to believe their spending can outstrip disposable income.

The result of such thinking has been a rise in household debt from 47 percent of GDP in 1980[25] to 85% of total output in Q2 2012.[26] As a result of this ever-increasing burden, the Fed has been forced into a series of lower lows and lower highs on its benchmark lending rate. Keeping rates low is an attempt to make debt service levels manageable and the consumer afloat. The problem is that this endless pursuit of unnaturally low rates has so altered the Fed's balance sheet that Mr. Bernanke will be hard-pressed to substantially raise rates to combat inflation once consumer and wholesale prices begin to significantly increase. Remember, an increase in the Fed's balance sheet implies an easy monetary stance. In order to rein in easy money, the Fed needs to reduce its balance sheet—but to whom are they going to sell and at what price?

Banana Ben has grown the monetary base from just $842 billion in August 2008 to a record high of $2,929 billion as of January 2013.[27]

But it's not only the size of the balance sheet that is so daunting; it's the makeup that's becoming truly scary.

Historically speaking, the composition of the Fed's balance sheet has been mostly Treasuries. And the Federal Open Market Committee would typically raise rates by selling Treasuries from its balance sheet into the market to soak up excess liquidity.

The Fed uses one of its superpowers called open market operations to control the Federal Funds rate, the rate at which large commercial banks lend cash to each other overnight to fulfill their reserve requirements to the Fed. Through the fractional reserve banking system (discussed in Chapter 1), the commercial bank is required to deposit a fraction of the money you deposit on loan with the Fed. It injects money into the bank by buying securities from them. Primary dealers are actually obligated to sell and to buy assets from the Fed. The Fed withdraws money by selling securities to commercial banks and receiving money as payment, thereby reducing reserves and removing credit from the system.

Historically, the Fed's open market operations have been confined to U.S. Treasuries. But utilizing a temporary additional power they gave themselves in August 1999, Fed officials now have the authority to not only purchase freely from commercial banks, but also purchase Ginnie Mae–, Freddie Mac–, and Fannie Mae–issued mortgage-backed securities (MBSs).[28] Those government-sponsored enterprises (GSEs) that the government had to take over because they made so many non-performing loans . . . well, guess what—those loans are now partially collateralizing your U.S. dollar.

So, because of the Fed's prior decision to purchase up to $1 trillion in MBSs and other unorthodox holdings, coupled with adding $85 billion more MBSs and Treasuries each month, without indication of when it will all stop, it will—supposedly someday—not only be selling highly liquid U.S. debt to drain reserves from banks. It will also be unwinding highly distressed MBSs and packaged loans of insurance corporation AIG. Not to mention the fact the Fed would have to break its promise of being a "hold-to-maturity investor" of such assets.

Moreover, not only are the new assets on the Fed's balance sheet less liquid, but the durations of the loans have been extended. The TALF was set up by the Fed during the crisis to spur consumer credit lending.

Under TALF, the Fed lent $1 trillion to banks and hedge funds at nearly interest-free rates—leaving the U.S. taxpayer on the hook for any losses. Because the money came from the Fed and not the Treasury, there was no congressional oversight of how the funds were disbursed. An act of Congress eventually forced the Fed to open its books. If you thought the federal government spent money in a reckless and inefficient manner, you should see how Ben negligently gave your dollars not only to banks and hedge funds, but also to foreign countries like Mexico, Bahrain, and Japanese car companies.[29] Money was lent at zero percent, making it easy for banks and hedge funds to buy U.S. Treasuries at 3 percent and make a quick profit. Not only did this program fail in its attempt to spur on consumer credit (we will see why in a minute), it also put both the U.S. taxpayer and the Fed in a precarious position going forward.

Unfortunately, when Ben finally decides it's time to fight inflation, the Fed will find it much more difficult to reverse course. The quality *and duration* of its balance sheet has deteriorated. Think about the Fed's "Operation Twist." The unwise goal of this program is to sell hundreds of billions of dollars in shorter-term debt to purchase mid- and long-term debt. Bonds that mature in 6 to 30 years have much greater price fluctuations than debt maturing in 3 years or less.

And because of the extraordinary and unprecedented (some would say illegal) measures Mr. Bernanke has implemented, only $1,665 trillion of the almost $3 trillion balance sheet is composed of U.S. Treasury debt.[30]

Our entire economy has become more addicted than ever to low interest rates. For example, because bank assets will now be collecting income at record low rates, when and if the Fed tries to raise rates, it will only be able to do so on the margin. If Bernanke raises rates substantially to fight inflation, banks will be paying out more on deposits than they collect on their income streams. Think about it—right now if your house isn't completely under water and you haven't destroyed your credit rating, you have refinanced your mortgage at a rate most likely lower than 4 percent. The problem is that banks borrow short and lend long. Assuming interest on deposits returns to a normalized rate of closer to 5 percent, banks will be paying their depositors more than the income they receive from those loans. Couple that with their already distressed balances sheets and look out!

Additionally, not only do the consumers need low rates to keep their financial obligation ratio low, but the federal government also needs low rates to ensure interest rates on the skyrocketing national debt can be serviced. Our projected $1.2 trillion annual deficits each year forever more, stems from the belief that the government must borrow more as the consumer begins to deleverage. In fact, both the consumer and the government need to deleverage for total debt relief to occur, or else we're just shuffling debts around and avoiding a healthy deleveraging entirely.

In order to have viable and sustainable growth, total debt levels must decrease, savings must increase, and interest rates must rise. But that would require an extended period of negative GDP growth—a completely untenable position for politicians of all stripes. Ben Bernanke would like you to believe that inflation will be quiescent and he can vanquish it if it ever becomes a problem. He failed to foresee the housing crisis. What makes you think this time he will get it right?

No Way Out—Starring Ben Bernanke . . .

When Bernanke's economy does ultimately land at the gates of celebrity rehab, it will detox along with fellow stars that also have seen better days. Ben may run into Sean Young, a celebrity rehab regular who starred with Kevin Costner in the 1987 hit movie *No Way Out*. In fact, that would be an appropriate movie title for the disaster that is mounting at the Fed today. I'm sure Ben and his Fed cohorts have been throwing movie titles around ever since the famed *Too Big to Fail* debuted on HBO. I can think of a few titles myself—*Reckless Endangerment, Absolute Power, Dangerous Minds, Apocalypse Now*—are all apropos for the cataclysm Bernanke is crafting in the economy. We can consider a comedy title such as *Dumb and Dumber* starring Ben and his predecessor Alan Greenspan as they troll around town with their suitcase of counterfeited money creating bubbles wherever they go while remaining completely oblivious to them. And, finally, we can imagine Ben as a poor man's James Bond in the action thriller—*License to Kill—The Economy*. I am sure that when they are not busy destroying the purchasing power of your dollar, Ben and his cohorts spar over who will "play them" in the next movie centered on the bubble in the bond market.

No Way Out is in actuality the most appropriate title for Ben's next movie—because, as we shall see, there is no viable exit strategy for the Fed. Instead of allowing the economy to go through the natural deleveraging process, the Fed has flooded the economy with cash and cemented our addiction to zero percent interest rates—every day that passes is another day closer to the reality that Ben has "No Way Out." Although Bernanke is correct that the Fed has the mechanical ability to stop draining its balance sheet, he falls miles short of understanding the economy's addiction to inflation and its consequences.

The problem with the addiction to money printing is that once a central bank starts, it can't stop without dire, albeit in the long-term healthy, economic consequences. And the longer an economy stays addicted to inflation, the harder the eventual debt deflation will become. As a result, the Federal Reserve is walking the economy on a very thin tightrope between inflation and deflation.

Once they finally step away from expanding the money supply, deflation rapidly takes hold. However, it then takes an ever-increasing amount of new money creation to pull the economy away from falling asset prices.

Since the summer of 2006, starting with an appearance I had on CNBC's Kudlow program, I have been making this case. I said that inflation would eventually prevail, but the economy faces massive deflationary forces that are based on deleveraging. The Fed would fight the deleveraging and deflation with a massive increase in its balance sheet. The Fed cannot control inflation directly because it is a function of the monetary base size and accompanying interest rate level—that the Fed controls directly—and banks' willingness to lend in order to satisfy the consumers demand for money. The Fed can't directly control the money supply and therefore has an impossibly difficult time hitting a specific inflation target.

When an economy is saturated in debt, the natural state of equilibrium between inflation and deflation is a general condition of stagflation, with deflation in the area of the economy that was previously in a bubble.

Let's take a look at the charts in Figure 3.1 to see how this works.

This is the monetary base—the amount of money in the economy plus bank reserves.

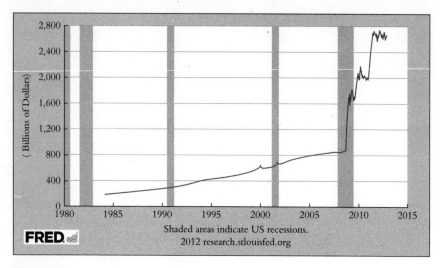

Figure 3.1   St. Louis Adjusted Monetary Base
SOURCE: Federal Reserve Bank of St. Louis.

We see a huge increase in this base when the Fed started their counterfeiting campaign. Bernanke can be vague and parse his words, but this chart tells the true story. Remember, the Fed, through its open market operations, can expand or contract this money supply, but not without risk.

The Federal Reserve prints dollars, or as Ben would prefer to say, electronically debits money into or withdraws it from, the economy, through open market transactions (i.e., the buying and selling of government bonds and now garbage MBSs). The Fed can also influence banking activities by manipulating interest rates and changing bank reserve requirements (how much money banks must keep on hand instead of loaning out to borrowers). We see the consequences of all Ben's superpowers in this chart.

The monetary base is the gas that drives an economy, as we learned in Chapter 2—often off of a cliff. An increase in the monetary base (MB) through the magic money multiplier via the fractional reserve private banking system can result in a much larger increase in bank money (M1, MZM, and M2). An increase of 1 billion currency units in the monetary

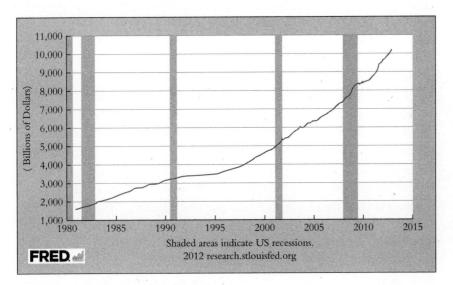

Figure 3.2 M2 Money Stock (M2)
SOURCE: Board of Governors of the Federal Reserve System.

base will allow (and often be correlated to) an increase of 10 billion units of "bank money" (see Figure 3.2).

Here's the dilemma the Fed has gotten itself into. Before the recession began in 2007, the ratio between M2 and the monetary base was about 10:1. Meaning that for every 1 dollar increase in base money, we have 10 dollars in M2 (notes and coins in circulation, demand deposits, savings deposits, and time deposits under $100k).

If the economy were to ever heal and the historical ratio of M2 to the monetary base were to return, M2 would explode upward toward $27 trillion dollars, from its $10 trillion today. The Fed couldn't allow the money supply to reach that level, so it would have to sell its assets—possibly in quick order—and send rates soaring even higher to fight inflation. Remember, rates would already be rising because of the inflation associated with the booming money supply and rising aggregate prices. And think of all the momentum investors following the Fed—what will happen when they are lured to follow the Fed's lead in the opposite direction. The Fed could actually be the catalyst that sets the bond bomb off. In this scenario, rates would soar and debt service costs would skyrocket and render the country insolvent. The United States cannot adequately service its debt as rates approach and then surpass their historical average (7 percent on the 10-year note). We will go much deeper into this crucial point in Chapter 5.

The increase of money in the banking system is equivalent to an artificial injection of credit—but who is getting this credit?

According to a recent *Wall Street Journal* article, ". . . banks remain reluctant to lend to households with even a hint of financial problems"[31]—and who would blame them? Government bureaucrats hound banks to make new loans and then subject them to congressional hearings if they make imprudent ones. Furthermore, "Fannie Mae and Freddie Mac, government-backed mortgage finance firms, tightened their standards and are returning any troubled mortgages."[32]

Federal debt has been accelerating as consumers attempt to rein in their debt. Unfortunately, Ben was anticipating that this new money would be engaged by the consumer, allowing them to perpetuate the Keynesian reverie of consumption. But, as you can see from the chart in Figure 3.3, the consumer is broke and still saturated with debt. Money is going to the federal government, creating a bubble in the Treasury market, and the residual is just sitting there like a ticking time bomb waiting to explode into runaway inflation.

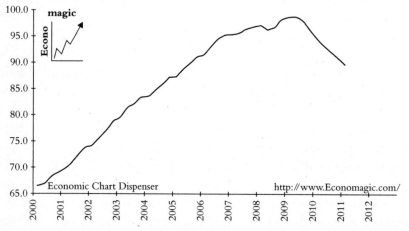

Figure 3.3 Housed Sector Debt as a Percentage of GDP

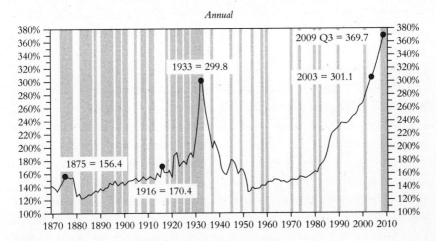

Annual

Figure 3.4 Total U.S. Debt as a Percentage of GDP
SOURCES: Bureau of Economic Analysis, Federal Reserve. Census Bureau: Historical Statistics of the United States Colonial Times to 1970. Through Q3 2009.

In Figure 3.4 we see that federal debt as a percentage of GDP has been rapidly accelerating since 1980—and has exploded in the last few years. So, while Ben has been counterfeiting in a futile attempt to get the consumer to borrow and spend, the federal government has been that obnoxious guy at a dinner party who doesn't let anyone get a word in, and soaking up the new money via deficit spending. The government is seen as the best creditor. Therefore, capital is squandered, feeding government fat cats at the table, and the real economy feeds off the crumbs. However, not too long ago, $150 billion deficits were a yearly figure; now they are a monthly figure. With Bernanke's easy money and low interest rates, the federal deficit has ballooned past a record $16 trillion dollars—that's 700 percent of the federal government's entire annual revenue! And our annual deficit is over 50 percent of federal revenue. Just imagine if your annual salary was 100k and you owed the bank a whopping 700k. Then go tell your banker that you are adding 50k each year—half of your entire salary—to your accumulated level of debt.

After your bankers recovered from their comas, they would summarily cut up your credit cards and remove all existing lines of outstanding credit. Our gross debt is over $16 trillion and that is supported by just $2.3 trillion of revenue. And we are adding well over a trillion dollars each year to the gross debt. Our international creditors will soon have no choice but to cut up our credit cards, which will send interest rates skyrocketing higher.

American's aren't feeling the full effect of these budget deficits yet because of the easy-money drip Bernanke has this economy riding. And our foreign creditors still mistakenly believe the United States has the tax base to pay off the debt. Buy when those rates go up—watch out!

Every addict has an enabler—we bear witness to this far too often in well-publicized celebrity addictions, and the economy is no exception. We will have to assume that when the economy does finally go to rehab and lies on the couch in deep therapy with celebrity addiction therapist Dr. Drew Pinsky, it will surely claim Ben Bernanke as its enabler. And we will see, like in so many high-profile cases, that Ben Bernanke is in fact the Howard K. Stern to the economy's Anna Nicole Smith, enabling the economy to engage in the reckless behavior of deficit spending.

The Thirty-Year Party in the Bond Market

As we discussed, the 1970s ushered in a decade of reckless monetary policy and incompetent government intervention and price controls that placed the economy in the throes of stagflation—high inflation and little to no growth. In the fall of 1979, Paul Volcker took the reins as chairman of the Federal Reserve. Volcker embraced his newly claimed title by raising the discount rate a full percentage point and put the markets on notice that killing inflation was his number one priority.

As you can imagine, interest rates soared. While the three-month Treasury bill was climbing from 8 percent in September 1979 to 12.5 percent by year-end,[33] long-term rates rose as well—the 10-year went from 9.1 percent in January 1979 to 12.64 percent by January 1980. Into early 1980 interest rates across the board continued to rise, and the economy tipped into recession. The inflation rate for the first quarter of 1980, as measured by the consumer price index (CPI), was 14.6 percent.[34]

This was awful news for the beleaguered incumbent Jimmy Carter, who subsequently lost in his reelection bid to Ronald Reagan. Volcker

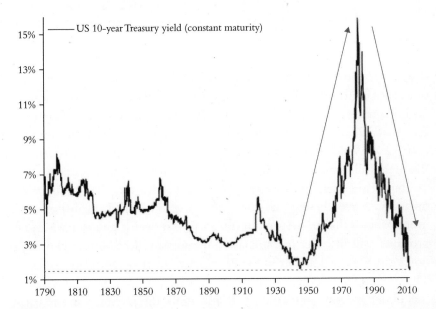

Figure 3.5 U.S. 10-Year Treasury Yield
SOURCE: © Global Financial Data.

did what few in his position had the strength to do—he raised rates and broke the back of inflation. By the middle of 1981, it was running at a 9.7 percent clip and for the year it was below 9 percent. Volcker was winning.

After Reagan won the election that November, Volcker continued to tighten interest rates. The federal funds rate, which had averaged 11.2 percent in 1979, peaked at near 20 percent in June 1981. The prime rate rose to 21.5 percent in 1981 and the 10-year was on its way to 15.84 percent.[35]

Reagan also understood the importance of ending the inflation threat and was willing to endure a deep recession to accomplish this. While Reagan was known to ask the question, "Why do we need the Federal Reserve at all?" he continued to allow Volcker to operate with little interference.[36]

In July 1981, the nation was in a deep and ugly recession. However, Reagan and Volcker didn't waver. They insisted that the nation "stay the course" and that it would emerge healthier and more prosperous in the end—and it did!

Paul Volcker remained convinced that a firm control of the money supply was the key to a sound economy. That's one of three pillars of a strong economy, the other two being low taxes and low interest rates that occur naturally from low inflation and high savings, not artificially produced by the central bank. He was right—inflation headed lower—a CPI that registered 13.3 percent for 1979 was to plummet to 3.8 percent for all of 1982.[37] The hard medicine had been taken, and through the courage of Volcker and Reagan, the economy was back on track and the great bull market in bonds, still in place today, was under way!

Now just imagine how we are to deal with our next battle with inflation. Never before has the Fed created so much high-powered money that is the rocket fuel for inflation. If it ever is unleashed—and it probably will in order to purchase our runaway debt—some Fed head down the road will be forced to raise rates in the manner of Mr. Volcker. The only problem is that the nation's debt is light years ahead of where it was under Reagan and Volcker. If you think the recession in the early 1980s was bad, think again. If Mr. Bernanke hangs around long enough, he will not only be able to call himself a student of the Great Depression but also get an opportunity to teach the class in real time.

We have engendered a 30-year bubble in bond prices—remember bond prices increase as rates decrease. Investors, seeking refuge in what they perceive as the safe haven of the U.S. Treasury, have been procuring U.S. debt despite record low rates. Interest rates have nowhere to go but up. Ben Bernanke has rendered our solvency as a nation dependent on the perpetual continuation of low interest rates. However, it is clear that Bernanke cannot keep rates low forever. Ben's misguided effort to counterfeit our way to prosperity coupled with the flawed Keynesian deficit spending model that our government too readily embraces, has led to record debts that will never be able to be repaid.

Sixteen trillion dollar Keynesian induced spending sprees and five-year easy-money drinking binges—like all good things—must at some point come to an end. And so, as we look at the 30-year party in the Treasury, we too see the revelry is near completion. Sure, partygoers have crowded the dance floor like never before. But if we open our eyes and look around, we can see the maître d' cuing the wait staff to start dismantling tables. And we come to the uncomfortable revelation that we are not too far away from the bartender announcing last call.

Notes

1. Murray N. Rothbard, *America's Great Depression* (Auburn, AL, Ludwig von Misses Institute, 2009).
2. Ibid., pages 4–9.
3. Ibid., pages 4–9.
4. Ibid., pages 4–9.
5. The Humane Society, 2012.
6. Joseph A. Schumpeter, *Capitalism, Socialism and Democracy* (New York: Harper and Row, 1950).
7. John M. Keynes, 1936 quote. The General Theory of Employment, Interest and Money, Create Space Independent Publishing Platform, November 15, 2011.
8. Paul R. Krugman, *End This Depression Now!* (New York: W.W. Norton, 2012).
9. Paul R. Krugman, *Fareed Zakaria GPS*, CNN, August 2011.
10. The Heritage Foundation, December 22, 2008.
11. Ron Paul, "The Bailout Surge," House of Representatives web site, http://Paul.house.gov, November 2008.
12. Ben Bernanke, *60 Minutes*, December 5, 2010.
13. Ben Bernanke, testimony on Capitol Hill, June 2010.
14. Ben Bernanke, interview on CNBC, July 2005.
15. Ben Bernanke, testimony before the Joint Economic Committee, Congress, October 2005.
16. Ben Bernanke, confirmation hearing before Senate Banking Committee, November 2005.
17. Ben Bernanke, House of Representatives hearing, February 2006.
18. Ben Bernanke, remarks before the Federal Reserve Board of Chicago, May 2007.
19. Ben Bernanke, response to a question after speech in Washington, DC, January 2008.
20. Ben Bernanke, testimony before House Financial Services Committee, January 2008.
21. Ben Bernanke, remarks before a banker's conference in Chatham, MA, June 2008.
22. Ben Bernanke, Southern Legislative Conference, August 2010.
23. Ben Bernanke, *60 Minutes*, 2010.
24. Ben Bernanke, *Washington Post*, op-ed, November 4, 2010.
25. Bureau of Economic Analysis, Federal Reserve Census Bureau. July 2012
26. Ibid.
27. Federal Reserve Bank of St. Louis. July 2012.
28. FederalReserve.gov. July 2012.

29. Mathew Taibbi, "The Real Housewives of Wall Street," *Rolling Stone Magazine*, April 12, 2011.
30. FederalReserve.gov. July 2012.
31. John Hilsenrath, "Fed Wrestles with How to Best Bridge U.S. Credit Divide," *Wall Street Journal*, June 19, 2012.
32. Ibid.
33. Brian Trumbore, "Paul Volcker part 2", Buyandhold.com, July 2012.
34. Ibid.
35. Ibid.
36. Ibid.
37. Ibid.

Chapter 4

Deflation Phobia and Inflation Philos

"By this means government may secretly and unobserved, confiscate the wealth of the people, and not one man in a million will detect the theft."

—*British Lord John Maynard Keynes on the Central Bank*

It is tradition that once a year after Americans partake in excessive amounts of turkey consumption, they converge to the mall to partake in excessive amounts of bargain consumption. This American tradition is termed *Black Friday*. Every year, we are reminded how savage American consumerism can be, as we ogle in horror at the Black Friday sales escapades. Black Friday is an idiom that retailers fashioned to indicate the arrival of the holiday season that hopefully carries them into profitability. The bargain hunting of Black Friday is just as much an American institution as Thanksgiving and apple pie.

So salient is the Fed's fear of deflation that it is curious why they don't push for Congress to outlaw Black Friday. Our central bank is petrified of falling prices. They would assume that the low prices disseminated from sharply discounted items would induce a consumption stoppage, a consumer strike of sorts. Instead of Americans trampling over each other to obtain merchandise at a lower cost, we would wait in hope and anticipation that prices would fall even more.

I can imagine we would peruse that 60-inch flat screen TV on Black Friday—wanting it, but mired in the possibility that the price of the TV could decline further. After all, prices for electronics tend to fall over time due to productivity enhancements, so why not wait? This quest for lower prices would leave us frozen, incapable of making the purchase. Day in and day out we lay pining for that TV, scouring newspaper circulars—confirming the price decline but again questioning if further discounts lie ahead. So there we sit in front of our 10-inch tube and trying to get the antenna in just the right place—paralyzed by our inability to make the purchase, consumed by our quest for lower prices. Time passes; major sporting events go by, and while we dream of how that big screen will enhance our viewing pleasure, we are transfixed by the possibility of further discounts and rendered unable to make the purchase. And so we wait, in frugal anticipation for the price to fall just a little more. While we are waiting, the entire economy falls to a standstill—our lack of consumerism is contagious. The entire economy would be held hostage in the awful throes of hyperdeflation—deferring our purchase in the hopes of shaving a few more dollars off the ticket price and living in absolute fear that prices will fall further. According to Fed-lore, once the deflationary monster comes, it is almost impossible to stave off.

So it must be assumed that after eating turkey, the men and women at the Federal Reserve fall into a tryptophan-induced coma and completely miss the coverage of Americans trampling over themselves in pursuit of deflated prices.

Of course, once the Black Friday sale ends, prices usually rise and shoppers are merely seeking to take advantage of those temporary bargains. And if there were an entrenched fear of protracted deflation among consumers, there could be an increased desire to defer some discretionary purchases. However, I will show in this chapter that inflation is not a better economic condition than deflation. In fact, it is the U.S. government's massive proclivity toward inflation that has caused the formation of the biggest bubble in global financial history.

In the following pages, I will put Keynesian Fed-lore like this to the test. In the previous chapter, Paul Krugman and I starred in the reality game show "End This Depression Now!" Watching Paul spend trillions of dollars an episode in a futile attempt to "end this depression now!" paired with my winning at the last minute by allowing the market to prevail was, as you can imagine, a huge ratings success. We were rumored to have nearly secured the front spot in the must-see Thursday night lineup, a spot held before by such heralded shows as *Cosby* and *Friends*. Unfortunately, network executives found the show's costs too prohibitive—unlike government, capitalism works on a for-profit model. Apparently, Paul cycling through a trillion dollars or more an episode creating nothing of value, followed by his whining incessantly that he would have been successful had the network allowed him to spend more money, failed to garner the support of the network hierarchy. I also heard through the rumor mill that the network was furious after being named in a lawsuit revolving around Paul's faux alien attack. That, I was told, was the last straw—the network cut their losses and canceled. It was getting a little redundant for me anyway—sitting there just spinning my thumbs—I am still trying to get the "Girl from Ipanema" out of my mind. For this chapter, I am running solo on my new series—a spin-off of the popular show on the Discovery channel called *Myth Busters*. My new show is called *Fed Busters*, and I am going to put popular Keynesian Fed-lore to the test. And by doing so, explain some of the misconceptions that have helped create the Greatest Bubble on Earth.

Fed Busters

There are widely disseminated legends, folklore, and wives' tales that influence judgment and are born out of beliefs held firm at the Federal Reserve; here, I take on these myths and decide if they are confirmed or busted.

Common Fed-lore Myth 1—The Myth of the Deflationary Death Spiral Monster

The monetary system employed in the United States is based on currency that can be created at a central bank's whim—by a mere touch of an electronic button. In charge of that button are the men and women at our Federal Reserve, who have a firmly entrenched belief that deflation is the worst of all possible monetary outcomes. Due to this belief, they have taken their mandate of stable prices to actually mean "slightly increasing prices." So to you and me, the word *stable* means not easily moved. However, to the men and women who control our money supply, it means increasing about 2 percent a year. So determined are they that the economy not be met by the evil deflationary monster that they create inflation of 2 percent (as measured by the phoniest of inflation measurements known as the Personal Consumption Expenditure Price Index). This is done as a buffer or wall to block evil deflation from coming in—because once that evil deflation monster enters the economy, they fear he will never leave.

The word *deflation* is a little nebulous in that it is used by economists in a technical way to describe a decline in the money supply. Most laypeople view deflation as a generalized decline in prices. *Inflation*, in turn, would refer to an increase in prices or, more technically speaking, an increase in the money supply or the fear of such a future increase in its supply that causes a decline in the purchasing power of the currency.

As a follow-up to my introduction on decreasing prices, I have decided to start my critique of Fed myths with the Keynesian Fed-lore of the "deflationary death spiral"; this Fed-lore is very widely held and promulgated. The men and women at the Federal Reserve believe that a slight increase in prices is a sign of a growing economy and falling prices are devastating.

Let's put this Keynesian Fed-lore to the test and see how it holds up.

In an economic environment of increasing productivity accompanied by a static money supply, one would assume that prices would slightly decrease. As an industry becomes more productive and makes better use of technology, those technological advances aid in the reduction of costs associated with producing the product. Profit margins improve, and in a competitive environment, businesses will pass most of these savings on to consumers. So with truly stable prices, the costs of many items would go down, and that would be a positive result; it would indicate that businesses were leveraging productivity to increase profit margins and decreasing the price of goods to consumers. However, outside of technology, we rarely see this materialize.

Those at the Fed view any deflation as harmful, regardless of the cause. Ben Bernanke has said that "deflation is in almost all cases a side effect of a collapse in aggregate demand—a drop in spending so severe that producers must cut prices on an ongoing basis in order to find buyers."[1]

And so, common Keynesian Fed-lore wisdom affirms—if consumers expect prices to fall, they postpone their purchases, causing prices to fall even further.

Let's put this theory to the test. If I'm hungry, I am not likely to starve myself in the belief that the salami sandwich I crave will reduce in price—eventually everybody has to eat. Gas prices go up and down, but I am not likely to troll around the neighborhood on empty waiting for the price of gas to decrease. But these are staple goods that some popular inflation models conveniently omit.

In technology, an industry whose efficiencies complement price declines, we fail to observe that the knowledge of the inevitability of lower prices thwarts consumption. Every computer and big-screen TV shopper understands that if they postpone their purchase for a year, they will more than likely get something bigger and better for the same amount or even less. If the Fed's deflation theory were accurate, we would have to assume that nobody would ever buy a computer, an iPhone, or a flat-screen TV; according to this wisdom, they would be waiting for the newer and cheaper model. According to common Keynesian Fed-lore, if people were aware that the price would go down, they would delay their purchase.

Now you may be thinking, "Pento, what about housing? Isn't everybody holding off on buying a house, anticipating that prices will go down?" Well, not really so much. The truth is that the mortgage-lending market has, thankfully, returned to some form of sanity and the job market remains anemic. If consumers had their erstwhile access to credit and a viable form of employment, people would be buying houses. Think about it. Let's say a newly married man tells his bride that he is postponing the purchase of their first home until prices bottom, and he thinks it could find a floor in just a few years. But in the meantime, since their rental doesn't come with a washer and dryer, his beloved needs to walk several miles to the laundromat—he told her car prices had a bit more to drop, too. The bride would be more inclined to walk to the nearest divorce attorney's office. And remember, housing is an area that the Federal Reserve and the federal government has yet to allow to form a bottom that can be supported by the free market. We saw the opposite in the stock market: without a tremendous amount of government manipulation, the stock market was allowed to bottom—that was a painful process. However, once the market found its bottom, it soared. People stopped waiting for stocks to go down and started worrying about missing the rally. The same thing would happen to housing if it were allowed to reach a true bottom.

The Truth about Price Deflation

Historically, we have seen long stretches in U.S. history when prices gently fell and wages remained stable. This price deflation didn't lead to disaster; on the contrary, it was consistent with real economic growth. After all, what's so bad about falling prices? We increase our standard of living when goods and services become more affordable through technological improvements. Declining prices increases our aggregate ability to spend and offers consumers that were shut out by those formerly high prices the opportunity to now raise their standard of living.

During the 30-year period 1870 to 1900, the United States experienced a period of true price stability coupled with a period of great prosperity. This period of the classical gold standard was marked by gently falling prices and increased productivity that raised living standards and gave us the first glimpses of globalization.

In fact, the 1880s were described by some to be our most ebullient and prosperous decade. While prices fell, the U.S. economy prospered. Industry expanded; the railroads expanded; physical output, net national product, and real per capita income all roared ahead. For the decade from 1869 to 1879, the real national product grew 6.8 percent per year and real-product-per-capita growth was described by Murray Rothbard, in his book, *History of Money and Banking in the United States: The Colonial Era to World War II* as "phenomenal" at 4.5 percent per year.[2]

This is a piece of history that Keynesian Fed-lore doesn't talk about. The Fed was created in 1913; this was a time before the Fed. There was no pseudo–government entity creating inflation under the guise of maintaining stable prices. There was just the gold standard and 30 years of stable prices coinciding with 30 years of prosperity and advancement.

As costs fall through innovation, profit margins remain. In contrast, far from achieving long-run price stability, the Fed has allowed the purchasing power of the U.S. dollar, which was hardly different on the eve of the Fed's creation from what it had been at the time of the dollar's establishment as the official U.S. monetary unit, to fall dramatically. A consumer basket selling for $100 in 1790 cost only slightly more, at $108, than its rough equivalent in 1913. But thereafter the price soared, reaching $2,422 in 2008).[3]

People associate deflation with the awful Great Depression, but most don't know that the consumer price index (CPI) steadily fell (albeit much more gently) from late 1925 through 1929, in the midst of the Roaring Twenties — hardly a time associated with economic stagnation.[4]

Furthermore, the 1970s dispelled the myth that inflation and high unemployment rate/recession can't coexist, as the pre-Volcker Fed of the 1970s thought they, too, could inflate their way to prosperity. They ended up creating a condition known as *stagflation*—rising prices and zero economic growth. This was largely responsible for the malaise of the 1970s (in case you thought it was caused by bell-bottom pants).

I'll have more to say about the relationship between inflation and the unemployment rate when I debunk myth 3.

Unlike the Volcker Fed—which crushed inflation with unprecedented hikes in the Fed Funds rate—Mr. Bernanke may find it nearly impossible to raise rates without causing massive economic carnage. The reason is clear: the level of debt outstanding in both public and private sectors has increased to the point where servicing it becomes impossible without artificially induced low interest rates that remain low forever.

In the first quarter of 1980, the financial obligation ratio (FOR)—a measure of household debt service as a percentage of disposable income, which includes rent and automobile leases—was 15.9 percent. It is now over 16 percent. So why worry? The number is the same simply because interest rates plunged from 20 percent to near zero percent. If interest rates were to normalize, that number would soar. To illustrate that point, the FOR pales in comparison to the level of household debt as a percentage of gross domestic product (GDP), which is now 85 percent of total output. Back in the early 1980s, by contrast, it was just 46 percent. On the public-sector level, the numbers are just as grim. National debt as a percentage of GDP has now reached 104 percent of output, while in 1980 it was a mere 40 percent.

Just imagine the stress on the consumer and the government that would be experienced if the Fed were to raise rates aggressively, as Volcker did. How could the consumer continue to service his or her mortgage and how could the U.S. Treasury finance the titanic national debt if rates were to increase much above today's levels?

The problem with inflation is real. That's the monster that the Fed is creating that should be feared. That's the monster that should be the cornerstone of Fed-lore because when the inflation monster comes, Bernanke's counterfeiting isn't going to slay it—it will feed it.

After Volcker slew the evil inflation monster—that monster that Fed-lore conveniently overlooks—throughout most of the 1980s and 1990s the U.S. exercised a strong dollar policy where we enjoyed a stable dollar, strong growth, and low unemployment, proving once again that a strong dollar, stable currency, and economic growth can all happily coexist.

However, today the Fed is exhaustively fighting a decline in prices, opting instead to keep prices at what their popular models would show as a modest inflation rate. The key point they totally miss is that deflation must occur to reconcile the imbalances created by decades of inflation. Asset prices must fall, money supply levels must shrink, and debt loads must decrease. But they are doing even more damage than just creating a huge bubble in the Treasury and bond market. As soon as they engage in another round of counterfeiting, the first thing to rise is food and energy. This is how it works: It first involves the purchase of an asset by the central bank. The Fed issues electronic credits to banks in exchange for their assets, which include Treasuries and mortgage-backed securities (MBSs). Their purchases drive up the demand for those assets, bringing about rising prices. In fact, Bernanke has clearly stated that the purpose of his "quantitative easing" (QE) program is to raise the rate of inflation, which in his mind is too low.

What the Fed is accomplishing is a reduction in the purchasing power of the U.S. dollar. It creates inflation by vastly increasing the money supply, and thus lowers the confidence of those holding the greenback. If international confidence in the dollar is shaken, most dollar-based asset prices will increase—with the exception of U.S. debt. When people perceive that the value of their dollar is decreasing, they cling to hard assets like gold, oil, and commodities.

Individuals with low to moderate income levels spend a disproportionate amount of their disposable income on food and energy; thus, a rise in commodities affects low to moderate incomes in a more substantive way. In contrast, those who are the owners of hard assets like gold and real estate see the value of their items increasing—they are the primary beneficiaries of the Fed's counterfeiting. Bernanke may think that by inflating away debt and reducing borrowing costs he is allowing consumers to deleverage. But he conveniently overlooks the negative side of that equation: the destroyed purchasing power of the low and middle classes. Lower wage earners typically don't own precious metals, stocks, and multiple homes. And they see the central bank's phony money last—if they do at all. Therefore, many are struggling today with falling real incomes and are unable to reap any benefit from the Fed's inflation. By not allowing low wage earners to benefit from what would naturally be the outcome of deflation—falling food and energy prices— the Federal Reserve has become the most pernicious redistributor of wealth—stealing the purchasing power from the poor in order to inflate the balance sheets of the wealthy.

The truth is that the Fed always has the means to inflate. Even if all the banks were unwilling to make one new loan to the private sector, the Federal Reserve could fund the federal government, which in turn could issue $100,000 checks to everyone. Not that I am supporting that, but if their only goal were to increase prices, they could easily accomplish that. After all, they could always partake in the now infamous helicopter drop of cash. It is easy for Bernanke to increase the price of goods. The problem is that the Fed appears to misperceive an increase in prices with economic growth—they shouldn't.

For every new dollar created by a central bank, there is not a dollar's worth of increase in the production of goods and services. Each new dollar created by fiat is merely a new dollar available for consumption, which can cause an increase in nominal GDP if the money doesn't sit at the Fed as excess reserves, but it doesn't necessarily grow the economy in real terms.

Here's why. The Fed's stock in trade is to engage in a legalized form of counterfeiting. But counterfeiting doesn't do a very good job of encouraging businesses into expanding the number of goods and services available for purchase, especially if the process has been well promulgated. Bernanke believes in Glasnost at the Fed. He wants everyone to know and understand the motives behind every action of the Fed. When everyone is aware that a massive round of counterfeiting is under way, it makes no sense to hire new workers or increase productivity. It is much easier to simply raise prices. If all are aware that the new money created isn't backed by anything and does not represent, or is not the result of, any increase in goods and services in the economy, rising prices becomes the primary outcome.

If I show up at the grocery store to buy gallons of milk with counterfeit money and I tell the manager that the bills came from my printing press located in my home's basement, he will have me arrested, not call his suppliers to have them ramp up the milk production supply chain. However, it is illegal not to accept the Fed's new money. Therefore, prices increase when the market has lost faith in the currency's purchasing power. Unfortunately, the Fed is working very hard to destroy the global confidence in holding the world's reserve currency.

When the Fed prints money, there are two sides to the ledger. On one side, money printing has the ability to temporarily, lower interest rates and reduce borrowing costs in the economy. That provides debt service relief to borrowers and can encourage people to take on even more debt. On the other side of the ledger, savers are punished and rising prices erode the purchasing power of the middle and lower income earners. When an economy is in a balance sheet recession, the economy must deleverage and will not take on much more debt at any interest rate. And if interest rates are already at zero percent, there can be no further relief on debt service payments that can be attained by more money printing. More QE at that point only exacerbates the negative side of the ledger by putting further pressure on the middle class. Real GDP contracts and inflation takes off.

So Bernanke shouldn't fear the evil deflation monster lurking under his bed at night—he should be afraid of the inflation monster he is creating. Like Frankenstein, Ben's "inflation creation" is the monster that will kill this economy and destroy our bond market.

The Keynesian Fed-lore myth of the evil deflationary monster— BUSTED!

Fed-Lore Myth 2: Japan Proves that Debt and Deflation Go Hand-in-Hand

Those at the Fed and in the mainstream media love to allude to Japan as an operative motivation for Bernanke's incessant counterfeiting. I am regularly challenging the "We will be Japan" perception. My favorite rebuttal is "The Fed is counterfeiting in an effort not to be Japan, but what they fail to realize is that we are more likely to be Argentina."

Fed Busters is going to investigate this "Turning Japanese Fear" by solving the mystery of Japan's flailing economy and ask the poignant question: are we Japan or Argentina?

As we learned in Chapter 2, currency-manipulating bureaucrats met at the Plaza Hotel in an attempt to deflate the U.S. dollar, manipulating the dollar downward, which in turn increased the value of the yen in respect to other currencies. The Bank of Japan countered with an easy monetary policy to inflate the yen.

The government attempted to offset the stronger yen by drastically easing monetary policy between January 1986 and February 1987. During this period, the Bank of Japan (BOJ) cut the discount rate in half from 5 percent to 2.5 percent, a 50 percent reduction in its key rate. Following the monetary stimulus, asset prices in the real estate and stock markets inflated, creating one of the biggest financial bubbles in history. The Nikkei nearly tripled from January 1985 to its peak in December 1989. From 1986 through 1990, Japan's money stock grew by an average of 10.5 percent per year. The government responded by tightening monetary policy, raising rates five times in 1989–1990 to 6 percent. After these increases, the market collapsed. From a peak of 40,000 in December of 1989 the Nikkei lost as much as 80 percent in nominal terms and sits at around 8,700 today.[5]

The elders who propagate Keynesian Fed-lore would love to suggest that the Japanese government did nothing, letting the free market prevail while Japan was engulfed into a deflationary spiral that to this day has immersed their economy on a downward trajectory. But due to the reckless spending spree the Japanese government embarked on, it is challenging for even the fairy tale of Keynesian Fed-lore to spin that tale. Therefore, Keynesian Fed-lore acknowledges that the Japanese government did eventually engage in deficit spending in order to alleviate the vicious deflationary spiral. But alas, they were too late and the stimulus too weak, and thus the economy of Japan was way too entrenched in a deflationary death spiral to break free. Had they partaken in more aggressive counterfeiting and reckless deficit spending sooner, they may have been able to pull Japan out of its deflationary hole. Now Japan is engulfed in the evil liquidity trap—and the only way out of this trap would be for the central bank of Japan to promise to keep inflating forever.

Now for the truth: First of all, the BOJ did not initially embark on the round of counterfeiting that Ben has at the onset of the crisis. One reason for this is that the Japanese are predominantly savers; the BOJ may have been more reluctant to increase the money supply when the crisis started, as inflation tends to favor debtors at the expense of savers. However, starting in 2000, they drew the last trick out of the Keynesian playbook and have enamored an affinity for counterfeiting that would even make Ben blush. For the past 12 years, the Japanese have been obedient Keynesians—counterfeiting and spending while losing decades.

Keynesian Fed-lore would have Japan be a warning to us all: once the deflationary death spiral monster takes hold, it is almost impossible to fight off—counterfeit as they may, spend as they will, it is just an overwhelming task for the government and BOJ. This is why the brave men and women at our Federal Reserve fight the deflationary monster every day—because as horrible as things may seem in our country, things could be worse; we could be Japan.

Let's take off the Keynesian-colored glasses and partake in an honest analysis of Japan to understand what really happened.

Doug French of the Mises Institute writes:

. . . for a brief moment in 1990, the Japanese stock market was bigger than the US market. The Nikkei-225 reached a peak of 38,916 in December of 1989 with a price-earnings ratio of around 80 times. At the bubble's height, the capitalized value of the Tokyo Stock Exchange stood at 42 percent of the entire world's stock-market value and Japanese real estate accounted for half the value of all land on earth, while only representing less than 3 percent of the total area. In 1989 all of Japan's real estate was valued at US$24 trillion which was four times the value of all real estate in the United States, despite Japan having just half the population and 60 percent of US GDP.[6]

When Japan's central bank–induced credit bubble finally burst, they went right to the Keynesian playbook. We can imagine at the onset of the crisis the government of Japan hastening to the crisis room. There, upon a marble pedestal like a valuable gem perched on a solid gold book stand protected by beveled glass, sat the "Keynesian Crisis Handbook." The sign above the book reads: "In case of economic crisis—break glass." A top government official clutches the small red hammer adjacent to the glass case and, with passionate fervor, strikes and breaks the glass. The Japanese officials stare in admiration as the "Keynesian Crisis Handbook" is raised off the pedestal, opened, and laid gently back on the gold-plated book stand. The book appears to illuminate the room with its Keynesian-based wisdom. The chamber falls silent in anticipation of the Keynesian wisdom soon to be uttered. The Japanese official speaks. . . .

Step 1: "The government should partake in reckless spending." The Japanese bureaucrats gesture in unanimity and without hesitation embark on their reckless government-spending journey.

In fact, between 1992 and 1995, Japan employed six spending programs totaling 65.5 trillion yen and also slashed income tax rates during 1994, and again in January 1998, they temporarily cut taxes by 2 trillion yen. In April of that year, the government unveiled a fiscal stimulus package worth more than 16.7 trillion yen, half of which was for public works—can you say "shovel ready" in Japanese? They thought this amount of Keynesian deficit spending would solve the problem—but it was apparent to them that it was too small. So again, in November 1998, another fiscal stimulus package worth 23.9 trillion yen was announced, and a year later (November 1999), another fiscal stimulus package of 18 trillion yen was tried. In October 2000, Japan announced yet another fiscal stimulus package of 11 trillion yen. So if you add them all up during the 1990s, Japan tried 10 fiscal stimulus packages totaling more than 100 trillion yen, each one failing to cure the recession.[7]

As I could have predicted, all this spending failed to cure their economic woes; however, it has bequeathed Japan with the world's highest debt-to-GDP ratio, at about 220 percent.

Japan has tried every trick in the "Keynesian Crisis Handbook" to no avail—the only solution that hasn't been endeavored is to stop intervening and allow the free market to self-correct. Unfortunately, that is the only course not mentioned in the "Keynesian Crisis Handbook," so Japan continues in its fruitless attempt to manage itself out of its recession, prohibiting free-market forces to avail.

The central bank of Japan has kept rates at zero for more than a decade; the Japanese banks are insolvent, yet are obstinate in their refusal to write down nonperforming loans. Banks continue to leave bad loans on their books, instead of allowing for those malinvestments to be liquidated, and so are referred to as zombie banks.

Centuries ago the famed Japanese samurai warrior would fall on his sword in ritual suicide when confronted with defeat. I am not suggesting that the Japanese literally fall on their swords; however, they should own up to failed business models and investments and purge them from the economy.

French notes:

> The idea that deflation is the villain of the piece misses an obvious fact: money supply continues to grow. However you slice it, be it M-1, M-2 or "broadly-defined liquidity"—they have all been growing every year since 1984, the earliest date provided by the BOJ data bank on its website."[8]

Deflation defined as a decline in the supply of money—clearly has not happened. Prices, as measured by the current fashionable indices have retreated. But, even so, the Japanese consumer price index decline has been quite mild.

So it seems to defy common sense to suggest that the problem with Japan is the small annual decreases in its CPI. Surely, if a mild 1 to 3 percent increase in prices is acceptable to mainstream economists, then a decrease of less than 2 percent ought to pose no dire problems.

The central problem of Japan is not deflation—the fundamental problem is a pattern of production ill-suited and ill-fitted to meet the realities of the marketplace.

In general terms, the Japanese wanted to protect their exporters, despite the fact that the marketplace had changed and moved against them. They wanted to persist in the belief that the blue chip debtors of yesteryear were still creditworthy. The Japanese economy failed to keep up with the new demands of their population. They engaged in the classic Keynesian digging and filling, protecting and supporting bad business models. Instead of allowing for the economy to rid itself of bad investments, they continually propped them up. It's not the deflation monster brought by the slight decline in prices that is burdening the Japanese economy, it's the economy's failure in sufficiently satisfying its population's needs.[9]

So the myth that Japan has lost decades due to the Keynesian Fed-lore deflationary monster has been BUSTED!

Despite the fact that deflation isn't Japan's problem, the Fed is counterfeiting in a futile attempt to not become the next Japan. Unfortunately, we are more likely to be the next Argentina. Let's put my Pentonomics-lore to the test. We are closer to being Argentina than Japan.

The bad news for Japan is that it is mired in debt; the slightly better news is that Japan owes its debt to Japanese families and businesses, who for the time being have been willing to plow their savings into government bonds. However, with the recent election of Shinzo Abe and his two percent inflation mandate; it won't be long before Japanese Government Bonds (JGBs) crash under the weight of a debt to GDP ratio of 237 percent and the skyrocketing interest payments that come along with inflation and rising interest rates. Thus far the lack of foreign ownership of JGBs has prevented Japan from becoming the next Greece—not that I want to dwell too much here on Greece, but some suggest that Greece should leave the euro and return to the drachma. Having Greece return to the drachma and defaulting on its debt through devaluation and money printing is a much worse option. Many are proposing that Greece inflate its way out of debt, just like Argentina did during 2002. However, this ignores the fact that the Argentines first defaulted on $100 billion of their external debt before removing their currency's peg to the U.S. dollar. Even though the peso lost about 75 percent of its value and caused a brief bout with high inflation, the Argentine central bank did not have to monetize its debt. Therefore, the amount of new money printed was greatly reduced and resulted in a quick rebound in the economy.

In sharp contrast, the Europeans, Japanese, and Americans still cling to the idea that inflation is the answer. PIIGS countries (the economies of Portugal, Ireland, Italy, Greece, and Spain) are pursuing an inflationary default that will increase borrowing costs and lead to a depression that will be far worse than if they simply admitted their insolvency and defaulted outright. Devaluing your currency to pay foreign creditors leads to hyperinflation and complete economic chaos. Paying off your debt by printing money was tried in Hungary during 1946 and Germany in 1923, but it resulted in complete devastation and hyperinflation.

If Greece does leave the euro and inflate its way out of debt, it will be the next Weimar Republic—lugging wheelbarrows of drachmas to buy a loaf of bread.

Japan is fortunate, for now, that it doesn't have to compete in the global market, where the effects of currency translation would pose the risk of increasing rates. The debtors of Japan are conveniently consumers of the yen—and that does buy them a bit more time.

Currently, the U.S. dollar enjoys its reserve currency status. The United States became the world's reserve currency via the agreement of Bretton Woods. At that time, there was an established exchange of the U.S. dollar for gold. That gold exchange no longer exists; currently, the world is permitting the United States to retain this status based on its confidence in our monetary system. Operating as the world's reserve currency puts the United States at an advantage in the debt market. Because contracts and prices worldwide are negotiated in the U.S. dollar, there is worldwide demand for dollar-denominated debt. As long as the world maintains confidence in the dollar, the United States gets preferential treatment in funding its colossal deficit.

The yen doesn't enjoy such status, but since Japan's debt is privately funded, it has survived massive credit downgrades while still enjoying low interest rates. The savers in Japan—whom Krugman would claim are the bane of the Japanese economy—are helping to alleviate the huge debt burden Japan has to service. The United States has no such savers; if we were to lose our status as the reserve currency, the U.S. dollar would have the same limited demand as any other currency and the interest rates in the United States would be at the mercy of the foreign markets.

Until recently, Japan has enjoyed a population that has a propensity to save. However, savings has retreated from 15 percent to a mere 2 percent.

This rate of savings was more sustainable when the population was younger, wealthier, and growing. Today's Japanese are old, stagnant, and saving less every year. The country will eventually find itself in a financial catastrophe when the public stops lending money at floor-scraping 0.75 percent rates. Interest rates will rise in Japan, and when they do, the government will be paying more than half of its revenue just to pay interest expense on its debt. This is a catastrophe waiting to happen.

Let's contrast to the United States: We can divide up the total national debt into three different categories—gross public debt, publicly traded debt, and intragovernmental holdings.

As I write, the U.S. government has more than $11.6 trillion dollars in publicly traded debt and an additional $4.9 trillion dollars in intra-governmental holdings. Intragovernmental holdings represent money that the federal government has borrowed from various agencies, such as Social Security. When Social Security payroll taxes are drawn from your salary, they don't actually go into a segregated account—they get lent right to the federal government. So your retirement security is nothing but a big fat I.O.U. from Uncle Sam. Why is this a problem? Isn't it all in the family?

In fact, Franklin Roosevelt said in a May 22, 1939, speech, "Our national debt after all is an internal debt owed not only by the Nation but to the Nation."

I would like to counter that statement with a quote by Ronald Regan:

> For decades, we have piled deficit upon deficit, mortgaging our future and our children's future for the temporary convenience of the present. . . . You and I, as individuals, can, by borrowing, live beyond our means, but for only a limited period of time. Why, then, should we think that collectively, as a nation, we are not bound by that same limitation?

Unfortunately, this quote is from Reagan's 1981 inaugural address, before he had to load up on spending to get his tax cuts through.

Let's take both men at their word—one saw debt as an asset of a nation and one saw it as a burden on future generations.

The implication from FDR is that we need not worry about the growing national debt because it is simultaneously both a liability and an asset. Roosevelt believed if we had to net out all our obligations, it amounts to a big zero. Therefore, since the obligation is to ourselves, there won't be any negative repercussions.

This is tantamount to saying to your new bride that you are going to trust her completely and give her 10 percent of your yearly after-tax income to invest toward a comfy retirement. You tell her you aren't going to check on this "investment" because you want to be surprised by its sum years from now. After several decades of wedded bliss, you sit down with her to see how much the retirement fund has grown and to discuss how to spend your nest egg during your golden years together. She then calmly tells you that there isn't any such retirement account because all the money she borrowed from you was lumped in with other income and then "invested" in the family budget—this is exactly what happens with all government trust fund money and public debt. After the husband pulls out any remaining hair on his head, he screams out, "What do we do now, we were counting on that money to exist for the remainder of our lives on this planet!" Then she tells you that even though it was our asset, it was also our debt, so in the end it's all a wash—see, it's not a big deal at all.

The truth is money owed to the husband cannot be counted as an asset if it isn't invested outside of the family. Otherwise, it is just your direct obligation to pay. If you were counting on that money to fund an individual or a nation's retirement, you will become greatly disappointed.

Savings is deferred consumption that is invested in an outside entity. This is true for both governments and individuals. The money that is supposed to be in trust funds for Social Security and Medicare should have been invested with foreign nations or even put in Al Gore's famed "lockbox." In fact, it would be more acceptable if the trust fund money were invested in a factory, mine, or utility that the government could point to and say, "Here it is. Look, this is what we did with your money." Or, better yet, what if we just let individuals plan and invest for their own retirement? Nevertheless, if the government had invested its pension fund in foreign governments, any profits could then be used to fund Social Security and Medicare. But, sadly, all we have done is pooled tax dollars into the general fund for Congress to fritter away on government largess. Nobody knows exactly where those tax dollars have gone except that they went to waste.

Government must have the tax base available to pay off all its debt if so desired and provide the international debt market with the confidence that it can do so at all times. Since our nation's debt has now eclipsed our entire yearly GDP and is 700 percent of our annual income, that premise is no longer tenable. And so, we do have this dire situation in common with Japan.

But, as we will see—we are not Japan, because foreigners now own 50 percent of our publicly traded debt, and we don't have the savings to fund it. So it has also become a debt owed by the nation to other nations, with massively negative currency implications. Despite FDR's ebullient attitude toward our debt, it has become the bane of the nation.

According to DaveManual.com, public debt is, for the most part, owned by these entities:

- Pension funds
- Foreign governments
- Mutual funds
- Foreign investors
- American investors
- Hedge funds

Of the $11.6 trillion in public debt, nearly half is owned by foreign entities, with China and Japan owning the largest amount.

DaveManual.com predicts that in 2015 the government will have to start paying out more than it takes in from Social Security. Not only will we have to start funding part of Social Security out of general funds, but we won't have Social Security's excess tax dollars to borrow from to fund our debt.[10] The United States will need to borrow nearly $10 trillion dollars *more* over the next decade to fund its deficit spending. Therefore, countries like China and Japan will play an important role over the next decade or so. But Japan has its own tragic fiscal problems to worry about, and the Chinese economy is suffering the worst decline in GDP in years. In 2007, the Federal Reserve owned $774.9 billion in U.S. debt. In just five years' time, it has more than doubled that holding to $1.75 trillion. But that could be just the beginning. If the Japanese and Chinese decide that owning U.S. debt is no longer a very smart investment, or if they simply don't have the savings to place into our bond market, then the printing presses in the United States will need to reach a level that is unprecedented.

Despite the fact that Bernanke has a "yen" to depreciate the dollar and to seek inflation. When foreign creditors start to question the status of our dollar as a reserve currency and interest rates skyrocket, he is going to wish we had the savings rate that Japan once enjoyed!

So there you have it. If Japan didn't have so many savers and weren't able to privately fund its debt, it would have already have gone the way of Greece—and that day is not far away. The BOJ may soon be forced to purchase most of its country's debt. Any country that has its central bank become the primary buyer of its debt will face runaway inflation. If Greece were to leave the euro and print drachmas to alleviate its debt burden, it would become the next Weimar Republic. And since the United States relies on foreign creditors to finance half of its debt, we would be lucky to be in the position Japan is in today with a privately funded debt. But, when the U.S. dollar loses confidence around the world and is no longer regarded as having reserve currency status, and we are forced to pay usury rates to our foreign creditors, it will be Sayonara Japan and Hola Argentina!

Pentonomics myth CONFIRMED.

Myth 3: The Keynesian Fed-Lore of the Phillips Curve

One common platitude held by economists is that a silver lining to this period of escalating unemployment is that inflation must moderate. Unfortunately, economics is not immune to the practice of accepting what is purported to be "common knowledge" as gospel truth. A perfect example of this is the theory of the Phillips Curve.

So I have set out to bust the myth of the Phillips curve. And question: do high rates of unemployment bring about low rates of inflation? And, conversely, do lower rates of unemployment engender higher rates of inflation?

I set out to find the origins of this Keynesian Fed-lore. It appears as though Fed elders have disseminated this myth based on the belief that employment rates dictate demand in the economy and thus directly affect inflation rates.

Even the mainstream *Wall Street Journal*'s chief economics correspondent Jon Hilsenrath reported that a rule of thumb in economics is that for every 1 percent higher in unemployment rates than the long-term average of 5 percent, there is downward pressure on inflation of 0.3 percent.[11] Apparently, Jon wasn't around for the 1970s' high unemployment and high inflation or the 1980s' and 1990s' low unemployment and high inflation. This shows how deeply ingrained this Fed-lore is. After all, doesn't that sound precise? There seems to be an exact science behind it. He went on to explain that this is because people who become unemployed create slack in the economy, which brings about deflation. Did you follow that logic? Fewer goods and services to absorb the money supply creates deflation?

Sounds convincing, Jon; now it's my turn. Economics is part science and part philosophy. But the Phillips Curve theory stands up to neither. Looking back since World War II, we find that the data do not support a correlation between employment rates and inflation. The highest rate in unemployment (10.8 percent) occurred in November 1982. At that time, the year-over-year increase in consumer price inflation was 4.5 percent. The lowest rate of unemployment (3.8 percent) occurred in April 2000. At that time, the CPI registered just 3.0 percent, so contrary to the popular Fed-lore, inflation was actually lower during the lowest period of unemployment than it was during the time of highest unemployment.

Taking a look from the standpoint of inflation, we see no apologies for the theory here either. Consumer price inflation hit an all-time high of 14.76 percent in March 1980. According to theory, we should expect to see a very low rate of unemployment. In fact, we see the rate was 6.3 percent, which is historically higher than the average of 5.0 percent. Later, inflation hit a low of 1.1 percent during June 2002. The Phillips Curve suggests that unemployment rates should have been historically quite high. But at that time, the rate of unemployment was 5.8 percent—slightly higher than the historic average and far below the high water mark of 10.8 percent.

The Phillips Curve doesn't hold up to historical data, and it doesn't hold water as a matter of economics or philosophy either. That's because inflation is a monetary phenomenon. And during times of government intervention—like today—excess money supply created by the Federal

Reserve in order to combat a recession has led to inflation. When people lose their jobs, the number of goods and services in an economy shrinks. In that case, excess money supply loses its buying power and prices rise. Conversely, during a robust job market, more goods and services are available to soak up any increased money supply.

All we have to do is look at the graphs shown in Figures 4.1 and 4.2 to see that this Fed-lore myth is easily BUSTED!

We know that the Fed has been mandated with price stability. However, since their creation we have lost 98 cents' worth of purchasing power on the dollar. Therefore, prices have been anything but stable. But the irony is that in 1977, at one of the most infamous times of price instability, Congress made the decision to task the Fed with an additional mandate of maximum employment. Just so you understand Fed/government semantics, as I mentioned earlier, by desiring stable prices, they mean prices rising 2 percent a year; and by maximum employment, they refer to an unemployment rate of 5 percent. Now I could write a soliloquy questioning why you would saddle an agency with an additional task after they have completely failed in carrying out their original objective, but this chapter is long enough, so just pause for a moment to revel in the irony and we will continue.

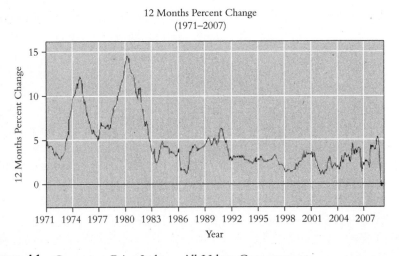

Figure 4.1   Consumer Price Index—All Urban Consumers

Labor Force Statistics from the Current Population Survey
Unemployment Rate for Age 16 years and over
(1971–2007)

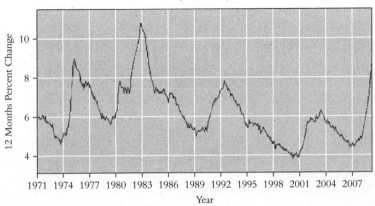

Figure 4.2 Philips Curve Graph
SOURCE: Bureau of Labor Statistics (www.bls.gov).

The Fed has a dual mandate of stable prices and maximum employment. But what may come as a surprise to most is that they have a distinct preference in their mandates. The Federal Reserve under Ben Bernanke has a clear bias toward fulfilling the goal of maximum employment. Given the situation where unemployment is high and prices are relatively stable, the Fed has opted to pursue a policy of higher inflation in the hopes of engendering lower unemployment rates.

What the Fed doesn't understand is that full employment can exist in perfect harmony with stable prices. That's because having more people producing goods and services can never by itself lead to an environment of rising aggregate prices. And, most important, an increasing rate of inflation actually increases the rate of unemployment. Not only do these facts make sense economically but also are borne out in the historical data.

Each and every time the Fed has increased the money supply and sent prices rising, the rate of unemployment has risen, not decreased. The simple reason for this is that inflation diminishes the purchasing power of most consumers. Falling real wages means fewer discretionary purchases can be made. Falling demand leads to increased layoffs, and unemployment rises as economic growth falters.

The 12.2 percent year-over-year (YOY) rise in the CPI that occurred in November 1974 led to the cyclical high of 9 percent unemployment during May 1975. Likewise, in 1979, the YOY increase in the CPI reached a high of 14.6 percent in March and April 1980, which was followed by another cyclical high 10.8 percent unemployment print in November and December of 1982. Once again, YOY CPI increased from 1.2 percent in December 1986 to 6.4 percent in October 1990. That again corresponded with the rise in unemployment that occurred from the 5 percent level in March 1989 to 7.8 percent in June 1992.

Today, we find that unemployment is ranging at about 8 percent due to the credit crisis and Great Recession. Bernanke believes he can bring that figure down by creating inflation. However, the unemployment rate just can't seem to respond to his Keynesian playbook. It is obvious he understands how to drive inflation. However, the rate of unemployment will only increase as long as the Fed mistakenly holds the belief that printing money can solve the employment situation.

Doubling down on this flawed theory, the Fed launched QE3 ($40 billion of MBS purchases every month) and stated that it will remain in effect until the labor market "improves substantially." He also promised that, "the Committee will continue its purchases of agency mortgage backed securities, undertake additional asset purchases, and employ its other policy tools as appropriate until such improvement is achieved. . . ." In other words, the Fed will continue to counterfeit money until there is a substantial decline in the unemployment rate. He since launched QE IV with a total of $85 billion of debt monetization with a specific target of 6.5 percent on the unemployment rate.

But there are two major problems with this measure. The first is that the Fed Funds rate has been near zero for the past four years and mortgage rates are at all-time lows. Also, the money supply (as measured by M2) is up over 10 percent from 12 months prior. Therefore, onerous interest rates cannot be the cause of our high unemployment rate. And the money supply is already growing well above productivity and labor growth, so there is already a superfluous amount of money creation. The other major problem with his plan is that the unemployment rate doesn't fall when the dollar is devalued. Rather the middle class gets dissolved and the inflation rate is rising.

The first round of QE began in November 2008. At that time, the unemployment rate in the United States was 6.8 percent. The second round of QE began in November 2010 and ended by July 2011. However, after printing a total of $2 trillion and taking interest rates to virtually zero percent, the unemployment rate had risen to 9.1 percent.

After four years of money printing and interest rate manipulations, the economy still lost 16,000 goods-producing jobs and 368,000 individuals became so despondent looking for work that they dropped out of the labor force in one month alone. And the unemployment rate has been hovering around 8 percent for over 43 continuous months. Mr. Bernanke must believe that $2 trillion worth of counterfeiting isn't quite enough and zero percent interest rates are just too high to create job growth, so he's just going to have to do a lot more of the same. But by undertaking QE IV, the Fed is tacitly admitting that QEs 1, 2 and 3 simply didn't work.

Here is why printing money can never lead to economic prosperity. The only way a nation can increase its GDP is to grow the labor force and increase the productivity of its workers. But the only "tool" a central bank has is the ability to dilute the currency's purchasing power by creating inflation. Central bank credit creation for the purpose of purchasing bank assets lowers the value of the currency and reduces the level of real interest rates. Interest rates soon become negative in real terms and consumers lose purchasing power by holding fixed income investments.

Investors are then forced to find an alternative currency that has intrinsic value and cannot be devalued by government. Commodities fill that role perfectly and prices rise, sending food and energy costs much higher. The increased cost of those nondiscretionary items reduces the discretionary purchases for the middle class. The net effect of this is more and more of middle-class incomes must be used to purchase the basics of existence. Therefore, job losses occur in the consumer discretionary portion of the economy.

The inflation created by a central bank also causes interest rates to become unstable. Savers cannot accurately determine the future cost of money, and investment activity declines in favor of consumption. Without having adequate savings, investment in capital goods like machinery and tools wanes, and the productivity of the economy slows dramatically.

The result is a chronically weak economy with anemic job growth. This condition can be found not only in the United States but in Europe and Japan as well. These stagflationary economies are the direct result of onerous government debts, which are being monetized by their central banks.

I predicted that QEs 1, 2, and 3 would not work. I now predict that QE IV and all the coming QEs will fail as well, causing the unemployment rate to rise along with the rate of inflation. In fact, I believe the unemployment rate will increase sharply over time. That will force Mr. Bernanke to choose which mandate (full employment or stable prices) takes precedence. I believe he will choose the former. That means this round of quantitative counterfeiting will last as long as he is chairman of the Fed.

What the Fed has accomplished is to enable Washington to amass $6 trillion of new debt since the Great Recession began in December 2007. It has not only prevented an economic recovery from occurring but has catapulted the United States toward a currency and bond market crisis in the next few years.

In reality, the Fed needs to uphold only one mandate—that of stable prices. Fulfilling that mandate by keeping in check the growth of money supply is the only way to ensure that our economy displays full employment and maximum economic growth.

Unfortunately, Bernanke is under the misconception that he can counterfeit his way to full employment—he can't. The only thing he has been effective in creating is an enormous bubble in the bond market. When this bubble is broken, unemployment will skyrocket—proving that Bernanke's inflation is not the facilitator of low unemployment but the linchpin to soaring unemployment.

The myth of the Phillips Curve—BUSTED!

Myth 4: You Can Rely on Government Statistics

Several times a week the market stands transfixed in anticipation of some government statistic to be announced. Figures such as unemployment,

CPI, PPI, or GDP often don't correlate to my perception of economic realities. I'm going to walk you through a thought process to demonstrate the inconsistencies of government statistics to reality.

Reflect for a moment on how the temperature feels outside. I am writing this chapter in July—so I know it's hot. I'm an economist and market strategist, not a meteorologist. But if I had to speculate, I would say it's about 95 degrees. What if I glanced at the temperature gauge and it read 70 degrees? My first assumption would be that it's broken. Then I get in my car and that gauge is also reading 70 degrees. I turn on the radio and hear "it's a comfortable 70 degrees out." Really? I don't feel comfortable—it doesn't feel similar to what I discern as 70 degrees. All my friends are complaining about the heat as well, but the official data doesn't corroborate what we feel and know to be true. To us, it's a heat wave! I pick up the paper and there is a headline that reads "Another day of moderate weather." I go on TV and make mention of the heat and the weather pundits argue, "Pento, it's 70 degrees out. What heat wave are you talking about?" I assume there is something wrong with me and my friends. Why are we boiling when every official piece of data I hear or read about dispels this as truth?

I consult the Internet to investigate my problem and find in an obscure publication that the government has changed the way it gauges temperature. They have made adjustments to the methodology and instruments to get what they think is a more accurate measurement. Of course! More government manipulation of data—this is just like inflation. Gauges of temperature, just like government statistics, are useful. But I don't need a thermometer to tell me it's hot, just like I don't need a government bureaucrat to tell me there is no inflation!

Take your family out to dinner and a movie. You don't need an inflation index to tell you a modest night out for a family of four is expensive and getting more so. I don't need some Washington number cruncher to factor in substitutions to make my grocery bill more palatable—I understand that feeding my family is becoming more expensive. I grasp the costs of my family's health insurance, auto insurance, cable bill, electric bill, water bill, property taxes, and the future cost of my children's college education. I know what my life costs—I live it! I inherently recognize that the cost of living my life is increasing in the same way I know that it's hot outside.

When I look at measurements of growth and inflation disseminated by government agencies, those measurements don't accurately reflect the reality I perceive. When I speak to people who are not in the profession of inundating themselves with government statistics, I garner their sentiment to be closer to mine. Therefore, I have set out to counter the myth of government measures of inflation—CPI—and growth—GDP.

The CPI is the broadest measure of consumer price inflation for goods and services. Over the past 30 years the government has shifted its method of reporting in an effort to depress reported inflation, making the CPI an inadequate measure of the costs needed to maintain a constant standard of living. A bias in CPI affects all sorts of things like estimates of growth in output and productivity, median income, and real wages; it alters the growth rates of government spending programs that are indexed to inflation like Social Security. CPI has major consequences for the prediction of government budget deficits and national debt. An incorrect calculation in CPI produces misleading estimates of inflation for monetary policy makers for whom the inflation rate is a critical target. CPI influences estimates of poverty rates, and it clouds comparisons of the comparative economic performance of nations.[12]

We hear all the time that fat has been replaced with the evil trans-fat, that sugar has been substituted for high fructose corn syrup, or that wheat isn't the same as it was 30 years ago—it is hybridized. It may surprise you to learn that the CPI, much like fat, sugar, and wheat, isn't the same as the CPI that you and I grew up with. This isn't your father's CPI. The ingredients in CPI have also changed.

In the early 1990s, Washington was inspired with the principled, albeit today novel, concept of a balanced budget. In an effort to reduce expenses, they moved to change the nature of the CPI. The Boskin Commission was established with the directive to prove that the CPI overstated inflation. The plan was to reduce cost-of-living adjustments for government payments to Social Security recipients and so on. The cuts in reported inflation were an effort to reduce the federal deficit without anyone in Congress having to do the politically impossible: to vote against Social Security. The changes afoot were publicized, albeit under the smokescreen of academic theories. The 1990s was a decade of growth and prosperity, and a balanced budget was certainly a noble cause. However, this highlights the unintended consequences of government manipulation. Given the strong and stable dollar of the 1990s, it is unlikely that the Boskin Commission could have predicted that over a decade later we would have a counterfeiter at the reins of the money supply of the likes of Ben Bernanke. They may not have anticipated a Fed that would recklessly print money using their now deflated inflation statistic as cover.

Muddling through the derivations of government calculations is about as dry as economics gets. So to have some fun with this, I am going to present a narrative in order to illustrate how CPI was doctored over the past 30 years.

Take a rather average man—we'll call him Herb. Herb lives by himself and is a creature of habit. Every month Herb makes no changes to his consumption—he eats the same foods, lives in the same place, watches the same amount of television; he lives a completely monotonous life. If a new product is introduced in the marketplace, it takes Herb at least 10 years to adopt it. Herb's consumption for this illustration is considered by the Bureau of Labor Statistics (BLS) to be a basket of goods. According to how the CPI had been calculated, if in 1980 Herb spent $500 a month to maintain his lifestyle and today he spends $1,000 a month to maintain that same exact lifestyle—that would be an easy measure of his inflation—it now costs an additional $500 for Herb to maintain a constant standard of living under the old calculation.

The BLS know that few in this country, if any, live the life of my fictitious Herb, and they distort the national basket of goods to their advantage. The actual calculation is, of course, more complex; local and regional surveys are taken, but this is just an illustration. Let's see how the new calculation of CPI affects Herb's life.

Herb washes his clothes exclusively with Tide detergent. Every month he purchases the same size bottle of Tide detergent for $5. One day he goes to the store and his regular Tide detergent has been replaced with "New and Improved Tide." The new and improved Tide also comes with a new and improved price of $6. Herb, being the creature of habit that he is, doesn't want the new and improved—he prefers the old and outdated. But Herb has no choice; he must purchase the Tide with the so-called improvements that he doesn't need and that don't really work. So he pays the additional $1 out of pocket for all the superfluous improvements. To Herb, his out-of-pocket expense just went up by $1, but to the BLS his basket remains unchanged—they don't view improvements as an increase in Herb's basket of goods.

Before the change, what a consumer paid out-of-pocket for goods and services reflected adjustments for quality changes that could be directly quantified in a monetary sense. So if Herb were to get an additional eight ounces of detergent—that increase in quantity could be directly quantified. The BLS expanded quality adjustments to include the concept of "hedonic" quality adjustments, altering the pricing of goods and services for nebulous quality changes that could not be priced directly and that often are not viewed or recognized by the consumer as a desired improvement. When the BLS deems a quality improvement, it adjusts the price lower to reflect the quality—even though the consumer may not deem the improvements to the product as improvements to their life.[13]

Poor Herb is still a little shaken from the improved Tide episode. He enters the meat aisle to get his favorite sirloin steak, and as he places his hand on his coveted steak, he comes to the shocking revelation that his sirloin has turned into chop meat. Herb, still stunned, notices there is a sign on the case that notes, "This item has been substituted in an effort to aid in the price moderation of your basket of goods." But this isn't a reasonable substitute for Herb. He loves his sirloin—he hates chop meat. Herb isn't pleased with his substitutions, but he is compliant. Unfortunately, this happens month over month and year over year, and soon Herb's new basket of goods barely resembles Herb's old basket.

Historically, consumer inflation has been estimated by measuring price changes in a fixed-weight basket of goods, in an attempt to measure the cost of maintaining a constant standard of living. Allowing for the substitution of lower-priced and quality goods effectively lowers the reported rate of inflation versus the fixed-basket method. The BLS introduced geometric weighting—a purely mathematical ploy that automatically reduces the weightings of goods rising in price.[14]

All these substitutions and improvements have Herb very shaken. Unfortunately, things are about to get a lot worse. Due to high gas prices, the BLS is demanding that Herb drive only out of necessity. Herb is a recluse—so the only time he drives is out of necessity. However, the BLS has a broad definition of what qualifies as necessity. When Herb attempts to utilize his car for his weekly excursion to the grocery store, which is already becoming very stressful, a bus pulls up. The driver instructs Herb to get in. Herb reluctantly complies, but to make matters worse, instead of heading to Herb's regular store the driver heads to the "outlet store" on the other side of town. The driver informs Herb that the BLS has determined that Herb needs to better utilize the discount and outlet stores in an effort to further reduce the cost of his basket.

Another change introduced was a reweighting of sales outlets (discount/mass merchandisers versus Main Street shops). The assumption is that consumers are making better use of discount and outlet stores, and therefore those price reductions need to be more appropriately applied to the price of goods in their CPI calculation.

As a result of government manipulation, Herb's stable, monotonous life has become almost unrecognizable. Herb peruses the local paper and reads the headline—CPI remains little changed year over year. To Herb, the basket has changed considerably and his standard of living has decreased—but to the bureaucrats concocting the figure, the basket showed little to no change. Funny how the government feels there is no need to factor in reverse hedonics into the calculation.

This illustrates the modification in the new way the CPI is calculated that challenges the theory of the "constant-standard-of-living measure" in favor of what the bureaucrats would define as a "constant level of satisfaction." The constant standard of living meant the consumer was able to consume the same goods in the same quantity, without having to trade off quality of living versus price. If you think things haven't changed over the past 20 years in the CPI calculation, tell that to Herb!

Now, you may be thinking: maybe Herb should lighten up or just get treated for his obsessive-compulsive disorder—what does this have to do with me? According to John Williams's Shadow statistics, an electronic newsletter service that exposes flaws in current U.S. government economic data and reporting, the true inflation (using the same methodology as 1980) runs as much as 7 percent above inflation calculated using today's metrics.[15] So a good "rule of thumb" is: When you walk outside and you perspire—it's hot. And when your reach for your wallet and it feels like you're paying more—its inflation!

A manufactured benign inflation number provides Banana Ben carte blanche to counterfeit under the guise of low inflation. allowing him to perpetuate a huge bubble in the bond market. A modest inflation reading also obfuscates another government measurement: GDP. GDP is the gross domestic product—the output of goods and services produced by labor and property located in the United States. It's a snapshot of a nation's prosperity.

One of the reasons it is imperative to accurately calculate inflation is that you need a true reading on price increases in order to get a true reading on economic growth. If we used an accurate inflation rate to deflate nominal GDP, it would have certainly settled the argument as to whether the economy is in recession. According to my calculations, we have never escaped our recession. Since most investors are bound by official government data, it is important to realize that GDP is calculated using the chain-type price index, which is an even more tortured inflation measurement than the CPI. Even though the CPI is a flawed number, it is a better estimate of inflation than the chain-type price index because the chain-type index allows substitution between categories, while the CPI is limited to substitution within a specific category. Using the chain CPI, when Herb reaches for a light bulb, they give him a Bic lighter.

Consumers are cognizant that their individual rates of inflation are much higher than the official reported data. The two most important points to take from that fact is that the economy is much slower and inflation is much higher than what is generally accepted.

Using his license to counterfeit, Bernanke can influence an increase in nominal GDP without propagating true growth. However, it is unclear from statements that he makes that he understands the difference between inflation and growth.

It is a sad situation when everything the man in charge of our central bank professes to understand about inflation is wrong. Mr. Bernanke does not know what causes inflation, how to accurately measure inflation, or the real damage inflation does to an economy. He, like most central bankers around the globe, persists in conflating inflation with growth. The sad truth is that our Federal Reserve believes growth can be engendered from creating more inflation.

However, in reality, economic growth comes from productivity enhancements and a growing labor force. Those two factors are the only way an economy can expand its output. Historically speaking, the total of labor force and productivity growth has averaged about a 3 percent increase per annum in the United States. Therefore, any increase in money supply growth that is greater than 3 percent has historically caused rising aggregate prices.

That's why money supply growth should never be greater than the sum of labor force growth plus productivity growth. Any increase greater than that only serves to limit labor force growth and productivity. Since Bernanke doesn't understand that simple economic maxim, he persists in his quest to destroy the value of the dollar. Perhaps that's why the Fed head has decided to keep interest rates at zero percent for at least six years, despite the fact that the growth in the M2 money supply is already north of 10 percent year over year.

Maybe Bernanke believes that a replay of the entire productivity gains from the industrial and technology revolutions will both simultaneously occur in this year. Or perhaps he feels that the millions of unemployed individuals laid off after the collapse of the credit bubble will all be rehired in the immediate future. What he also fails to understand is that consumers are in a deleveraging mode because their debt as a percentage of income is, historically speaking, extremely high. So regardless of how much money Bernanke counterfeits into existence, it won't lead to more job growth or capital creation—just more inflation.

There is little doubt that global economic growth is faltering. Most of the developed world is mired in an incipient recession. If inflation were reported more accurately by our government, the United States would also be in recession.

But this is the age of a very dangerous global phenomenon, where central bankers view the market forces of deflation as public enemy number one and inflation as the panacea for anemic growth.

There is an all-out assault on the part of global central banks to destroy their currencies in an effort to allow their respective governments to continue the practice of running humongous deficits. In fact, the developed world's central bankers are faced with the choice of either massively monetizing sovereign debt or to sit back and watch a deflationary depression crush global growth. It's clear that Bernanke has blatantly chosen to ignite inflation, and his adamant proclivity for inflation is not only leaving our economy in the throes of stagflation, it has also created a colossal bubble in the bond market.

The myth that you can trust government statistics—BUSTED!

Myth 5: The Fed Was Created for Your Benefit

Let's finish this chapter with the myth of the Fed's creation. Fed-lore would implore you to believe that the Federal Reserve was created for your benefit. To prevent a run on the bank, so you don't lose money. To maintain price stability, so your dollar retains its purchasing power. To provide maximum employment, so you have a job. As I've already mentioned, you have already lost 98 cents of every dollar, and as I write, unemployment is near 8 percent, so clearly the Fed isn't accomplishing its stated objectives.

So why does it exist?

The Federal Reserve—whom author G. Edward Griffin so aptly referred to as the "Creature from Jekyll Island"[16] was created to bail out banks and be a ready buyer of government debt.

When AIG requested $80 billion from Ben Bernanke, why was Ben so eager to oblige? Ben is in the business of counterfeiting—he is a wholesaler of money, and his customers are the banks. After Lehman's collapse, Ben feared a systemic failure could be triggered by AIG's inability to pay the counterparties to all the sophisticated instruments they had sold. And who were AIG's counterparties? Ben's best customers—Bank of America, JPMorgan Chase, Citigroup, and on it goes. Not only was the AIG bailout a way to hide an enormous second round of cash to the same group that had already received Troubled Asset Relief Program (TARP) money, it became unmistakable who Ben was working for: his customers—the banks. If I'm wrong, then tell me why Bernanke and Co. didn't get permission—using the emergency powers of the Fed—to climb into his helicopter and pass out $100 bills to you and me?

Today, Bernanke is printing money in what I would assume to be a futile effort to keep housing prices elevated and facilitate the funding of the enormous government debt. By doing this, he is creating a bubble in the debt market that he will soon be unable to control. This is not a myth—this is reality. The myth is that ignoring the disaster that lies ahead is better than preparing for it. The myth is that ignorance is bliss. Were you blissful if you missed the warning signs of the Nasdaq bubble and lost the value of half your portfolio? Were you ebullient if you failed to decipher the housing crisis before your house lost half its value? I wasn't fooled by either of those bubbles and was warning people specifically of the impending housing crisis in 2005. You can still find my debates and commentaries in print and on TV years before the crisis hit.

Now I'm warning investors that the Fed, which was created to boost commercial bank earnings and monetize U.S. Treasury debt, is not going to be able to prohibit the bond bubble from bursting. In the wake of the upcoming bond devastation, you will not have a direct line to Ben Bernanke for a bailout. You will be on your own. The good news for you is that you're now arming yourself with valuable information. You are obtaining the information to protect everything you have worked hard for, and when the bond bubble bursts, you may even be poised to profit from it.

So there we have it.

The myth that the Fed was created to protect you—BUSTED!

The notion that you are wisely gathering information from this book to protect your assets—CONFIRMED!

Notes

1. Ben Bernanke, "Deflation: Making Sure It Doesn't Happen Here," 2002. Speech.
2. Murray Rothbard, *History of Money and Banking in the United States: The Colonial Era to World War II* (Auburn, AL: Ludwig Von Mises Institute, 2002).
3. George Selgin, "Has the Fed Been a Failure?" Cato Institute, December 2010.
4. Robert P. Murphy, "The Sphinx Speaks," *Mises Daily*, April 29, 2011.
5. Benjamin Powell, "Explaining Japan's Recession," *Quarterly Journal of Austrian Economics* 5(2), Summer 2002.
6. Doug French, "Illusions of the Age of Keynes," *Mises Dailey Index*, January 25, 2010.
7. Powell, "Explaining Japan's Recession."
8. French, "Illusions of the Age of Keynes."
9. Ibid.
10. DaveManual.com, July 2012.
11. Jon Hilzenrath, "Okun's Confounding Law . . . Here We Go Again," *Wall Street Journal*, March 10, 2011.
12. Shadowstats.com, July 2012.
13. Ibid.
14. Ibid.
15. Ibid.
16. G. Edward Griffin, *The Creature from Jekyll Island: A Second Look at the Federal Reserve* (Boston, MA: American Media, 1998).

Chapter 5

The Bubble Reality Check

"The U.S. government has a technology, called a printing press (or today, its electronic equivalent), that allows it to produce as many U.S. dollars as it wishes at no cost."

— *Ben Bernanke, November 21, 2002*

"One myth that's out there is that what we're doing is printing money. We're not printing money."

"The money supply is not changing in any significant way. What we're doing is lowering interest rates by buying Treasury securities."

— *Ben Bernanke, December 2010*

These are some of Bernanke's Bubble Blowing Blunders.

Over the past four chapters, we have laid the foundation for the economic environment that lead to the conditions where a bubble of this magnitude could exist. In this chapter, we construct a case that establishes the Federal Reserve, private banks, Wall Street, and Washington as working in concert to create a massive and unprecedented bubble in the U.S. debt market overall, and most importantly in U.S. Treasuries.

The Investor Reality Check

An economic reality is that money supply growth in excess of labor force growth plus productivity growth must lead to rising prices. Excess money supply growth is the product of going off the gold standard and the fractional reserve banking system, which allows for the creation of new money courtesy of the Federal Reserve and private banks. When the banking system engages in easy monetary policies, the money supply growth exceeds the growth of labor and productivity. And superfluous money supply growth tends to concentrate in one, or just a few asset classes. In the 1970s, it resulted primarily in rising food and energy prices; in the late 1990s, it went into equities; and in the 2000s, it moved into real estate. The assets that the banking system's excess money tends to favor are stocks, real estate, and commodities; these assets have historically been the beneficiaries. However, today—quite counterintuitively—the beneficiary is U.S. debt.

Money moving through an economy flows like water—maybe that's why they call it *liquidity*. Anyone who has experienced a flooded basement or leaky roof understands that too much water often ends up collecting in one place, causing damage. Similarly, we see throughout history, when banks get out their garden hose and start "watering" (read counterfeiting), the excess money gets pooled in a particular asset class.

My children have a water toy that allows them to assemble a variety of plastic conduits, enabling the water to channel and move a plastic boat in a variety of directions. When the Fed starts pumping liquidity, there also are a variety of elements that help to direct money, enabling it to accumulate in a specific asset class that eventually leads to a bubble. Tax rules and regulations work as one of those channels. Bill Clinton reduced the capital gains tax (a good thing); however, when Greenspan got out his garden hose, the money flowed into venture capital and equities, where investors took advantage of low tax rates to yield high after-tax returns. Seventy-five years of legislation directed at providing greater accessibility to home ownership led Fed and private banks' easy money in the early and mid-2000s to pool into housing.

Today, Basel III, the upcoming worldwide banking regulation, acts as an enormous incentive for banks to purchase and hold sovereign debt. Basel III serves as a replacement to Basel II, a regulation successful in facilitating the flow of capital into mortgage derivatives. Basel is an international standard for banking regulators to control how much capital banks need to put aside to guard against the types of financial and operational risks banks face. There is an effort on the part of regulators to maintain adequate consistency of regulations so that this does not become a source of competitive disparity among internationally active banks.

Most banking regulations are born out of the inadequacies that stem from our fiat currency and fractional reserve banking system. Think for a moment of a person who has a benign brain tumor pressing on the part of his brain that controls motor skills, leading him to periodically bump into walls. Every time he bumps into a wall, he pads the wall so it will "never happen again." He can pad his entire house, but that's not going to solve the problem of the tumor in his brain. Regulations like Basel II and III only serve to pad the walls—they don't remove the tumor from the banking system. The only valid solution for regulating the banking system is a return to the gold standard and a 100 percent fractional reserve banking system. But as we witness throughout history, regulations not only fail in solving the problem, they too often channel the Fed and the banking systems' excess money creation into favored asset classes, creating a repository for bubbles.

Basel II encouraged banks to amass collateralized debt obligations (CDOs) and mortgage-backed securities (MBSs) by allowing them to meet reserve requirements utilizing these high-yielding debt instruments. It permitted the outsourcing of financial risk management to credit rating agencies who, enticed by fees, liberally provided AAA ratings. This led AAA ratings to be donned on MBSs and credit default swaps that, in the end, proved to be extremely bad credit risks. Now they have concocted Basel III, which skews asset distribution to sovereign debt—obviously encouraged by the fact that sovereigns, such as the United States, don't have to default because they can print money. And when the bubble in sovereign debt explodes in their faces, they will reconvene and formulate Basel IV.

I don't want to get too far into the weeds with this regulation, but there are important components of Basel III that are directing bank money into sovereign debt that support the premise of my argument. The Basel III accord allows banks to purchase sovereign debt without any reserve requirements. In essence, banks have been greatly incentivized to purchase unlimited amounts of Treasuries instead of making "more risky" loans to the private sector. This has managed to hold the collapse of the bond bubble in abeyance. However, it has also at the same time vastly exacerbated the problem by encouraging yet more monetization of the bubble from private banks. Basel III increases the amount that the banks have to hold in reserves and greatly favors U.S. Treasuries as an asset class.

Investor psychology is another important factor driving the Fed's excess liquidity into the Treasury.

For the past two decades, the U.S. private and institutional investor has been at the mercy of Fed-induced bubbles. Real savings and investment are the building blocks to a strong and vibrant economy. When capital is created as a result of a person's hard work, it is invested cautiously in businesses believed to be solid long-term investments. This fosters business formation in new industries and grows an economy in real terms. Due to reckless monetary policies employed by the Federal Reserve over the past two decades, savings and investment have been completely distorted. Hedge funds willing to take huge risks chase bubbles all the way up and short them all the way down. This strategy, if well implemented, can make a hedge fund a lot of money; however, it does not grow an economy in the same way real savings and investment does. And so we witness that money creation via the Fed's manipulation creates a short-term boost in gross domestic product (GDP) by artificially propping up stocks or housing. Unfortunately, the real economy, or the Main Street economy as it is often referred to, for the past two decades has stagnated. Counterfeiting via the Federal Reserve creates massive imbalances in the economy, destroying the middle class; their purchasing power gets savaged, and it punishes savers and discourages investment as well. Therefore, viable growth cannot occur.

Savvy market participants are enticed to follow the Fed's every move, instead of establishing solid long-term investments. Volatility in the market led by hedge funds, high-frequency traders, and day traders has deterred investors from equities, repositioning them into the bond market like never before. Let's take a fun look at investor psychology over the past two decades.

In the late 1990s our investor fell madly and passionately in love with Internet stocks. His love affair with dot-com was a hot and heavy romance, leading him to chase every tail on Nasdaq. The Nasdaq was everything he ever wanted in an investment—she was young, hot, fast, and sexy—and he jumped in with both feet. Sadly, our investor quickly found out that dot-com and Nasdaq were not the investment he thought they would be, and he lost his heart along with a ton of money. Heartbroken, he lay in bed in the fetal position, swearing he would never invest in another stock as long as he lives.

Then in 2001, Greenspan initiated another round of easy money, and love was in the air again. This time he realized the love of his life, the investment of his dreams, was right in front of him—she was there all the time! Maybe he had to chase Nasdaq stocks, like Dorothy had to go over the rainbow, to realize there was no place like home. This romance was different—this investment didn't get him all worked up and then leave him hanging—she gave back. In fact, as interest rates went down and home prices went up, she threw off a tremendous amount of excess cash. His love affair with his house was so profitable, he picked up another one or two or three. This wasn't the same crazy, hot, fast romance he had with Nasdaq—this romance had a solid foundation; brick and mortar, real estate stood the test of time—it wasn't ephemeral. In fact, he was told that housing prices never went down. With the investment in housing, he was safe. Unfortunately, 2008 came and we learned otherwise—again, our investor was scorned, broke, and heartbroken and had just about given up on investing all together.

Now our investor has parked his money with the plainest Jane in town—this investment is boring, simple, and completely ubiquitous—and with interest rates already low and getting very close to zero—she seems to get more unattractive by the day. She puts out only twice a year, but he doesn't care, he's done with love, he just wants safety. She's the U.S. debt market—she's not as hot and fast as Nasdaq, she's not a domestic goddess like real estate, but she's backed by the U.S. government and the man with a printing press who knows how to use it. If you're not safe with this investment, you're not safe anywhere.

And so we see that after investors have taken so many shocks in recent years—the Nasdaq bubble, the real estate bubble, Madoff, the flash crash, the LIBOR scandal, MF Global, the Facebook initial public offering. They are seeking refuge in bonds. But don't take my word for it—TrimTabs also attributes the flood of money into savings vehicles and bond funds to a variety of factors:

> Poor stock market returns in the past 15 years, a weak economy, an aging population, stock market trading glitches, and increasingly aggressive central bank market manipulation. The typical American household isn't doing well financially, and retiring Baby Boomers are seeking safety rather than growth. Also, I think investors are wary of a market dominated by high-frequency trading and central bankers who are trying to take advantage of the trading robots by jawboning all the time about bailouts and money printing.[1]

And like the Sirens that sing a song so irresistible that none can hear it and escape, bubbles lure investors in. Investors seeking safety in bonds and the U.S. Treasury fail to realize that with interest rates so low, they are in fact making a very risky investment! They are being lured by the Sirens' beautiful song of safety to the Fed's next bubble in U.S. debt.

Remember from Chapter 2—one of the three factors that engender a bubble is that the asset in question is massively overpriced. This fact is always undisputed; think of the Nasdaq romance that had Internet stocks with no earnings trading at a million times eyeballs that view a Web page, investors' love affair with homes that led to prices rising 10 percent each year, and now think about bonds yielding nothing. Yielding negative real returns, far less than inflation! Everyone knows prices of these assets have become ridiculous, yet in each case they find justification for the madness. "Online purchases will replace brick-and-mortar stores." "Home prices have never and can never fall on a national basis." Today, we hear, "The world has no place else to park its savings but in our dollar and bond market, and there is no other safe and liquid place to put your money."

There is no way that bonds trading at historic lows are a safe investment—when bond yields go up, the price of bonds goes down. To make the argument that bond yields will never go up stands in the face of economic physics—there is no way that bond yields are going to remain at these low rates indefinitely. And when bond yields start to rise back toward historic norms, not only will investors realize what a poor place they chose to park their money, the U.S. government will realize it has lost control of our enormous debt and deficits.

You have to think for a minute about the bond investor, he may be a retiree looking for a safe vehicle to park his money. When interest rates initially begin to rise and his principal begins to fall, he may decide to wait it out, knowing he will eventually get his money back and accept the below market return on his investment. But that will not be the case if he or she owns a bond fund. These investments never mature. However, the major players in the bond market are seasoned professionals. As interest rates begin to rise, and worse if there is a market consensus that rates will rise even further, the bond professional isn't going to wait out underperforming bonds. After all, these professionals don't own bonds for their paltry yield—in fact, nobody really does. Once prices start going against them it won't take a big move in principal to wipe out that tiny yield. These bonds will become hot potatoes, bouncing around the market with nobody wanting to touch them. This will exacerbate the situation and drive rates higher—couple this with the Federal Reserve unwinding their balance sheet at the same time and watch out—interest rates will soar and the principal of low-yielding bonds will plummet!

Unfortunately, that Siren song, as soothing and comforting as it may sound, leaves many skeletons in its wake. Investors may not view this as a long-term commitment; in fact, they may view it as someplace to park their money until something better comes along. The only problem is that the parking lot is full and cars are now parking on the grass. And if you have ever tried to leave a parking lot after a big sporting event or concert, you know it can get ugly when everyone's attempting to exit at once.

The truth is that everyone doesn't have to leave the lot at once for the bubble in the Treasury to burst. In fact, there are many who argue with me and say that "U.S. debt can't be in a bubble because it is the largest and most liquid bond market and the world has no other choice but to park their savings in U.S. debt."

This assumes that there must be a mass selling of Treasuries from existing holders in order for them to fall in price. However, the U.S. debt market is like a stock that must issue a massive secondary offering each and every year. If XYZ Corp. had to come to the market in order to dilute its shares by 10 percent every year, the problem would become the need to find new buyers in perpetuity who were willing to pay the current market price. If the secondary offering failed to find buyers close to the prevailing price, the shares would begin to tumble even though there wasn't any selling from the existing shareholders. But the new price of the secondary would apply to all existing shares of the company. If the secondary offering failed, prices would need to fall until new buyers came in. If new buyers aren't incentivized to purchase XYZ unless the price were to fall precipitously, existing holders of the stock would realize immediately that the value of their asset was crumbling. That could start a panic out of XYZ shares and send prices plummeting. It is the exact same situation when dealing with U.S. Treasuries. The mass exit from U.S. debt would cause the dollar to tumble as foreigners sold greenbacks to repatriate into domestic currencies. When foreigners no longer view the greenback as the "safe haven," demand for our debt would plummet and interest rates would soar. Some people will say, "Of course, that could never happen with U.S. debt—right? After all, you're talking about America now, and the laws of mathematics, physics, and economics don't apply here." Keep reading and you will find out how it's virtually guaranteed to occur!

The Interest Rate Reality Check

Now, you may be thinking, "Pento—interest rates aren't going to soar—you're crazy. Bernanke and the Fed will keep rates low for a prolonged time and then gradually increase them and we will have a painless exit from the bond market." John Maynard Keynes famously said, "In the long run we will all be dead." Maybe that's what Bernanke is hoping for—that he can keep rates low until we are all dead. Unfortunately, that's not the way the market operates; when people lend you money, they eventually are going to want to get paid a return.

In forecasting the consequences of current economic policy, many pundits are downplaying the risks associated with the surging national debt and the rapid expansion of marketable Treasury securities. Their comfort stems from the belief that a staggering debt burden will be manageable as long as interest rates remain extremely low; and, as they believe the Fed is in complete control of setting rates across the yield curve, they see no danger of rates ever rising past the point of comfort. Those who subscribe to this fairy tale forget that, in real life, there are many more hands on the interest rate steering wheel.

The Congressional Budget Office estimates that the 2012 deficit will exceed $1.1 trillion, and total U.S. debt now stands at over $16.4 trillion (105 percent of gross domestic product [GDP]). That's a lot of debt that needs floating. Yet, as I write, the 10-year note is yielding 1.5 percent, which is 6.2 percentage points below its 40-year average. Experience teaches that even moderately long-term investors should be expecting rising rates. The simple truth is that unless the United States has entered into a multidecade deflationary depression, interest rates must at least mean revert in the near future. In fact, historically, we see that the average yield on the 10-year going back to 1969 is 7.3 percent. Regardless of the extreme and obvious misalignment of fundamentals and bond prices, the mantra from the dollar shills remains firm: "The U.S. dollar will always be the world's reserve currency, and the U.S. bond market will always be regarded as the safe-haven depository for global savings."

With interest rates having been so low for so long, it's under-standable that many people have forgotten that central banks are not ultimately in control of interest rates. It is true that the Fed can be highly influential across the yield curve and can be especially effective in controlling the short end. But, in the end, the free market has the last word on the cost of money.

Although the Fed has certainly created enough base money to send aggregate prices soaring, deleveraging forces and the problems over in Europe are, for now, disguising the evidence of runaway inflation. But when inflation finally erupts into the daylight, it will be impossible for borrowing costs to stay low. And no one can realistically be able to loan money below the rate of inflation forever. To attract buyers, the Treasury will soon have to offer a real rate of return.

Since our publicly traded debt level is increasing while our personal savings rate is not, we must inevitably rely more and more on foreign creditors to purchase our bonds. The problem is that the Chinese have been losing their appetite lately, and the Japanese savings rate is chasing ours down the tubes. Europe is also clearly suffering through its own sovereign debt issues. If not the Fed, who, then, will buy?

At this point, many economists breathe a sigh of relief. Since the Fed has no investment objectives, it could care less how much it loses by buying low-yielding Treasuries from banks. Given that the Fed has an unlimited supply of dollars to buy such debt, it could simply choose to pressure rates lower indefinitely, so long as that policy stance is deemed necessary to remedy a weak economy.

I concede that the Fed can always place bids for U.S. Treasuries. With Bernanke's license to counterfeit, the Fed could potentially buy all of the auctioned Treasury debt if it wanted to in order to keep rates low, but does that mean all debt markets will follow suit? All other interest rates; from bank loans, to municipal debt, to corporate debt, to the interest rates a bank pays their depositors would skyrocket. Will private banks continue to offer rock-bottom mortgage rates when inflation skyrockets? Given that the U.S. taxpayer is on the hook for losses at the government-sponsored enterprises (GSEs), maybe the Fed will be compelled to buy all MBS's to keep mortgage rates low. What about municipal debt? If rates on municipals soared, the Fed may need to buy all that debt as well. How about the corporate bond market? Can the Fed order a bank to loan to a company at a rate the bank does not find profitable? The only way to keep rates in all debt markets in line would be for the Fed to buy all kinds of debt in mass quantities, not just Treasury debt—hello Zimbabwe!

The truth is that such a policy has never been considered, let alone attempted, by any major economic power. And what will our foreign creditors think about such a strategy? Anyone with the ability to move investments outside the U.S. dollar would clearly do so, to avoid the wholesale debasement that such an inflationary policy would create. Once you take the argument to its logical conclusion, it is plain to see how futile, ignorant, and dangerous an attempt to hold all rates down by the Fed would be.

Ask any historian of Hungary, Germany, Argentina, Bosnia, or Zimbabwe why interest rates skyrocketed during their respective battles with hyperinflation. Why were their central banks unable to control borrowing costs?

In the end, central banks can only temporarily distort the savings-and-demand equation. The more the Fed prints, the higher the eventual rate of inflation will be. If mainstream pundits truly believe the Fed can supplant the entire public and private market for debt indefinitely, then I don't want to be around when that fantasy inevitably becomes a nightmare.

The truth is that there are three primary factors that determine the interest rate level a nation must pay to service its debt in the long term:

the currency, inflation, and credit risks of holding the sovereign debt. All three of those factors are very closely interrelated. Even though the central bank can exercise tremendous influence in the short run, the free market ultimately decides whether the nation has the ability to adequately finance its obligations and how high interest rates will go. An extremely high debt-to-GDP ratio, which elevates the country's credit risk inevitably leads to massive money printing by the central bank. That directly causes the nation's currency to fall while it also increases the rate of inflation.

It is true that a country never has to pay back all of its outstanding debt. However, it is imperative that investors in the nation's sovereign debt always maintain the confidence that it has the ability to do so. History has proven that once the debt to GDP ratio reaches circa 100 percent, economic growth comes to a halt. The problem is that the debt continues to accumulate without a commensurate increase in the tax base. Once the tax base can no longer adequately support the debt, interest rates rise sharply.

Today, our debt is a staggering 700 percent of income. And our annual deficit is about 50 percent of our entire annual federal revenue. If the U.S. government were an individual, his or her banker would remove any and all access to future credit in haste. This is unsustainable; the sad truth is that the United States has such an onerous amount of debt outstanding that the hope of continued solvency rests completely on the perpetual condition of interest rates that are kept ridiculously low. It isn't so much a mystery as to why the Fed is working overtime to keep interest rates from rising. If rates were allowed to rise to a level that could bring in the support of the free market, the vastly increased borrowing costs would cause the economy to falter and deficits to skyrocket. This would eventually lead to an explicit default on the debt.

But the key point here is that continuous and massive money printing by any central bank eventually causes hyperinflation, which mandates yields to rise much higher anyway. It is at that point where the country enters into an inflationary death spiral. The more money they print, the higher rates go to compensate for the runaway inflation. The higher rates go, the worse economic growth becomes, and the greater the debt-to-GDP ratio grows. That puts further pressure on rates to rise and for the central bank to then increase the amount of debt monetization, and so the deadly cycle repeats and intensifies.

The bottom line is that the United States will eventually undergo a massive debt restructuring the likes of which history has never before witnessed. Such a default will either take the form of outright principal reduction or, alternatively, the central bank will set a course for intractable inflation. Unfortunately, history illustrates that the inflation route is always tried first.

If history were a guide, it would reveal how quickly Bernanke could lose control of interest rates to the free-market forces requiring a higher return. In 2009 the Greek two-year note was trading at 1.3 percent; by December of 2011 it was at 153 percent, and now it is in the neighborhood of 225 percent. Even at 225 percent are you going to back up the truck and load up on Greek debt? Probably not; despite the huge return, you have most likely lost faith in the Greek government's ability to ever pay you back. That's what happens when the market decides your debt burden has grown too onerous. Remember, this is Greece, not Zimbabwe. Greece is the cradle of civilization, creator of the Olympic Games. In 2004, they hosted the Olympic Games—this isn't some obscure banana republic. Greek debt is issued in euros, not drachmas. The euro is the currency of the second-largest economy on this planet.

It is a bitter pill the market prescribes when they deem your debt to be unmanageable. In fact, just look at the chart of the Greek 10-year in Figure 5.1 and see how fast the market can turn. And imagine what would happen if the U.S. 10-year note ever went anywhere near 40 percent.

In the long run, Bernanke's low interest rate mirage will disappear when the market demands higher rates, exposing the enormous bubble in the bond market. Investors, who sought refuge from a volatile market or sought a safe lot to park their money, will realize that the U.S. Treasury at historically low rates was not safe. When the markets lose confidence in the government's ability to manage and pay back their debt, Bernanke will lose his control of interest rates and they will skyrocket. Investors will realize how full that lot was and that getting out isn't going to be painless.

So now we know that the economic reality is when money supply growth becomes excessive, the economy becomes unbalanced and inflation gets concentrated in certain asset classes—we saw this with tulip

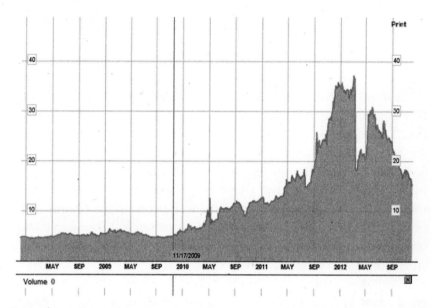

Figure 5.1 Greek 10-Year

bulbs in the 1600s, with real estate and equities in 1980s Japan, with Nasdaq in the late 1990s, and with real estate in the 2000s. But it gets worse—in the late 1990s Alan Greenspan used a garden hose to shower the economy with money, fostering the Nasdaq bubble. A 1 percent Fed Funds rate helped to drench the economy in 2000s, producing the real estate bubble. The man in charge of our Federal Reserve today doesn't use a garden hose to water the economy—he has a fire hose and is drowning us in money. The desire investors have for safety combined with regulations like Basel III are steering capital into the U.S. Treasury. A 1 percent Fed Funds rate that existed for two years created the massive real estate bubble that brought down the economy of the entire planet. A zero percent Fed Funds rate that will have existed for at least six years will ensure that this Treasury bubble is the biggest bubble in history!

The Teaser Rate on U.S. Debt—Reality Check

I'm going to suspend reality for a moment and turn everything that I know about economics, which I reverently refer to as Pentonomics, on its head. We are about to enter the twilight zone and imagine Pentonomics is completely erroneous in order to prove that I am still right about the bubble in U.S. debt. Confused? You won't be in a minute. . . .

Assume Pentonomics is wrong. In this anti–Pentonomics paradigm, Ben Bernanke is the omnipresent all-knowing kingpin of interest rates. Paul Krugman won the "End This Depression Now!" game show, and the increase in government spending and counterfeiting revives this flailing economy. The government increases our debt load from $16 trillion to $20 trillion in two years (that is actually not an unbelievable number) and we achieve nirvana—the heavens have parted, the economy recovered, the Keynesian utopia has arrived! Pentonomics was wrong—you can spend and counterfeit your way to prosperity—we can all breathe a sigh of relief. Not so fast. . . .

With the economy booming, unemployment plummets—more good news! Yes, but in this is the counter-Pentonomic reality: inflation soars due to all these new spenders entering the economy. What do you think the omnipotent master of interest rates, the all-knowing Ben Bernanke, would do? Prevailing Fed wisdom tells me that in any economic paradigm, he will have to raise interest rates significantly in order to sop up all the excess base money he saturated the economy with to achieve his objective. Channeling Paul Volcker, Bernanke raises rates in order to wring out the inflation caused by all the jobs in the economy—following so far? Even a move in interest rates to a more normalized level of 7 percent would send debt service costs soaring. In 2011, we paid $454 billion to service our debt, and that was with interest rates at historic and unprecedented lows. Add a few more trillion in debt and an additional five or six percentage points and we are still in trouble—despite a healthy rebound.

Now, before the Krugman types cause a stir—I am going to admit the following—an increase in growth will certainly increase revenues from taxes, and removing people from the public dole of unemployment and food stamps will reduce government spending. Even with the increase in revenue and decrease in spending, we will still not be able to manage the enormous costs of servicing our debt. Why? Because the government has taken an adjustable-rate $20 trillion dollar mortgage out on this economy!

In order for the bubble in U.S. debt not to burst, you have to both suspend economic reality and believe Bernanke is in complete control of rates, assume the economy will be in a deflationary depression for the amount of time it takes to refinance our debt to a 30-year fixed rate, and then also get future spending under control. Unless Treasury refinances all the debt for 30 years at these low rates—assuming there are enough lobotomized buyers to lend to the government in the low single digits for 30 years—any increase back to more normalized levels will expose our nation's insolvency and the bubble in the Treasury. So I am right even when I'm wrong!

That's why it troubles me greatly to know that while the 30-year Treasury bond is yielding as little as 2.8 percent, we are not locking in that low rate for our newly issued debt. Any thinking American knows it would be best to take advantage of that ridiculously low yield and finance the Treasury's borrowing at the long end of the curve.

However, much like those homeowners who chose to think in terms of weeks, not years, when evaluating their long-term finances, our government has subjected us all to what amounts to the mother lode of all subprime adjustable-rate mortgages.

The fact that the Treasury Department must issue a record amount of debt in the ensuing years will put upward pressure on interest rates. Add to that a record-low Fed Funds rate and a $3 trillion monetary base that is growing by a trillion dollars each year, and the prospects for higher inflation and rising interest rates are fairly certain. So why are those in power refusing to ensure the future solvency of our country?

Here are the relevant facts to make you aware of just how significant this problem really is. In an average week the United States can sell somewhere in the neighborhood of $109 billion in auctions—the most troubling aspect isn't the sheer volume of debt that must be sold; it is the fact that most of it is being sold on the short end of the yield curve.

The overall debt picture is subject to the same fiscal irresponsibility. According to a 2011 report issued by the Treasury, of the total marketable securities held by the public, 59 percent will mature in the next four years! Mitch Stapley, chief fixed-income officer at Fifth Third Asset Management in Grand Rapids, Michigan, explained it this way: "There has never been a single example in the history of finance where financing long-term liabilities, which we are, with short-term debt, ends well."[2]

If Pentonomics is correct, the Fed's lucky streak of luring bond investors with low interest rates will eventually draw to a close and expose that the extended period of low borrowing costs has bred a new breed of investor. To the bulls and bears, we can now add the ostriches—those who bury their heads in the sand of declining debt service ratios while refusing to face up to intractable levels of total U.S. government debt. If these ostriches were to actually look at the numbers, they would realize that it is their investments that are made of sand.

As the issuer of the world's reserve currency, the U.S. government has thus far enjoyed the benefits of low interest rates despite its inflationary practices. When we run a trade deficit with foreign countries, they have a strong incentive to "recycle" our deficit back into our dollars and Treasuries. This practice has hidden what would otherwise be much higher borrowing costs and much lower purchasing power for the dollar.

However, even if I am wrong and the free market doesn't force rates up in the near future, when Bernanke's counterfeiting campaign accomplishes its goal of cementing inflation into the economy, the Fed will be forced into raising rates to mollify the sting from skyrocketing food and energy costs. But, either way, holders of the U.S Treasury have been led astray by the low debt service ratio that has masked our economy's underlying insolvency. Even if interest rates simply revert to their average level—not a stretch, given rising commodity prices, robust money supply growth rates, and endless Fed money printing—the debt service expense could easily reach over $1 trillion, or about 40 percent of all federal revenue collected today. Now imagine what would happen if rates were to rise to the level of Spain or Italy. Don't forget: as interest rates rise, GDP growth slows, sending the debt-to-GDP ratio even higher. Either way, we end up unable to manage our enormous debt burden.

It remains a mystery why our government refuses to lock in a low interest rate for our ballooning debt obligations. Maybe they just know there aren't enough long-term buyers out there. But isn't it worth a try? Of course, the initial outlay of interest would be higher, but wouldn't that be worth it to know we are locking in a rate that is near an all-time record low? My guess is that the current budget deficit would be significantly higher if the debt were sold longer term. Therefore, it is just more politically expedient to mortgage our future instead. Maybe

Treasury fears a 30-year auction with nobody showing up. This failed auction will create panic, exposing the bubble in the Treasury.

There's no denying the huge gamble that we have undertaken. Because our surging debt load must be rolled over more frequently, we have made a bet that rates will stay low for a very long time. However, we now have in place what amounts to the perfect recipe for creating intractable inflation, a currency collapse, and a bond market debacle— artificial and temporary low interest rates, free and easy money, and runaway debt. All of which virtually guarantees interest rates will be much higher in the future.

The options subprime mortgage borrowers hoped for of either being able to refinance at a lower rate or sell their homes at a profit never materialized. Instead, many were forced to declare bankruptcy and/or walk away from the properties. Unfortunately, if the U.S. Treasury does not get its fiscal house in order, we may be forced to effectually walk away from our debt, either through default or by paying it back in worthless dollars.

It wasn't just the nominal level of debt that suddenly sent Euroland into insolvency but, much more significantly, a spike in debt service payments. Right now, the U.S. national debt is the biggest subprime adjustable-rate mortgage of all time. Much like homeowners who thought they could afford a mortgage that was 10 times their annual incomes, investors are blinded by deceptively low current rates of interest. These ostriches won't poke their heads up to see the writing on the wall: skyrocketing debt and quantitative easing cannot coexist for long in the context of low interest rates. As rates continue to rise, the reality of U.S. insolvency will be revealed and the bubble in the Treasury will be exposed.

Banker Reality Check

In Frank Capra's 1946 film *It's a Wonderful Life*, we are introduced to the noble but beleaguered George Bailey, whose dream to travel the world is squashed by his commitment to his family's Building and Loan Association. *It's a Wonderful Life* is not only a heartwarming Christmas classic but also provides an interesting glimpse into banking of the early 1900s.

In December 1816, the first depository savings bank, the Philadelphia Savings Fund Society, launched an industry that changed the face of banking and the American economy. Savings and loans accepted cash deposits from customers, made loans to borrowers, and financed a rapidly growing consumer sector of the economy. They enabled a growing middle class to obtain the American dream of owning a home or a car.

During the depression, the government played an active role in all areas of the economy, including banking and housing. The typical mortgage before the government intervened was five years in length, ending in a balloon payment (principal plus interest). These loans were usually renewed for another five-year term. The National Housing Act of 1934 changed the structure of the typical American mortgage, allowing Americans to lock in to rates for a longer period. This encouraged home ownership—in 1930, about 33 percent of American households owned their own homes; by 1990 Americans enjoyed 67 percent home ownership. Government programs such as the Federal Housing Administration, its FHA-insured loans, and the GI Bill also increased the availability of 30-year fixed-rate mortgages.

In 1938, as part of the New Deal, we were introduced to the now infamous housing beauty Fannie Mae (the Federal National Mortgage Association). Fannie Mae started out in life as a government-sponsored enterprise (GSE) whose purpose was to expand the secondary mortgage market by securitizing mortgages in the form of MBSs. We have since learned that government sponsored means the risk of loss was on taxpayers, while executives bestowed themselves lavish private-sector salaries. Fannie provided local banks with federal money to finance home mortgages and created a liquid secondary mortgage market. In the first 30 years following its inception, Fannie Mae held a monopoly over the secondary mortgage market and allowed lenders to proliferate their lending.

It would take until 1970 to meet her equally charming brother, Freddie Mac (the Federal Home Mortgage Corporation). In the late 1960s, Washington decided that Fannie needed some competition, so they gave her a sibling, apparently anticipating that a little sibling rivalry would produce more mortgages and more home ownership—and it did! In a move that would later come back to haunt them, they allowed these quasi-government agencies to be listed as publicly traded companies, completely blurring the public/private line.

With the government in the driver's seat, the pre–depression era mortgage had been completely replaced with the 30-year fixed. This mortgage gave Americans the ability to repay in small amounts over time and provided a great boost to house affordability.

If George Bailey continued at the Building and Loan, he would have eventually realized it was "a wonderful life." According to Dale Steinreich, "The idyllic life of a savings and loan banker from the end of World War II to about the mid-1960s conformed to the rule of 3–6–3: pay your depositors 3 percent, earn 6 percent on their home loans, and be on the golf course by 3:00 P.M.".[3]

Unfortunately, that sublime life was about to take another tragic turn; in the 1970s that angel may have had to reprise his role and talk our lovable George Bailey off the ledge of the bridge again. This time it wasn't the evil Mr. Potter antagonizing George; it was the Federal Reserve and government regulations.

It's important to note that banks are in the business of borrowing on the short end of the yield curve and lending on the long end. Since interest rates are generally lower for shorter time durations, banks make profits by capturing the spread. But if the gap between long-term and short-term rates narrows, or sometimes vanishes completely, banks have a much harder time operating. Rapid and dramatic changes in interest rates also expose banks to money-losing risks. The truth is that low and stable interest rates are paramount toward maintaining a strong and stable economy. That condition gets obliterated under a fiat currency system.

In a free market, whenever the supply of savings contracts the cost of money tends to increase. And the opposite is also true. Theoretically, when the townspeople of *It's a Wonderful Life's* Bedford Falls save more in aggregate, George will have lots of money to lend, so he will lower borrowing rates and increase the demand for borrowing. Conversely, if the bank were low on deposits, they would raise rates to entice savings and thus increase the propensity of the townspeople to save. Consequently, in a free economy, market forces tend to stabilize interest rate volatility. However, in the United States, interest rates are anything but free.

Here's why—when interest rates are set by a few people behind closed doors, as they are by the Federal Reserve, massive distortions can occur in the supply-and-demand metric. We saw this in the last two bubbles, where the easy money gave entrepreneurs a false signal to borrow and spend and we got the Nasdaq bubble and the housing bubble. In the 1970s, the loose monetary policies endorsed by the pre-Volcker Fed brought about the savings-and-loan (S&L) crisis of the early 1990s.

Rising interest rates, which were a direct response to rising inflation, soon found S&Ls paying out more on their short-term borrowed funds than they were collecting on their long-term assets. The consequences for those imbalances caused by our central bank rendered nearly 1,000 banks insolvent.

Following World War II, interest rate on 10-year T-bonds was 2.8 percent in 1953 and 4 percent by 1963. This was a banker's steep yield curve with short-term rates falling lower than long-term rates. However, by 1982, the rate on 10-year T-bonds was 13.9 percent, and, even worse for S&Ls, the rate on 1-year T-bills was 14 percent—leaving not only higher rates but, worse, a banker's dreaded inverted yield curve. The banks were upside down in their lending. According to Steinreich, "For S&Ls, the rule of 3–6–3 had turned into 8–6–0, quickly sinking them into heavier and heavier losses."[4]

But for George and his fellow S&L bankers, it gets even worse. The Fed used Regulation Q (its authority to set maximum rates on time deposits given to it by the Banking Act of 1933) for the first time to lower (instead of raise) deposit rates in 1967. The Federal Deposit Insurance Corporation (FDIC) and the Federal Savings and Loan Insurance Corporation (FSLIC) extended the rate ceiling over every institution they had jurisdiction over. If I were a saver in 1967, my option on choosing a bank at that time was who gave out the best toaster oven; banks didn't compete with interest rates, they competed with kitchen appliances.

Necessity is often the mother of invention. While banks were locked into the same substandard interest rate, the money market fund (MMF) was born. MMFs were not subject to Regulation Q, and brokerage houses like Fidelity, Dreyfus, and Merrill Lynch jumped in to fill the higher interest rate demand. The cash that was sitting making little at banks quickly fled to MMFs for higher rates.

In 1980, deregulation eliminated Regulation Q, but it was already too late—most S&Ls were steeped in huge losses. Congress played legislative catch-up and enticed S&Ls into the business of funding strip malls. Positive pro-growth tax policy instituted by the Reagan administration to lower the rates and broaden the base took away many tax loopholes, leaving strip mall investment less desirable. The elimination of tax incentive loopholes put the final nail in the S&L coffin. By 1989 the S&L crisis was in full throttle, leaving over 1,000 banks in its wake.

And so we saw that after the S&L crisis, banks have gotten smarter—to mitigate this problem, early in the last decade banks began turning more and more to securitization as a way to unload the mortgages on their books by packaging and selling loans to outside investors. Not only does securitization bring in fees and reduce banks' risk exposure, but it also sucks in more capital to the real estate market, while increasing financial-sector profits. It's no wonder that the securitization market grew to over $10 trillion in the United States before the credit crisis of 2008. On paper, this was a good solution to the problem, but additional government involvement in the securitization market threw in a monkey wrench.

Given the size and diversity of the investment market in the United States and around the world, there was adequate private demand for securitized mortgages. With relatively low risk and more generous yields than government debt, pension funds and other institutional investors bought heavily. However, as the Federal Reserve continued to lower rates and as the government-engineered housing boom finally went bust, this private-label demand dried up almost completely. By September 6, 2008, it was clear that Fannie and Freddie encouraged too many subpar lenders to obtain the American dream and they could not survive without a government takeover and were forced into conservatorship.

The GSEs now provide financing for 9 out of 10 mortgages. Therefore, the real estate market today is virtually 100 percent distorted and manipulated by government forces. The GSE business model faced inherent conflicts due to its combination of government mission and private ownership.

The Federal Reserve's manipulation of interest rates, in conjunction with shortsighted government regulation always bears unintended consequences. Such unintended consequences created the S&L crisis in the late 1990s and helped spawn the banking crisis in 2008, and are creating a huge bubble in U.S. debt today. The chairman and CEO of North Jersey Community Bank (NJCB), Frank Sorrentino, agrees that regulations force behavior that wouldn't normally occur, often leading to dire consequences. "Think of what happened in 2008 with subprime, how many banks were forced to make bad loans because of CRA? Those banks didn't get a bail-out—they got a welcome to the FDIC and they were closed."[5]

Regulations such as the Community Reinvestment Act (CRA) persuaded banks to make risky home loans they would not have otherwise made. Today, government policies such as Basel III are encouraging the accumulation of sovereign debt in a similar way Basel II encouraged the accumulation of CDOs and MBSs. Although Basel III is not directly affecting Mr. Sorrentino's decision making, he confers that regulations like CRA and Basel III "force behavior that wouldn't normally occur" and therefore will "stoke behaviors that the regulators aren't really contemplating." In an effort to conform to regulations, decisions are "not based on economics, they (regulations) force banks to do things that they wouldn't normally do and there are often unintended consequences."[6]

In 2008, the banking industry went through an enormous shock—the Fed's low interest rates coupled with regulations such as CRA had banks making questionable loans. Regulations like Basel II encouraged banks to accumulate the optimistically rated AAA MBSs and CDOs. Today, the zero percent Fed Funds rate and regulations such as Basel III are creating similar unintended consequences—an enormous bubble in the U.S. Treasury.

With the Fed Funds rate at an artificial zero percent, it is difficult to imagine how banks are currently managing their balance sheet and how they would respond to a sudden dramatic move up in interest rates. Mr. Sorrentino agrees that the Fed's low rate environment has been making it harder on retail banking establishments.

NJCB is an anomaly, admits Sorrentino, ". . . it has always been making loans and continues to do so." Once upon a time, he notes, banks would leverage a steep yield curve by taking in deposits and investing in government securities and be on the golf course by 3 o'clock." In a zero percent rate environment, Sorrentino acknowledges, "banks can't play that game anymore."[7]

Although banks such as NJCB felt the Fed's initial liquidity was necessary, Sorrentino wonders, "At what point have we gone too far? At what point do we no longer need low rates to boost the economy and instead let interest rates normalize to where they need to be. Fed's low rates not only punish banks like us, but also every saver and pension fund, damage is clearly being done. How far are they willing to go with it? At some point you will be unable to undo the damage."[8]

Mr. Sorrentino is confident his bank would manage if interest rates took a sudden spike up. He explained that 30 percent of his balance sheet is interest rate neutral and a significant portion of his loan portfolio adjusts with rates; he is aware that not all banks his size are managing their balance sheet as well.

NJCB is compensating for the Fed's ultra-low interest rate policy by increasing its balance sheet—we are making "every loan that makes sense for our bank." However, he is aware that larger institutions such as Goldman Sachs and JPMorgan Chase are loading up on Treasuries instead of making loans. Despite the record low Treasury yields, it is evident by data provided by the Federal Reserve on assets held by banks, big banks such as JPMorgan Chase and Goldman Sachs are increasing their exposure to U.S. Treasuries; they "make it up in fees they collect from the government, from the sale of government securities."[9]

In fact, a recent article in Bloomberg confers that as banks' deposits are rising, so is their proclivity for government securities. Bloomberg notes:

> As deposits increased 3.3 percent to $8.88 trillion in the two months ended July 31, business lending rose 0.7 percent to $7.11 trillion, Federal Reserve data show. The record gap of $1.77 trillion has expanded 15 percent since May, the biggest similar-period gain since July 2010. Banks have already bought $136.4 billion in Treasury and government agency debt this year, more than double the $62.6 billion in all of 2011, pushing their holdings to an all-time high of $1.84 trillion."[10]

Over the past four years, too-big-to-fail banks such as Goldman Sachs and Citigroup have grown larger into what I like to call "too big to succeed." They appear willing to purchase low-yielding government securities, enticed by fees they collect. Accounting rules don't require banks to mark Treasuries to market if they are held to maturity, and there is no capital reserve requirement for holding them either, so big banks have piled in head-first. However, if the market's lack of confidence in the dollar and the government's ability to manage its debt caused a huge spike in interest rates, holding a Treasury at cost wouldn't compensate these banks for their underperforming debt. Their balance sheets would become completely upside down, similar to the S&Ls after Volcker's rate hikes. But these banks are huge—this would be the S&L crisis on steroids! I assume that, if questioned, Jamie Dimon or Lloyd Blankfein would contend they are properly hedged against this risk. OK, Jamie—does AIG and the London Whale ring a bell?

Holders of MBSs in 2006 would have argued that they were properly hedged by the credit default swaps (CDSs) they purchased from AIG. However, AIG required a bailout from the Federal Reserve in order to make due on their CDS obligations. If interest rates are spiking from a worldwide lack of confidence in the value of the dollar, how is the market going to perceive a Fed bailout for bank counterparties from whom they've bought protection? This move would send the dollar into free fall.

If the main driving force of dramatically rising rates is perpetuated from the market's loss of confidence in the United States' ability to manage its debt, how will the market perceive our government piling on new debt to bail out insolvent banks? You can take a clue from what's going on over in Europe, but I'll have much more to say on that in Chapter 7.

Despite this, Mr. Sorrentino feels confident that "too big to fail isn't going to be allowed to fail at this moment—however there are at least 6500 other banks that are not going to meet the same fate."[11]

But that still leaves me to ponder—if rates soar due to investors' lack of confidence in the U.S. dollar and the government's ability to manage their debt—how are the banks going to get bailed out? The Federal Reserve will certainly come to the rescue and counterfeit—sure, we'll all get our deposits back, but the real question is: will those dollars be worth anything? Such is the consequence of allowing a few people the right to dictate the most important price in a free-market economy: the cost of money.

The China Reality Check

There is a funny colloquialism describing the relationship of bankers and borrowers: "If you owe your bank $1 million, that's your problem; if you owe them $1 billion, it's their problem." Following this logic given our $1.2 trillion dollar indebtedness to China, we could conclude that is one major problem—for us and for them.

You can't have an economic analysis about the bubble in U.S. debt without exploring China's role in abetting it and their possible contribution to prompting its burst.

The United States is a nation of consumers—Americans love to buy "things." Stroll through a Wal-Mart or a Dollar Store—Americans' love affair with buying, our proclivity for purchasing a large quantity of items for a low price, is on vulgar display. Americans love to buy—we love our "things."

As proficient as Americans are at purchasing "things," the Chinese are equally skilled at mass producing "things." Unfortunately, Chinese goods are often not only inexpensive; they are also cheap in quality. Think about it—would you ever fly a plane that was built in China or drive a Chinese-manufactured car? Of course not! Lucky for them, many Americans like cheap "things," regardless of the quality, and all of the cheap things feed Americans' desire for more "stuff."

But it gets better—when Americans consume merchandise made in China they pay with U.S. dollars, the government of China takes those dollars and prints yuan, then repatriates those dollars back to the United States as debt. This enables our addiction to cheap plastic goods and knock-off designer handbags by keeping our currency strong and interest rates low, while also stoking our compulsion for consumption, reckless deficit spending and debt.

This is the currency manipulation that China engages in. But make no mistake—the United States is a currency manipulator as well. After all, what do you call printing $2 trillion in the last few years alone?

The key point here is that not only does China work as an enabler by buying our debt and allowing the U.S. government to spend beyond its means, but it also has led to an enormous bubble in the Treasuries.

There is no doubt that our onerous and uncompetitive policies have hurt our balance of trade. Since 2000, the United States has seen its manufacturing sector as a percentage of GDP drop from 14.5 percent to 12.2 percent.[12] More troubling is the jobs picture. The number of manufacturing jobs lost in the United States since 2002 is 3.12 million. And the number of goods-producing jobs lost is 4.03 million![13]

Here's proof that the answer for the U.S. manufacturing dilemma can't be found by simply forcing the Chinese to appreciate their currency or by devaluing the U.S. dollar. History clearly shows any such currency manipulation strategy to be a complete failure. They tried it between 2005 and 2008. In 2005, China announced it would increase the value of its currency and abandon its decade-old fixed exchange rate to the U.S. dollar in favor of a link to a basket of world currencies. Later, in 2008, China then returned to a peg against the dollar. However, during that time frame the yuan rallied from 0.1208 USD to 0.1467 USD (a move of over 20 percent). But the falling dollar had a negligible effect on U.S. exports. For all of 2005 the U.S. deficit with China was $201.5 billion. In 2008, three years into the dollar devaluation and yuan appreciation, it soared to $266.3 billion (more than a 32 percent increase). The truth is that there is nothing as important as the state of labor, taxes, and regulations within a given country. So, eventually, the Chinese should wake up and abandon their foolish currency peg. It creates domestic inflation, doesn't help the trade balance, and stupidly hinges Chinese wealth on the continued lofty valuations of our currency and bond market.

The irony is that communist China employs more growth-oriented principles such as low taxes and reduced regulations. The United States has the most productive labor force in the world; the Chinese can't compete with us on human capital. However, they kill us on low taxes and less regulations. They foster a more favorable environment than the United States in starting a business. But don't get confused—China is a completely managed economy.

China employs a mercantilist, statist, centrally planned, top-down approach to manage their economy and trade. Such centrally planned statist economies tend to forgo benefits to individual citizens in an effort to enhance the state. China boasts huge GDP figures—albeit at a reducing rate—and plans world domination by owning foreign countries' debt.

Economists define these protectionist policies that devalue currency in attempt to boost exports as beggar-thy-neighbor. The goal of a beggar-thy-neighbor policy is to increase demand for a country's exports while also reducing demand for the countries imports. To be clear, I believe that China manipulates its currency, they engage in the beggar-thy-neighbor currency devaluation race to the bottom. However, the U.S. dollar is winning the currency debasement derby, and for some stupid reason the Chinese have gone along for the ride.

If the Chinese don't want to sell dollars and drive up the value of the yuan, then perhaps we need to consume less and/or produce more as a country. Because of the vast quantities of Treasury holdings the Chinese possess, I believe we just aren't in the position to force them to do much of anything.

Besides, do the Commerce and Treasury Departments believe that a yuan revaluation will cause factories to sprout up in the United States like spring dandelions? If devalued currency alone were the recipe for economic growth and manufacturing, then Zimbabwe would be the manufacturing capital of the world! Are they? Why don't you walk around your house and turn over some stuff and see how many items you can find with "Made in Zimbabwe" stamped on the back. Not many? I didn't think so! To paraphrase Bill Clinton's 1990 slogan, "It's not just the currency manipulation stupid," it's also tax, labor, and regulations. Contrary to what many think, the United States should lower taxes and reduce regulations if it wants to compete better with the Chinese. We should also concentrate on boosting our high-tech manufacturing output and not necessarily seek to just supplant China's textile industry.

A trade and currency war with China will have a detrimental effect on both countries, but less so for the Chinese. For China, it will mean fewer exports and a lower value on their current Treasury holdings. However, a rising yuan will also boost living standards for all Chinese citizens. Just think about the benefits received from reduced prices on their metals and energy-related imports. Eventually, the Chinese will grow its middle class and be able to consume its own production.

Many still believe we have the upper hand on China—with all the money we owe them, they are indebted to the solvency of our country if they ever expect to be repaid. So they simply don't have any other choice but to squander their savings in U.S. dollars and debt. But I don't buy into that reasoning. When our dollar and bond market starts to crumble, China will find that it's nonsensical to continue to park their savings in the United States.

If the Chinese were to stop recycling their trade deficits with the United States and let their currency appreciate, shrinking the deficit, it would mean a much higher interest expense on our debt as the Treasury Department scampers to find a replacement for China's support of our bond market. In this fragile world economy, the United States might have a hard time finding another foreign buyer with such large pockets. It would also send interest rates up to a level that would cripple our still overleveraged private sector and now massively indebted public sector. And, unlike the Chinese, it would mean the return of inflation in earnest for all U.S. consumers—especially given our heavy reliance on imports.

In 1989, we saw the uprising in China's Tiananmen Square. Grievances over inflation and limited freedoms sent young Chinese to the streets in a massacre that may have left as many as 2,600 dead. During 1987–1988 the official CPI jumped from 7.3 percent to 18.5 percent and then to 28 percent in early 1989.[14] Unrest in China over soaring consumer prices is still simmering under the surface; however, Chinese citizens appear willing to accept inflation as long as the manufactured economic boom in China carries on.

To maintain their currency peg, the People's Bank of China had to print trillions of yuan and perpetually hold more than 1 trillion U.S. dollars in reserve.

The simple fact is that a strong currency offers the benefit of greater domestic consumption, while a weaker currency offers nothing but inflation.

The Chinese government should take the path that preserves and balances their economy while enriching their entire population, rather than go down the road to never-ending inflation in a foolish attempt to boost exports. For China, the realistic hope is that the greater purchasing power of a strong currency will enable its growing middle class to supplant U.S. consumers as the end market for China's own manufacturing efforts. However, for the United States the challenge will be to develop a diversified manufacturing base in an expeditious manner before surging interest rates, a plummeting dollar, and soaring inflation overwhelm the economy.

If China makes the decision in the future against inflation, it will be a great move for its people. But at the same time it would be detrimental for the United States because of our reliance on repatriation of the trade imbalance to fund the enormous debt. If the Chinese choose not to inflate their currency, they will no longer be in the business of repatriating U.S. dollars. And the United States is in jeopardy of losing its best foreign customer of U.S. debt.

The United States can't afford to lose China as a buyer of our debt—inflation, trade wars, uprisings, and a growing middle class are all looming as possible reasons for China to scale back on U.S. debt. However, there is one more dark cloud looming over China, and this one could be big.

China is a command-and-control economy that has a horrible monetary strategy and weak renminbi policy. The Chinese economy defies the laws of basic economics that rewards a stable currency, land ownership, and a bottom-up economic structure. However, due to their enormous manufacturing base and $3 trillion in currency reserves, many investors chose to ignore the rules of economics and remain extremely enamored with the Chinese economic paradigm. Today, China stands as a bit of an anomaly in economics—however, there is growing concern that its centrally planned utopia is on the verge of collapse. And so we shall explore some issues with the Chinese economy that may not only threaten their vision of world domination but, more important, impede their ability to continue as the largest foreign consumer of U.S. debt. As we will see, China may have more problems than inflation to worry about. According to some, China has a massive real estate bubble waiting to burst.

Those who love to extol the virtues of a free-market economy often don't apply those principles to China. How is it that they believe the only place on Earth where an oligarchy can micromanage the allocation of capital with impunity is China?

In 2008, spurred on by the economic crisis in the United States, the Chinese government employed massive monetary expansion, a favorite Keynesian remedy for times of economic hardship. The government of China was trying to increase domestic investment and consumption, as well as to compensate for the slowdown in exports. In November 2008 the government announced it would invest $586 billion for the purpose of stimulating growth.

However, as any Keynesian knows, *investment* is always a code word for spending and counterfeiting. As we saw with my "End This Depression Now!" game show—when a government engages in digging and filling in order to spur economic growth that investment is never allocated in the most efficient way. In Chinese, digging and filling appears to translate to building and not occupying—another reason to hate China's one child policy.

Just like the United States in 2008, the Chinese real estate market is plagued by over construction. This over construction is not limited to megacities like Shanghai, Beijing, and Shenzhen. "Brand-new ghost towns have sprung up all across China in recent years, the most famous of which is perhaps Kangbashi in Ordos, Inner Mongolia. That city's housing capacity can currently accommodate well over 300,000 residents, yet only one tenth of that number actually live there. Numerous other lesser-known cities also boast swaths of high-rise apartments and majestic public buildings while appearing to be entirely devoid of residents."[15]

Similar to the United States in the mid-2000s, we see enormous speculation in real estate in China. With high inflation and low bond yields, Chinese citizens have been enticed to invest in high-return condos in these Chinese ghost towns. Inflation is greater than the yield on the 10-year. It is extremely difficult for the Chinese citizen to find investments that yield more than inflation.

China imposes tight restrictions for returns on bank accounts, government bond yields, and other domestic investments. When the easy-money policies took charge after the worldwide crash of 2008, the excess cash flowed into the only place with big returns—real estate.

> The regulated Chinese banks, run primarily through the government, require high down payments and discourage the ownership of multiple homes. However, unregulated financing activity is running rampant throughout China. According to *SocGen's Wei Yao:*
>
> Trillions of Yuan in capital have been raised through investment trusts, underground money markets and high-yield retail investment products to sustain short-term liquidity for those who are cut off from the formal credit market, especially

small- and medium- enterprises, private property developers, and more recently, local government financing vehicles.[16]

Writing for the Casey Report, James Quinn described China's economy as "a house of cards," and pointed out that "Fitch downgraded the country's credit rating and warned there was a 60 percent chance the Chinese banking system will require a bailout in the next two years."[17]

In the same issue, Doug Casey wrote,

It's not just Europe, the United States and Japan that are riding for a fall but also the Chinese. What's coming up, in other words, is a worldwide financial and economic cataclysm.[18]

Investor Jim Chanos takes this one step further—

The Chinese government's balance sheet directly does not have a lot of debt. The state-owned enterprises of the local governments and all the other ancillary borrowing vehicles have lots of debt and it's growing at a very fast rate. The assumption is that the state stands behind all this debt. We see that the debt in China, implicitly backed by the Chinese government, probably has gone from about 100 percent of GDP to about 200 percent of GDP recently. Those are numbers that are staggering. Those are European kind of numbers if not worse.[19]

Chanos also notes that China may very well become "Dubai times 1000."[20]

Much like America in 2006, we see that China is plagued by staggering levels of credit expansion, speculation, malinvestment, and toxic loans. There is a belief that the central planning bureaucrats in the Chinese government can manage this situation—that may be a dangerous assumption. The laws of economics are ubiquitous and they cannot be over ridden by force. China is going against the natural tide of economics, applying top-down central planning to an economy that is driven by bottom-up market forces. We have seen through history that reckless credit expansion always leads to the same things: price inflation, malinvestment, and bubbles. The good thing for the Chinese is they still have a huge pile of savings parked in foreign currency reserves. The United States enjoys no such pleasure.

There are several factors prevalent to hinder the Chinese enthusiasm for U.S. debt. Given that the entire planet is saturated in debt, the United States will not be able to replace China as a debt consumer should they employ a major scale-back in debt purchases—or, worse, sell U.S. debt in retaliation of a trade war.

Currently, the U.S. Treasury is the most popular "party" in town—when the Treasury throws an auction all the A-list players show up. China is on the A list—but what if Treasury threw a bash and no one came? It was just Tim and Ben standing next to a huge keg of Treasuries that nobody wanted. The United States can't afford for their A-list customer to be a "no show"—we are one bad auction away from the bubble in the Treasury bursting. If China fails to show up to an auction or, worse yet, they sell some of the estimated $1.2 trillion they have in U.S. debt—watch out!

The bottom line is that when a government like the United States becomes so embroiled by burdensome debts and enormous deficits—they are at the mercy of deep pocket countries like China to keep the spending engine going. And it's not that Vietnam, or some other Asian country, will simply supplant China in the recycling of our debt if they hit a wall. The point is that the value of those U.S. dollars will plummet along with bond prices.

Knowing this, why would any international investor seeking a "safe haven" choose to park assets in U.S. sovereign debt? If Bernanke is to be believed, continued economic weakness in the United States will cause low-yielding Treasuries to lose value due to inflation while the weakening dollar erodes the underlying value of the bond in real terms. This is a one-two punch that sane investors will seek to avoid. It is no coincidence that a record percentage of U.S. Treasury auctions are now being bought by central banks, for whom sanity is a lowly consideration.

The fact is that without Chinese support, the dollar would be a dead duck. Then, future Treasury auctions and the $1.2 trillion in U.S. debt the Chinese already own will become our very big problem.

Washington's Addiction to Debt—Reality Check

On Sixth Avenue in Manhattan, there is a billboard-sized display called the national debt clock. The clock presents an escalating tally of our national debt, and estimates each American family's share. Reinforcing that debt our elected officials so ardently bestowed on this nation is a burden to all American families. The clock made its debut in 1989, when national debt sat at $3 trillion dollars. When debt hit the $10 trillion mark in 2008, it was rumored the clock ran out of digits. That rumor proved false, and five years later in 2012 that clock vividly displays this nation's reckless spending as in excess of $16 trillion dollars.

I would like to propose the clock be moved from the streets of Manhattan into the halls of Congress. Then our elected officials can have a constant reminder of what an atrocious job they are doing managing our nation's finances. From the redundant and seemingly never-ending debate in Washington, it appears unclear if Congress ever plans on confronting the colossal national debt they have engendered. We raise the debt ceiling as if it was our patriotic duty to do so.

Over the past decade and a half, our economy has floated up on a succession of asset bubbles, all made possible by the Fed and private banks. Our central bank lowers borrowing costs far below market levels. Commercial banks then expand the money supply by making goofy loans to the government or to the private sector, mostly to inflate asset prices. As a consequence, debt levels and asset values soar. Without fail, asset prices and debt levels soon become intractable, and the Fed and commercial banks are forced to cut off the monetary spigot, either on their own volition or because the demand for money plummets. The economy is forced to deleverage, and consumers are forced to sell assets and pay down debt. A healthy recession ensues. . . .

In 2008, Americans confronted the reality that their household debt was insurmountable and made modifications to their lifestyle in an attempt to reduce their debt burden. Unfortunately, government deemed if they allowed a serious recession to ensue and let free-market forces properly purge malinvestments from the economy, the situation would become politically untenable. Instead, they chose the Keynesian path of deficit borrowing and spending.

While it is true that "W" was a paragon of fiscal irresponsibility, Barack Obama's administration is the Bush administration on steroids. While you were sacrificing and paying down debt over the past four years, they were accumulating debt at an historic rate that doubled the past administration's equally remarkable debt levels. The thing is, when *they* load up on debt, *their* debt is also *your* burden. The problem with all this debt and fiscal profligacy is clear. Every dollar of debt is a promise made by government on behalf of the American people to repay that same dollar—with interest. For years, the debt debate centered on future generations—the burden we are leaving to our kids and grandkids. With debt accumulating at such a rapid pace, markets aren't going to wait for my son and daughter to collect a paycheck—markets are going to force the American people to tackle this debt soon. The markets will eventually do what the Congress refuses to.

To put the pace of our debt in perspective the United States collected $2.4 trillion in tax payments in 2011 and over spent by about $1.3 trillion—that's nearly 50 percent of revenue and it is unsustainable! The budget deficit for the entire year of 2002 was $158 billion dollars; we had monthly deficits in 2012 reaching $150 billion—our yearly budget deficits have now become our monthly budget deficits!

A country cannot rescue the private sector by moving the debt to the public sector. In truth, we haven't bailed out the private sector at all, just mortally wounded the public sector. But there will be no one around to bail us out in the future. We have delayed and exacerbated the inevitable confrontation with our debt.

Democrats believe we need to raise taxes in order to balance our budget. The American economy produces $15.5 trillion in GDP per annum but has $120 trillion in unfunded liabilities. With a hole like that, no amount of taxes could balance the budget. Raising revenue from the 14 percent of GDP, as it is today, to the 20 percent it was in 2000 would barely make a dent toward funding our Social Security and Medicare liabilities. Therefore, we need to cut entitlement spending dramatically. But the Democrats refuse to face the obvious facts.

With the Tea Party gaining traction in Congress and causing nightmares for incumbents, Republicans engaged in a battle in the summer of 2011 to raise the debt ceiling (although they raised it seven times under George W. Bush). That fight ended with Congress agreeing to make $1.2 trillion dollars in future cuts—I'll believe that when I see it!

In my opinion, the best news for the long-term future of this nation is the Republican "cut, cap, and balance" plan, which should also include a limit on government spending as a percentage of the economy.

Unfortunately, the country needs a taste of brutal reality before such bitter medicine has a chance of going down.

Both parties have opted to stay drunk to avoid a hangover—but the severity of that hangover is growing greater by the day. We see the same stalemate play out in perpetuity—Democrats aren't going to reduce entitlements without raising taxes on "the rich," and Republicans aren't going to raise taxes when the unemployment rate is near 8 percent and the economy is stagnating.

On August 5, 2011, the United States was downgraded from AAA to AA+ by S&P, Moody's left the AAA but has placed U.S. debt on negative alert. After having failed utterly to warn investors of the dangers associated with the toxic debt of entities like Enron, Fannie Mae, Freddie Mac, and AIG, as well as the perils of investing in mortgage-backed securities and sovereign debt of various bankrupt countries, the credit ratings agencies (CRAs) have now apparently decided to be more vigilant.

The squabbling over the debt deal finally prompted Standard & Poor's (S&P) to wake up to the reality of the U.S. government's fiscal calamity. The truth is with or without a deal on the debt limit, the CRAs should have already lowered their debt ratings on U.S. debt. In fact, the rating should be lowered again each time the debt ceiling is raised. And it should be lowered still further if we eliminated the debt ceiling altogether. To lower the rating because the limit is *not* raised is like cutting the credit score of a homeless person because he was denied a home equity loan.

The irony is that even after the downgrade, bond prices rallied. This provides further evidence of the bubble. It appears that U.S. debt is the beneficiary of any worry in the market—even if the worry is about U.S. debt. This is one of the classic signs of a bubble where investors ignore fundamentals in favor of the trend. It is the lemming—the "group-think" investor mentality that we saw with dot-com stocks in the late 1990s and more recently with housing.

The prevailing wisdom of today now yields to the conclusion that getting your debt downgraded automatically renders a boost to your currency and bond prices. Therefore, why worry? Their comfort is ridiculously based on the notion that the United States has a printing press and can create unlimited amounts of inflation. Therefore, interest rates will never rise and debt service won't ever be a problem.

I think that's also what the government of Hungary believed after WWII. They had a printing press also and it was used to pay debts accumulated during the war. But their *daily rate* of inflation hit a global record of over 200 percent.

The U.S. government seems completely inept at taking even the smallest baby step toward lowering our annual shortfall in revenue over spending—let alone paying down the debt.

Recent examples of the paralysis in Washington include the myriad of debt ceiling increases, the Simpson Bowles Committee, and sequestration punt. Time after time, D.C. manages to decide to increase the debt without cutting spending. If we continue with this posture, we will eventually receive the real debt downgrade, which will come from our foreign creditors.

Liberals fight for more spending in health care, education, and infrastructure. And in similar fashion, many conservatives refuse to give an inch on defense. During the September 12, 2011, Republican presidential debate in Tampa, Rep. Ron Paul (R-TX)—a Libertarian, who is a staunch advocate of limited government and a more modest military footprint—offered a stunning statistic about the reach of the U.S. armed forces.

> We're under great threat, because we occupy so many countries. We're in 130 countries. We have 900 bases around the world. We're going broke.[21]

Political fact checks found small inconsistencies with Paul's numbers in what constitutes a country and if a military presence exists with less than 10 people. However, they concluded that Paul represented our overall military presence with accuracy.

We have enough bombs to blow the world up five times over, yet we feel the need to have a military presence in 130 countries. Republicans understandably don't want to hamper America's ability to defend herself—however, national insolvency will not make us safer.

Federal Reserve Chairman Ben Bernanke has also failed to recognize that the true nature of the problem is our debt. Instead of allowing the nation to deleverage, he viewed taking on more debt as a panacea. This failure in vision will lead to a crisis far more severe than the one most think we have avoided by taking on all this government debt.

It is clear to me that the overleveraged condition, which brought the economy down in 2008 still exists today—only worse. For all the suffering and displacement that has gone on, all we have accomplished is an unprecedented transfer of private sector debt onto the Treasury's balance sheet. The Fed has been able to keep yields this low through relentless devaluation and a propaganda campaign that convinced the majority of investors that deflation was a credible threat (kinda like those phantom Iraqi weapons of mass destruction).

But Washington's ability to continue that ruse will eventually come to an end. The unrelenting growth of the Fed's balance sheet, increasing monetary aggregates, surging gold and commodity prices, soaring food prices, and trillions of dollars of new debt projected for the near future will serve to vanquish the deflationists. Eventually, any echoes of those once prominent voices will barely be heard amid the thunderous roar of oncoming inflation.

The truth is that only a central banker could afford to own bonds that are yielding rates well below inflation for very long. And that negative yield is growing even more so. The fact is that yields on Treasuries will eventually have to rise to the level at which they provide a real return for investors.

The bottom line is that a massive increase in the supply of debt coupled with a rising rate of inflation will always place upward pressure on interest rates. However, if the Fed steps aside from buying nearly 100 percent of the Treasury's current auctioned output, it will leave a gaping hole—sending bond yields rising. Will the Fed ever be able to sell all those Treasuries and unwind their humongous balance sheet without sending bond yields soaring?

And for those Pollyannas who claim Bernanke can keep printing forever and force rates low for as long as he wants, I want to know how the Fed can buy every bond issued without creating hyperinflation?

All the elements of a bubble in the bond market are in place, just as they were for the real estate market in the middle of the last decade. And now, if we do not aggressively cut spending on the federal level, the bond market may be ready to enter a multidecade bear market in prices.

The trigger for this secular move higher in yields will be the resurgence of inflation and the overwhelming effect supply has on bond prices.

The true fiscal cliff will come when the bond market and the dollar are crashing, and investors realize our country is insolvent. If the politicians in Washington are unwilling to deal with the massive debt they have accumulated, the markets will.

Notes

1. Charles Biderman, "Trim Tabs Say Mattress Remains Most Popular Destination for Investor cash," Trim Tabs Money Blog—Biderman Market Picks, August 20, 2012.
2. Karen Brettel, "As Debt Maturities Loom, U.S. Needs to Extend," Reuters, September 1, 2011.
3. Dale Steinreich, "75 Years of Housing Fascism," Ludwig von Mises Institute, July 9, 2009.
4. Steinreich, "75 Years of Housing Fascism."
5. Taken from a personal interview with Frank Sorrentino, Chairman and CEO of North Jersey Community Bank (NJCB), on August 6, 2012.
6. Ibid.
7. Ibid.
8. Ibid.
9. Ibid.
10. Cordell Eddings and Daniel Kruger, "Banks Use $1.77 Trillion to Double Treasury Purchases," August 20, 2012.
11. Taken from a personal interview with Frank Sorrentino, Chairman and CEO of North Jersey Community Bank (NJCB), on August 6, 2012.
12. BEA.gov, 2011.
13. Ibid.
14. B. Markus, "Bust Looms as China Booms," Ludwig von Mises Institute, March 9, 2011.
15. Ibid.
16. Tyler Durden, "Exposing China's Mysterious Multi-trillion Shadow Banking System," Zerohedge.com, July 19, 2011.
17. Doug French, "The China Model Is Unsustainable," Ludwig von Mises Institute, October 3, 2011.
18. Ibid.
19. Jim Chanos, Bloomberg TV, September 2011.
20. Markus, "Bust Looms as China Booms."
21. Ron Paul at the Republican Presidential Primary debate, September 12, 2012.

Chapter 6

The End of an Empire

". . . the bright light of all the world was put out, or, rather, when the Roman Empire was decapitated, and, to speak more correctly, the whole world perished in one city."

—From a letter by St. Jerome

"Who would believe that Rome, built up by the conquest of the whole world, had collapsed, that the. mother of nations had become also their tomb; that the shores of the whole East, of Egypt, of Africa, which once belonged to the imperial city, were filled with the hosts of her men-servants and maid-servants, that we should every day be receiving in this holy Bethlehem men and women who once were noble and abounding in every kind of wealth but are now reduced to poverty?"

—From a letter by St. Jerome

"The bright light of all the world was put out." These words were penned in response to the August 24, 410, sack of Rome—the final blow to the Roman Empire by the Visigoths—a nomadic tribe of Germanic descent referred to as the Barbarians. Although the sack itself was said to be mild, as far as sacks go, the psychological blow to the Romans was more painful.

The shock of this event reverberated from Britain to Jerusalem—the great Roman empire of Julius Caesar, an empire that reigned for five centuries had fallen.

In that same year, we hear of Britain's plea for assistance against local Barbarian incursions, called the "Rescript of Honorius." The Romans, after nearly four centuries of occupation, abandoned Britain, telling them, thereafter, to look to their own defenses. The civilized world that was known for centuries had ended—the "Dark Ages" had arrived.

Taking a look back through history we realize the Roman Empire didn't end in one fatal blow as much as in a long drawn out deflating balloon. Rome had been in decline for centuries before that fatal sack, it was a wonderment it stood for so long. When the Barbarians pillaged the city, they didn't find the glorious Rome of centuries past—men in togas lounging in bath houses—la dolce vita. The Barbarians found a starving citizenry—Rome for all purposes was already dead—the sack marked the time. The feudal system had begun generations before. Outrageous taxes to pay armies and fund the empire had led Romans to flee the cities and in favor of the servitude of large land owners whereas indentured servants, they found a more sustainable existence.

For two centuries the Roman Empire enjoyed its golden years, characterized by the *Pax Romana*, a period of unprecedented peace and prosperity. The accession of the emperor Commodus in 180 A.D. marked the descent "from a kingdom of gold to one of rust and iron."[1] This has led some historians to mark Commodus' reign as the beginning of the decline of the Roman Empire.

Rome was buckling under the burden of the costs of running its colossal empire. And like civilizations centuries before, it turned to debasing its currency in an attempt to make its money stretch.

"During the fifty-year interval ending with the rule of Claudius Victorinus in A.D. 268, the silver content of the Roman coin fell to one five-thousandth of its original level. With the monetary system in total disarray, the trade that had been hallmark of the empire was reduced to barter, and economic activity was stymied."[2]

The middle class was almost nonexistent, and the proletariat was already sinking to the level of serfdom. The world had appeared to have fallen into an intellectual and moral morass. Emperor Diocletian set about the task of reorganizing the empire with great vigor—his quest for "hope and change" outweighed his basic knowledge of economics.

Since money was completely worthless, he devised a system of taxes based on payments in kind. This system had the effect of destroying the freedoms of the lower class—they became serfs and were bound to the soil in order to ensure that the taxes would be forthcoming. "The political zeitgeist of intervention and coercion was alive when he took office but under him it grew and evolved far beyond attempting to influence the availability of comestibles or reducing the freedom of Roman citizens to negotiate prices."[3] Diocletian was what we would refer to in modern days as a central planner.

Diocletian then set out to reform the currency, by issuing a variety of new coins and ended up with a denarius that consisted of mostly copper, a metal thought to be of lower value than what was previously held. Instead of letting the market price this new currency, Diocletian set prices by decree, thus significantly overvaluing the currency. The principal reason for the official overvaluation of the currency, of course, was to provide the wherewithal to support the large army and massive bureaucracy—just like we see today with central banks counterfeiting in an attempt to preserve bloated bureaucracies of the governments they support.

"Diocletian's choices were to continue to mint the increasingly worthless denarius or to cut 'government expenditures' and thereby reduce the requirement for minting them. In modern terminology, he could either continue to 'inflate' or he could begin the process of 'deflating' the economy."[4] Diocletian was faced with the same dilemma as our world governments—the choice of counterfeiting and creating inflation or making cuts to spending—what is referred to today as austerity.

Diocletian, like so many of today's politicians, found the deflation route intolerable, reducing the costs of civil and military government, was impossible. On the other hand, he knew to inflate would be equally disastrous in the long run. Inflation had brought the Empire to the verge of complete collapse.[5]

Desperate, Diocletian made the decision to continue to inflate, but in a way that would, he thought, prevent the inflation from occurring.

He decided to institute price fixes for goods and services, instead of allowing the market to determine what the currency was really worth. It was most ambitious, setting price ceilings for over 900 commodities, 130 labor wages, and freight charges that were published broadly throughout the empire in both Greek and Latin.[6]

Obviously, Richard Nixon was not well versed on his Roman economic history, as he proposed similar price fixes in response to his round of counterfeiting—the difference being that Diocletian prescribed the penalty of death for anyone who disposed of his wares at a higher figure. The emperor didn't quite grasp the concept that asking Romans to provide a good or service that cost them more to produce than they were allowed to sell it for wasn't a very good incentive. One would also have to assume that Nixon might have thought to legislate the penalty of death—if he thought he could have gotten it through Congress.

A historian notes, in the end—"Diocletian had failed to fool the people and had failed to suppress the ability of people to buy and sell as they saw fit."[7]

When Nixon instituted price fixes it too led to supply shortages and long lines for gas—Diocletian's shortages led to much bloodshed, shortages that increased the dearth so much, that at last after many had died by it, the law itself was finally set aside.[8]

It is not known how long the price fixes remained in force, it is known that citing the strains of government and poor health, Diocletian abdicated four years after the statute on wages and prices was promulgated. Less than four years after the currency reform associated with the edict, the price of gold in terms of the denarius had risen 250 percent. Coincidentally—or maybe not so—Richard Nixon also abdicated the role of presidency after closing the gold window and since his tenure; the price of gold has skyrocketed.

Diocletian's "attempt . . . resulted in complete regimentation under a totalitarian state."[9] Over subsequent decades, despite the limited currency reforms of Constantine, taxes were incrementally increased and the vague semblance of private enterprise progressively crushed. Over two centuries people left the cities—they fled higher taxes and preferred a life as an indentured servant. Centuries before the Laffer curve, a curve that shows a worker's tax tolerance, Roman citizenry was proving that at a certain point you would rather be a veritable slave to a large land owner than succumb to an empire's onerous tax policies.

The End of a Monetary System

Now, you may ask why I am reviewing some obscure piece of Roman history. How does the reign of Diocletian or the fall of the Roman Empire affect the bubble in the bond market? Economics is a social science—it is part philosophy and part science. As in science, economics has fundamental rules that are absolute and cannot be broken. We see these rules hold true for centuries.

As civilizations evolved, economies utilized a system of barter. If I have a horse that you need and you have two goats and a chicken that I want, we could make an exchange. Market participants inherently understood the value of commodities they were exchanging. The horse was my currency, and if I promised you a horse, and handed you a horse's head you would realize immediately my currency was greatly devalued. Humans throughout time are acutely aware when their currency has been degraded. The barter system was ultimately inefficient—I had a horse that you wanted, you had three pigs and a chicken, but I want two goats and a chicken—so we would have to find additional trading partners.

To solve these inefficiencies, currency was created. I can imagine somebody could have proposed to pull a leaf off a tree, scribe a number on it, and exchange it; market participants could agree this was currency. Leaves are plentiful and easily gathered, that's why money doesn't grow on trees. However, with today's fiat currency worth nothing and created without limit—leaves from a tree would at least be finite—today's central banks are not even limited by the confines of the natural world. The Irish novelist James Joyce described infinity with an analogy of a seagull carrying a grain of sand in its beak in a pile that extends to the sky—you have to stretch your mind in a similar way to realize the infinite pile of money backed by nothing central banks are propagating today.

Historians trace the use of metal for money all the way back to Babylon in about 2000 years B.C. However, the standardization in the form of coinage did not occur until the seventh century B.C.[10] Metals such as gold, silver and copper logically became the most efficient currency—it needed to be mined; it required labor to extract it from the ground.

And interestingly enough, as soon as we witness the creation of a standard monetary system—we observe government's inclination to debase. Metal currency would flow into the government whittled down and its metal content diminished. This hasty manipulation of the mints was just as effective as our modern printing presses, with their floods of worthless, or nearly worthless, paper money.[11]

Currency devaluation never fools anyone for long and inflation always ensues. Centuries of history prove that economies that succumb to the debasement always fail; and their economies end up in ruins.

Michael Rostovtzeff, a leading Roman historian, summed up Diocletian's experience in these words:

> The same expedient had often been tried before him and was often tried after him. As a general measure intended to last, it was certain to do great harm and to cause terrible bloodshed, without bringing any relief. Diocletian shared the pernicious belief of the ancient world in the omnipotence of the state, a belief which many modern theorists continue to share with him and with it.[12]

Today, it is clear many in power share the pernicious belief in the omnipotence of the state and central bank—it is only a matter of time before they too realize their debasing is the same expedient tried centuries before. Like Mother Nature—the laws of economics will not be fooled.

In the early 1930s, industrialized countries such as Germany, Japan, the United States, and France went off the gold standard. After World War II, in an agreement at Bretton Woods, this new international monetary order was conceived and then driven through by the United States in mid-1944. The Bretton Woods system provided a better solution than what had been established in the 1930s, but it still worked as another "inflationary recrudescence of the gold-exchange standard of the 1920s and—like the 1920s—the system lived only on borrowed time."[13]

With the Bretton Woods system, the dollar, valued at 1/35 of a gold ounce, was to be the only key currency. The dollar was no longer redeemable in gold to American citizens; instead, the dollar redeemable in gold only to foreign governments and their central banks. In an Executive Order signed on April 5, 1933, by U.S. President Franklin D. Roosevelt "forbidding the Hoarding of Gold Coin, Gold Bullion, and Gold Certificates within the continental United States," U.S. citizens were actually banned from owning gold. The order criminalized the possession of monetary gold by any individual, partnership, association, or corporation.

In the Bretton Woods system, "the United States pyramided dollars (in paper money and in bank deposits) on top of gold, in which dollars could be redeemed by foreign governments, while all other governments held dollars as their basic reserve and pyramided their currency on top of dollars. The United States began the postwar world with a huge stock of gold (approximately $25 billion) there was plenty of play for pyramiding dollar claims on top of it."[14]

At the time the dollar was artificially undervalued and most other currencies overvalued. The world was thought to be suffering from a dollar shortage—that shortage was to be footed by the U.S. taxpayer in the form of foreign aid. Exiting World War II, the United States had a huge economic advantage; they had an enormous surplus of gold and had an intact manufacturing base. In the 1940s, foreign aid such as the Marshall Plan sprouted up. "The actual legacy of the Marshall Plan was a vast expansion of government at home, the beginnings of the Cold War rhetoric that would sustain the welfare-warfare state for 40 years, a permanent global troop presence, and an entire business class on the take from Washington. It also created a belief on the part of the ruling elite in D.C. that it could trick the public into backing anything, including the idea that government and its connected interest groups should run the world at taxpayer expense."[15]

The baton had been passed—there was a new world sheriff in town, the sun was setting on the British Empire—it was time for the United States to take the reins.

Setting off to be the "new world power" in town, the United States government embarked on its post-war policy of continual monetary inflation, a policy still ardently pursued today. By the early 1950s, the continuing American inflation began to turn the tide on international trade. As the United States was inflating and expanding money and credit, some European countries still held firm on a hard currency, which led to imbalances. The rules of Bretton Woods insisted that countries have to continue piling up dollars in reserve and use these dollars to inflate their own currency and credit. The Europeans felt locked into a system in which there was nothing much else they could do. Europe did however, have one option—the option of redeeming dollars for gold at $35 an ounce. And as the dollar became overvalued relative to gold, European governments began exercising that option and gold flowed steadily out of the United States. In his book, *The History of Money and Banking*, author Murray Rothbard notes

> Economic law has a way, at long last, of catching up with governments, and this is what happened to the inflation-happy U.S. government by the end of the 1960s. The gold exchange system of Bretton Woods—hailed by the U.S. political and economic Establishment as permanent and impregnable—began to unravel rapidly in 1968.[16]

As dollars piled up abroad, gold continued to flow outward, and the United States found it increasingly difficult to maintain the price of gold at $35 an ounce in the free gold markets at London and Zurich. Thirty-five dollars an ounce was the keystone of the system. American citizens were banned from owning gold; European citizens had no such ban and also started selling U.S. dollars for gold in the free gold market. The tables had turned; the United States was hemorrhaging gold.

A crisis of confidence in the dollar on the free gold markets led the United States to effect a fundamental change in the monetary system in March 1968. Hence was born the "two-tier gold market." The idea was for central banks to ignore the gold markets and trade among themselves.

Economists in the Keynesian and Friedmanite camps "were now confident that gold would disappear from the international monetary system; cut off from its "support" by the dollar, these economists all confidently predicted, the free-market gold price would soon fall below $35 announce, and even down to the estimated "industrial" nonmonetary gold price of $10 an ounce.[17] These economists' believed their fiat currency would prevail. They had the hubris to assume that gold, a currency that held the test of time for thousands of years, would suddenly succumb to the economic force of gravity and fall while the dollar would rise—but the true laws of economics can't be fooled.

On August 15, 1971, President Nixon, perhaps channeling Diocletian, imposed a price-wage freeze in a vain attempt to check
bounding inflation. In a fit of haste, Mr. Nixon also brought the postwar
Bretton Woods system to a crashing end. As European central banks at
last threatened to redeem much of their swollen stock of dollars for gold,
President Nixon closed the gold window. "For the first time in
American history, the dollar was totally fiat, totally without backing
in gold. Even the tenuous link with gold maintained since 1933 was
now severed. The world was plunged into the fiat system of the
thirties—and worse, since now even the dollar was no longer linked to
gold. Ahead loomed the dread specter of currency blocks, competing
devaluations, economic warfare, and the breakdown of international
trade and investment."[18]

And so after the Smithsonian Agreement, a system hailed by Nixon
as the greatest monetary system ever, was a complete failure. The
world's central banks sought to defy the laws of economics once more
and embarked into complete fiat monetary system with floating
exchange rates. Central banks, which had been a complete failure in
managing a quasi-gold standard, decided they knew better than centuries of history that pointed to the contrary and pursued a fiat currency.

Forty years later we are witnessing a collapse of that fiat currency
experiment. The free price of gold never fell below $35, and by early
1973 had climbed to around $125 an ounce. The higher free-market
price of gold simply revealed the accelerated loss of world confidence in
the reserve currency of the dollar and the entire fiat currency system.[19]
Today as I write, gold is trading in the neighborhood of $1,700 an
ounce. I don't assume this is a result of merely an enormous demand for
gold jewelry. Instead, it represents the utter lack of confidence by
market participants to maintain the value of our money. The market is
speaking—they are rejecting the fiat monetary system and anticipating
the end of the failed experiment in phony money.

Central banks of the world today work with hubris in their belief
that economic forces can be controlled. An object is restricted by
gravity—it succumbs to the physical laws of the universe that cannot be
altered. Monetary policy is restricted by the universal laws of economics—laws that have passed the test of time, and cannot be disputed.
A currency of a nation, a worldwide economic system cannot run

indefinitely on money created out of thin air. Eventually, the laws of economics—the gravitational pull of monetary law will prevail. We see this battle playing out all over the world today and it is becoming clear— the economic forces are winning. But don't just take my word for it—this is what some other notable monetary theorists are saying. . . .

Monetary scholar Edwin Vieira contends that "every 30 to 40 years the reigning monetary system fails and has to be retooled. The last time around for the United States was in 1971, when Nixon cancelled the convertibility of dollars into gold. Remarkably, the world bought into the unbacked dollar as its reserve currency, but only because that was the path of least resistance. But here we are 40 years later, and it is clear to anyone paying attention that the monetary system is irretrievably broken and will fail."[20]

DollarDaze.org did a study of 775 fiat currencies and found "there is no historical precedence for a fiat currency that has succeeded in holding its value. Twenty percent failed through hyperinflation, 21% were destroyed by war, 12% destroyed by independence, 24% were monetarily reformed, and 23% are still in circulation approaching one of the other outcomes."[21]

> The average life expectancy for a fiat currency is 27 years, with the shortest life span being one month. Founded in 1694, the British pound Sterling is the oldest fiat currency in existence. At a ripe old age of 317 years it must be considered a highly successful fiat currency. However, success is relative. The British pound was defined as 12 ounces of silver, so it's worth less than 1/200 or 0.5% of its original value. In other words, the most successful long standing currency in existence has lost 99.5% of its value.[22]

And Jeff Clark argues that "history has a message for us: No fiat currency has lasted forever. Eventually, they all fail."[23]

Now you may be thinking this kind of thing only happens to third world countries. You'd be wrong. There is no discrimination as to the size or perceived stability of a nation's economy; when government leaders abuse their currency, their country pays the price.

When confronted with centuries of history that proves the fiat monetary system will not last, today's leaders like to point to technology as a factor, rendering thousands of years of monetary data obsolete. We can look to the cave man and note when he placed his club on the ground it remained on the ground, stationary—it didn't float about through the air. Scientist's centuries later developed the laws of physics and gravity that explain this phenomenon—and those laws are indisputable. The introduction of more sophisticated material, composites and plastics don't violate the laws of gravity—they remain the same and are absolute. You don't hear arguments of "this time it's different"—the laws of gravity don't apply to this piece of matter.

For the past 40 years, the world economies have stared the most fundamental law of economics in the face and expected it to levitate. Centuries of information and history that tells us that when nations move away from a metal backed currency, when nations debase their currency it doesn't end well—it never ends well. We are in the midst of the collapse of the fiat monetary system. This law of economics is absolute. This law doesn't change because the technology allows for mass counterfeiting at a press of a button any more than new materials don't challenge the laws of gravity. The fundamental laws of hard and stable currency cannot be debated.

Why are central banks and fiat currencies the bane of an economy? And what does a central bank and a fiat currency have to do with a bond bubble? They have served as the primary enablers for their governments to run up massive debts that have engendered their insolvencies. They have caused rampant inflation and the dissolution of their middle classes. They have eroded the incentive to save and invest and caused productivity rates to crumble. And they are the culprit behind every currency and bond market crisis in history.

We are now at the cusp of a collapse of the fiat currency system that will spur on a worldwide recession/depression. You just can't separate the fact that a bond market crisis goes hand-in-hand with a currency crisis. When the bond market starts to collapse, it will be accompanied by a vastly weakening U.S. dollar. Market participants will lose faith in most fiat currencies—but the dollar, the world's reserve currency will collapse the hardest, which will bring down our bond market and the world with it. Due to the worldwide distribution and abundance of dollars this event will be unprecedented in history. As the dollar loses its purchasing power, it will take many more dollars to buy the necessities of life. Food and energy prices will soar in dollar terms and will absorb much of the dollars left over and not being used to purchase U.S. debt. We will see foreigners selling dollars and buying back their own currencies to invest domestically in hard assets. The falling dollar will create runaway inflation here in America. Hard assets, most commodities and non-discretionary items will be in huge demand. Market participants will flee the worthless paper money in favor of hard assets that can't be debased by central banking bureaucrats whom they have lost all faith in. Gold, oil, and a basket of other commodities will rise, as demand for bonds and the dollar will plummet.

The Economic Laws of Debt

For hundreds of years, the sun never set on the British Empire—its span across the globe ensured that the sun was always shining on at least one of its numerous territories. On July 1, 1997 the United Kingdom transferred sovereignty of Hong Kong to the People's Republic of China PRC, officially ending 156 years of British colonial rule, marking the technical end of the British Empire. However, the allegorical sun had set on the British empire after World War II, if not before.

By 1922 the British Empire held sway over about 458 million people, one-fifth of the world's population at the time. The empire covered more than 33,700,000 km^2 (13,012,000 square mile), almost a quarter of the Earth's total land area.[24]

Despite British victory from the Second World War, the effects of the conflict were weighty, both at home and abroad. Much of Europe, a continent that had subjugated the world for several centuries, was in ruins; the balance of power had shifted to the United States and the Soviet Union. Britain was bankrupt; insolvency was forestalled in 1946 with a $3.5 billion loan from the United States.[25]

Britain, in contrast to France and Portugal, adopted a policy of peaceful disengagement from its colonies. Like the Roman Empire in its day; the British Empire had a profound effect on all aspects of the world. England introduced the concept of the fractional reserve banking, a system in effect today.

In mid-seventeenth century England, there were no banks of deposit until the outbreak of the civil war. Before the war, merchants stored their surplus gold in the king's mint. Shortly before the outbreak of the Civil War, Charles I needed money and confiscated a huge sum of £200,000 of gold, under the guise of a "loan." The merchants eventually got their gold back, but decided not to redeposit it in the mint. Instead, they chose to deposit their gold in the coffers of private goldsmiths. The warehouse receipts of the goldsmiths were soon used as a substitute for the gold itself. Eventually, the goldsmiths fell prey to the temptation to print pseudo-warehouse receipts not covered by gold and lent them out; fractional reserve banking had arrived in England.[26] In fact, paper money, as we know it today, originates from the European fractional reserve banks of the seventeenth century, where the search for more money by governments was the main driving force.

In the 1720s, Prime Minister Sir Robert Walpole's introduced the funding system "scheme" in England. And from then on, government debt never needed be repaid. "It was enough to create a regular and dependable source of revenue and use it to pay the annual interest and the principal of maturing bonds." For every retired bond sold, a new one was issued. In this way, a national debt could be made perpetual. Walpole's system proved its worth in financing British expansion in the eighteenth and nineteenth centuries. "The British Empire was built on more than the blood of its soldiers and sailors; it was built on debt."[27]

The British Empire concluded its empire-ship mired in debt, today we find the United States facing a similar plight. Nations cease to grow when debt to gross domestic product (GDP) ratios close in on the 100 percent level. Now I'm not saying that as soon as the debt to GDP ratio hits that level sirens sound and economic growth stalls. However, 800 years of data demonstrates economies saddled with onerous debt loads exceeding 90 percent of output always suffer anemic growth rates.

U.S. Debt—This Time It's Different

Carmen M. Reinhart, a senior fellow at the Peterson Institute for International Economics and Kenneth S. Rogoff, a professor of economics at Harvard University are co-authors of *This Time Is Different: Eight Centuries of Financial Folly*. While I don't agree with the politics in

their book—I am in complete concurrence with their research conclusion—this time is different; this time debt and deficits do matter
simply due to their size. This economy now has a debt to GDP ratio
ranging around 105 percent. According to Reinhart and Rogoff's study,
"Growth in a Time of Debt," they found relatively little association
between public liabilities and growth for debt levels of less than 90
percent of GDP. But, when burdens reached above 90 percent they
were associated with one percent lower median growth. Their results
were based on a data set of public debt covering 44 countries for up to
200 years. Their annual data set incorporated more than 3,700 obser-
vations spanning a wide range of political and historical circumstances,
legal structures, and monetary regimes.[28]

Furthermore, they noted "off-balance sheet guarantees and other
creative accounting devices make it even harder to assess the true nature
of a country's debt until a crisis forces everything out into the open.
(Just think of the giant U.S. mortgage lenders Fannie Mae and Freddie
Mac, whose debt was never officially guaranteed before the 2008
meltdown.)"[29]

Their empirical work concentrates on central-government obligations because state and local data are limited across time and countries,
and government guarantees, as noted, are difficult to quantify over time.
But, they do note that consumer, state and local debt are important
because they so frequently trigger federal government bailouts in a crisis.
Recently, we have seen a rash of municipalities filing for bankruptcy.
What if the federal government had to step in at some point to stop
the bleeding?

The authors go on to note that it isn't "unusual for governments to
absorb large chunks of troubled private debt in a crisis and the United
States has an extraordinarily high level of overall U.S. debts, public and
private."[30]

In addition to hidden liabilities, the authors point out that their "90
percent threshold is largely based on earlier periods when old-age
pensions and health-care costs hadn't grown to anything near the size
they are today. Surely this makes the burden of debt greater."[31]

Now we know that 800 years of data proves debt to GDP levels
matter, let me take a minute and explain why growth suffers when debt
ratios begin to exceed 90 percent.

When the United States or any nation has to borrow enormous amounts of money every year to fund its debt, it has the means to ensure it gets funded before the private economy. The U.S. government—like any other government—draws money out of the private economy and redistributes it in an unbalanced and inefficient way. First, it uses funds to service its debts, it funds the military so roads and bridges can be built in Afghanistan, and it redistributes money domestically in the form of transfer payments. Now Keynesians make the frequent argument that transfer payments such as food stamps and welfare increase growth. Their argument being, it places money in the hands of people who will immediately spend it. This shows a fundamental lack of understanding of how an economy grows. When the federal government takes savings out of the productive economy, a bank doesn't make a loan in order for a business to expand and a nation's savings aren't utilized to fund a new business. This borrowed money is placed in the hands of a person who spends it at Wal-Mart, not on capital goods such as tools and machinery. Wal-Mart may be a great American company, but it is a veritable outlet for Chinese made goods. The Chinese take our dollars and repatriate them back into the United States by purchasing our debt and the cycle continues. Americans consume and foreigners produce. We find ready buyers of our debt and get low interest rates. However, what we are doing is selling away our progeny, as every dollar borrowed is a future promise to tax or print another one; with interest. Wal-Mart may increase its hiring of a minimum-wage cashier or stock person, but that's not what grows an economy. In any scenario, government deficit spending is an inefficient use of an economy's savings.

When so much of an economy's savings is redirected to government, growth in the private sector fails to manifest. In the 1970s, Steve Jobs and Steve Wozniak created a computer in their garage that changed the world. In order to bring this invention to market, they needed capital. They had a few options—obtain a bank loan, seek venture capital money, or pursue acquisition opportunities at an existing company. All three avenues have one thing in common—investment. Someone has to save for investment to funnel into the next revolutionary industry that will change the world. When a nation's savings are funneled into the redistribution whims of government instead of the garages of small upstarts, revolutionary businesses aren't born. Think of all the jobs that came out of the technology revolution. There was an advertisement that aired a few years ago where Steve Ballmer, the CEO of Microsoft, told of his mother inquiring about his decision to work at Microsoft. She questioned what software was and why a person would ever want to own a personal computer. Years later, that question seems ironic—as people today don't want to own just one personal computer but several. Three decades ago, people didn't demand a personal computer; an economy doesn't grow based on low-income wage earners making demands to consume via government transfer payments. It grows with investment—a nation's savings voluntarily and freely redistributed to companies, businesses, and upstarts in the hope of making a profit.

When a nation's savings is funneled to government, they make their different "investments." Over the past few years, we have been reminded that government is not led by a profit motive, as if making decisions in an attempt to garner financial success was evil. I have news for those who discredit the capitalist model of investment for profit—government is far from pure in their investment motives. Governments are made up of a group of men and women who are motivated by campaign contributions and votes; they are singularly focused on winning their next election. Investment dollars are funneled into Solyndra—where campaign contributors are the winners and the American taxpayer foots the bill. Funds are syphoned to the next government welfare program, where government seeks to create dependencies and therefore garner a group of loyal voters.

When government engages itself in an industry, we see huge price distortions. Think about housing, health care, and higher education, industries where government has emerged as a competitor or partner with private enterprise we witness prices rise as the supply demand model is altered.

Let's imagine that government decides to provide vouchers to low income wage earners to purchase a netbook in order to increase availability of internet access. Government influence distorts any market, and here's why. When the market anticipates a huge demand in netbooks; they change direction to accommodate this new need. The supply/demand price model becomes distorted—component pricing for netbooks skyrockets as demand increases with buyers who are not price sensitive when somebody else is footing the bill. As technology companies refocus their staff away from new technologies such as tablets, supply of those new products plummet and prices also rise; instead of market forces driving technological advances, companies reposition themselves to follow the government's lead. The net effect is slowdown of technological advances and an increase in price. If you don't like my netbooks example, try substituting the words *real estate market*.

Is Austerity a Bad Thing?

In addition to witnessing the collapse of the fiat currency system, we are also witnessing a worldwide deleveraging. Governments around the world have spent too much—debt to GDP levels have violated the 90 percent range where 800 years of data tell us a countries growth rate will falter. Governments all around the world, including ours need to scale back—these measures of cutting costs and raising taxes are referred to as austerity. The prevailing view amongst Keynesians is that the austerity measures being taken in Europe to prevent a complete currency and bond market collapse is the cause of their current recession. But blaming a recession on the idea that an insolvent government was finally forced into reducing its debt is like blaming a morning hangover on the fact that you eventually had to stop drinking the night before.

There is now a huge debate over whether the developed world's sovereigns should embrace austerity or increase government spending in an effort to boost demand and avoid a full-blown economic meltdown. Not too long ago, I read a commentary titled, "We Should Not Imitate the Austerity of Europe" written by former U.S. Secretary of Labor and current professor of public policy at the University of California, Robert Reich. In it, Mr. Reich contends we should simply: "Blame [the recession] on austerity economics—the bizarre view that economic slowdowns result from excessive debt, so government should cut spending." He continued, "A large debt with faster growth is preferable to a smaller debt sitting atop no growth at all. And it's infinitely better than a smaller debt on top of a contracting economy."[32]

It is clear Mr. Reich is not familiar with 800 years of data that would explain to him why the large debt is responsible for the anemic growth rates. But why should the former Labor Secretary let centuries of historical data get in the way of his compelling, albeit delusional, tale of woe where austerity is the bane of Europe's problems. I would like to ask Robert a question. If government spending increases GDP growth greater than the accumulation of new debt, how is it possible that a nation's debt to GDP ratio can become a burden in the first place? After all, the United States has been running tremendous annual deficits that are around 10 percent of GDP for the last several years. Therefore, since government spending is supposed to grow GDP faster than deficits (at least in the mind of Mr. Reich), why isn't it the case that the debt to GDP ratio is falling? Instead, the opposite is true. Our debt to GDP ratio is rapidly rising.

Mr. Reich and those like him who vilify austerity measures are also ignoring the reality that investors in periphery European sovereign debt had already declared those markets to be insolvent. Sharply rising bond yields in southern Europe and Ireland were a clear signal that their debt to GDP ratios had eventually eclipsed the level in which investors believed the tax base could support the debt. Once sovereign debt has risen to a level that it cannot be paid back, by definition, the country must default through hyperinflation or restructuring.

However, in the unlikely scenario that the bond market actually has it wrong, a dramatic reduction in government spending gives sovereigns their only fighting chance before admitting defeat and pursuing one of the two default strategies.

If these governments can quickly balance their budgets and lower the level of nominal debt outstanding; it gives them a chance to restore investors' confidence in the bond market, bolsters the confidence in holding the euro currency and offers the hope that the private sector can rapidly supplant the erstwhile reliance on public sector spending.

Keynesians must realize that it was the high level of government spending, which was supported by a compliant central bank, that initially caused these debt-to-GDP ratios to rise to the point where governments were deemed to be insolvent.

Mr. Reich fails to recall that these governments already tried over borrowing and spending and it didn't work. How is it possible to believe that adding even more public sector debt, most of which is printed, can fix the problem? As we have just discussed, public sector spending doesn't grow an economy; it just adds to the debt and thus, increases the debt to GDP ratio. Yet more government spending, or investment as they like to call it, guarantees the bond market will be correct in judging European nations to be bankrupt. Keynesians fail to acknowledge what we have just discussed. Additional public borrowing not only increases debt but steals more money from the private sector that would have otherwise been used to pare down onerous household debt levels; or been invested in a more productive matter. The private sector is the only viable part of the economy that can support real growth. More borrowing would also cause the European Central Bank (ECB) to print more money and create more inflation; resulting in a further reduction of economic growth and the standard of living.

The truth is that austerity will come to the United States, regardless of whether it is voluntary, or because the bond market demands it. Pursuing voluntary austerity measures gives Europe, and indeed the developed world, their only chance before defaulting on the debt. Indeed, Japan and the United States now have a better opportunity than Europe to make austerity measures work. That's because both their bond markets are currently quiescent; despite that fact that both of their debt-to-GDP ratios are far worse than those in the Eurozone—EU (17) debt to GDP is hovering around 87 percent, while the United States has 105 percent and Japan has 237 percent public debt-to-GDP ratio. But the bottom line is that austerity is the market-based mechanism to countervail decades of profligate government profligacy and is a nation's best option and only hope.

Without embracing austerity, the debt continues to increase inexorably and GDP contracts, which will render the United States insolvent. This cycle, if not broken by debt restructuring and default, would ultimately lead to 100 percent of federal revenue used to service our enormous debt load. And when the entire amount of revenue an economy procures goes to service its debt, it is a mathematical certainty that the bond market will collapse. However, investors in America's debt will sniff this out way before debt service expenses approach anywhere near 100 percent of revenue. *It is my belief that the United States will spend about 30 to 50 percent of its entire revenue on debt service payments by the year 2016. And that could be the catalyst for the entire collapse.* As bond holder's sense this inevitability they will demand higher rates to hold

U.S. debt thus exacerbating the cycle. When will this happen? I can't tell you the exact date, but the fundamentals are in place—we are on track to have a severe crisis in the debt market and it could commence before the end of 2015. The Fed's continual counterfeiting that appears to the markets as a respite is actually creating a huge bubble and enabling this bubble in the Treasury to be an unprecedented event in modern times. The longer those in Washington chose to ignore the inevitable, the longer they fool themselves that austerity is the cause of the problem and not the solution in Europe; the longer they believe we can print, borrow, and spend our way out of this, the closer we come to the crisis becoming a done deal.

Where Will All the Money Go?

In my discussions with pundits, market participants and friends about the coming crisis in the U.S. debt market, I am often asked the question—where will all the money go?

There are two answers to this question, depending on what the questioner is really attempting to ascertain. The first reflects a basic lack of understanding in the fundamental concept that there is no money in the market. When the dot-com bubble burst and the real estate bubble collapsed you heard this question—where did the money go? It seemed like in a matter of days and weeks money just disappeared. The truth is . . . the money was never there to begin with.

Let's walk through a transaction and see how this plays out. You buy 100 shares of Enron back in 1998 for $85 a share. You transfer $8,500 from your account and purchase the shares from an existing holder— let's call him Joe. The money has moved from your account to Joe's account, and Joe blows all the money on a series of wild nights out with friends. And what do you have? You own 100 shares of Enron whose market value has been estimated based on the last transaction that other people have performed. There is no actual money in those shares and the shares won't buy you anything unless you can find a buyer. You get statements every month that reflect the final transaction at the close of business at the end of the month. But that stock has no monetary value until you locate a buyer and the money is transferred into your account.

Even the closing price is misleading because it doesn't represent the price all holders of Enron would get if they all decided to sell in unison. When the holders of Enron woke up the morning of the November 28, 2001, they found Enron was pursuing bankruptcy and their stock was worthless—the money didn't "go anywhere" it was already gone—Joe already blew all his money on women and booze years ago and his cash is still floating around the economy. Now, some may say, "A stock can go bust but that can't happen to American bonds that are backed by U.S. dollars." But history has clearly shown us that a country's debt and currency can lose its value in the same way as Enron shares lost their worth. Once a currency collapses it takes many more units of it to purchase goods and services. In the case of the United States, it will simply take many more dollars to buy food, energy, commodities, and the foreign currencies of our creditors.

Now let's think about what a bond is—your decision to buy a bond is different than the decision to buy a stock. You bought Enron stock for growth but you bought their bonds based on a belief the company will have the cash flow to make the interest payments and pay you back at the end of the maturity. When you bought the bond from Enron—where did the money go? Well, in Enron's case they took the money and shifted it into one of their sham holding companies. Therefore, Enron filed for bankruptcy because they didn't have the cash flow to pay the interest or principal on that bond. As an unsecured creditor you ended up in bankruptcy court at the end of the line—you are lucky if you got a penny on the dollar.

Now think about how the federal government funds its debt. The federal government issues debt in various maturities bills, notes, Treasury Inflation-Protected Securities (TIPS), and they rely on all of this debt to be rolled over. The purchasers of government debt make their decision based on the revenue stream of the U.S. taxpayer and the belief that the U.S. government can manage its finances. In reality, U.S. debtholders are unsecured creditors of the U.S. government—the debt isn't collateralized by the Washington Monument or the Lincoln Memorial—it is based in the faith of the credit of the U.S. government and its taxing authority. And if that faith were to erode, they would demand higher interest rates similar to any other holder of debt. It is true that a country never has to pay back all of its outstanding debt. However, it is imperative that investors in the nation's sovereign debt always maintain the confidence that it has the ability to do so. As we noted, history has proven that once the debt to GDP ratio reaches circa 90–100 percent, economic growth begins to falter. The problem being that the debt continues to accumulate without a commensurate increase in the tax base. Once the tax base can no longer adequately support the debt, interest rates rise sharply.

The U.S. government can print money—so debt can be repaid, albeit with worthless dollars. And this gets me to my next point—the U.S. dollar is backed by nothing but confidence and perception. Its value depends on our collective belief in its current and future purchasing power, and the hope that its supply will be restricted. When its supply is increased, users of the currency lose faith in its buying power.

As a corollary, if dollar holders believe that the United States will have no choice but to monetize trillions of dollars of Treasury debt in the near future, the currency will falter. In this manner, currencies that are backed by nothing but confidence tend to behave like stock prices. The share value of a corporation represents the strength of the company. Likewise, the value of a currency represents the strength of a sovereign state.

Looked at through this prism, the fate of the U.S. dollar in the future may not be all that different from the fate of those Enron shares in 2001. In the 1990s, Enron was one of the most respected corporations in America, and the share price soared. But once the accounting scandal broke, and Enron's profits were proven to be illusory, the purchasing power of its shares plummeted. Eventually, the shares became worthless.

The shares did not collapse simply because Enron issued more shares and diluted value. The big change came when investors lost faith in Enron the company. Likewise, the U.S. dollar may lose value because of garden-variety dilution, but the real leg down will occur if holders of U.S. government debt lose faith that they will be paid in full and in real terms.

This brings me to the next part of the question—what other debt the buyer would purchase if not U.S. debt. It is true that the countries that own much of our debt would fare better than us in a U.S. debt crisis. But one shouldn't assume that a U.S. debtholder would have to roll all that money into another sovereign debt issuer. This argument assumes that the United States needs to only be the "best house in a bad neighborhood." Or as I like to say, "the amoeba with the highest I.Q."

I don't buy into the assumption that a decision away from U.S. debt would be a commensurate decision toward another sovereign. On the contrary, I think the crisis of sovereign debt will metastasize throughout the developed world. Europe doesn't have to exit the crisis zone for the United States to enter. The same goes for Japan. These three sovereigns can be in crisis at once. And this would coincide with a collapse in the fiat currency system.

All fiat currencies can fall simultaneously in relationship to hard assets. I am reminded a lot about the dollar's valuation in regards to the euro. People assume that the dollar is strong if it is rising against the euro or other fiat currencies. This isn't the case, let's say you and I strap on parachutes and decide to jump out of a plane. My parachute completely fails to deploy and yours has deployed half way. I may look up at you and for a moment it may seem that while I am crashing you are flying—but the truth is we both crashing into the ground—I just may get there a little sooner. Some argue Europe is providing a temporary relief to rising U.S. interest rates. This may offer the United States a temporary respite but at the same time is further extending the bubble in rates. I would like to give this advice: selling euros to seek safety in the U.S. dollar is like exchanging your ticket on the Titanic for a ride on the Hindenburg.

As the dollar loses its purchasing power in relation to commodities we will see food and energy prices soar. Hard assets, most commodities, and nondiscretionary items will be in huge demand and that is where much of the money that used to be in the bond market will end up. So as former bond market participants decide to park their dollars in a hard asset such as gold, oil, or a basket of commodities, interest rates would rise as demand for bonds plummet.

It is hard to know at what moment or what series of events will inspire an epiphany on the part of bond holders to stop accepting negative interest rates. I have to admit that I cannot predict the exact day; however, I know that all the fundamentals are in place.

The Bell Is Ringing for the Bubble in the Bond Market

They always tell you no one rings a bell when a market top or bottom is reached. But if a bell is now ringing for the end of the 30-year bull market in U.S. debt I would have to say that bell ringer may be our very own U.S. Treasury Department!

The U.S. Treasury Borrowing Advisory Committee, which brings together dealers and Treasury officials, has already unanimously agreed that the Treasury should start permitting negative interest rate bids for T-bills. In other words, newly issued T-bills from the Treasury would offer investors a guaranteed negative return if held to maturity. The mania behind the U.S. debt market has reached such incredible proportions that investors are now willing to lend money to the government at a loss—right from the start of their investment. This is a clear signal that the bond market can't get any more overcrowded, over owned or overpriced.

Of course, many in the Main Stream Media contend there is justification for today's ridiculously low bond yields and that a bubble in U.S. debt is impossible. But those are some of the same individuals who claimed back in 2006 that home prices could never decline on a national level and any talk of a bubble in real estate was nonsense. These are also the same people who assured investors in the year 2000 that prices of Internet stocks were fairly priced because they should be valued based on the number of eyeballs that viewed a Web page.

We will go into Europe in the next chapter, and we can easily see the future of U.S. Treasuries from viewing what is occurring in Portugal and Greece today. Portugal and Greece were able to borrow tremendous amounts of money because they converted their domestic currencies to the euro and, therefore, had the German tax payers behind them. If these two countries had to borrow in escudos and drachmas instead, yields would have increased much earlier, forcing a reconciliation of the debt years before a major crisis occurred. Therefore, their current debt-to-GDP ratios would be much more manageable. But now their bond bubbles have burst. The yield on the Portuguese 10-year was 5 percent but went as high as 17 percent in January 2012. Greek 10-year bonds once yielded 5 percent. However, they reached over 35 percent just prior to Greece's officially defaulting on its debt in March of 2012. The bottom line is that these counties were able to borrow more money than their economy was able to support simply because their interest rates were kept artificially low.

Likewise, the United States was, and still is, able to borrow a tremendous amount of money—far more that can be sustained by its income and revenue—because interest rates have been artificially low for far too long. Not only has the Fed pegged interest rates at zero percent since December 2008, but the U.S. dollar has been the world's reserve currency for decades. These two factors combined have deceived the United States into believing it can add about 8 to 10 percent of GDP to its debt each year. And since the end of 2007, the amount of publicly traded debt has increased by nearly $6 trillion; that's over a 100 percent increase!

U.S. Treasury debt accumulation will be inexorably north of $1 trillion each year for at least the next decade to come. That's an increase of at least $10 trillion added to the current $16.5 trillion total. Along with that increasing debt supply, there is tremendous inflationary pressure coming from the expansion of the Fed's balance sheet and a Fed Funds rate that will end up being at zero percent for at least six years in total. Those two factors alone paint a very ugly picture for the direction of bond prices. And as I said, there isn't any money in the bond market. There is just an assumption of value based on recent transactions, which represent a very small percentage of total assets.

Manias can last a very long time and become more extended than reason should allow. But eventually investors will have an epiphany and demand higher rates. Once the bond bubble explodes here as it did in southern Europe, it will destroy the dollar along with it. That's because foreign sellers of U.S. debt will be forced to abandon dollar based holdings completely. That will mark the end of the U.S. dollar as the world's reserve currency and the restoration of gold as the global store of wealth.

The bond market needn't go through a massive sell-off from existing bondholders either. Bond market participants in new auctions just need to demand a higher interest rate. Those perpetual secondary offerings of U.S. debt would reprice all holders of Treasury debt.

Interest rates at more normalized levels—the average interest rate on the 10 year note is 7.3 percent going back to 1969—would automatically render the United States insolvent. How about the 10-year returning to 15 percent. This isn't out of the realm of possibility. In fact, it has already occurred here. Still unsure if the U.S. debt market can collapse? How is it that the 10-year went to 15 percent in 1980, from below 6 percent just a few years earlier? The United States was at that time the world's reserve currency and we were also the world's pre-eminent superpower. However, we weren't running up trillion dollar deficits then. And we didn't have a $3 trillion Fed balance sheet either that is growing by 33 percent this year. So if it happened then why can't it happen now? Investors managed to find alternative investments for their money in 1980. What do you think would happen to the real estate market, household debt service payments and government interest expenses if interest rates were to increase by 100s of basis points now?

On a September 10, 2012, appearance on Squawk box, none other than former FDIC Chairperson Sheila Bair expressed concerns about rates going to 4 percent in a six-month period—a rate she admits historically is not unrealistic. Bair acknowledges, "It scares the heck out of me, when you look at the banking system, banks are more and more funding with insured deposits—it's cheap money right now so it improves their net interest margins. But those deposits will re-price—and I do worry about inflation risk. I do worry about the Fed's ability to control the interest rate environment when that happens." She then goes on to categorize the bond market as a bubble and concedes, "The thing with bubbles, everyone calls them too soon—we are in the mother of all bond bubbles—let's face it, it's just a matter of time."[33]

The question you need to ask yourself is: how long will investors accept negative interest rates? More important, how long will foreign investors continue to accept those rates? They do not have to support bonds at this level—they will eventually demand a real interest rate. Demand for the Treasury will attenuate and yields will rise . . . in dramatic and devastating fashion.

Eventually, bondholders will have that epiphany—like the former FDIC chairwoman stated—it's just a matter of time. Investors will wake up and realize there is great risk in holding bonds yielding next to nothing. Foreign investors will see their principal falling and that they are losing value by holding the U.S. currency, which will be falling as well. Once they change their mind set this will be a prescription for panic. The sell-off may compel the Fed to purchase nearly every bond issued in an effort to keep yields down; but this will trigger a negative feedback loop. The economy will tank, tax receipts will plummet, debt to GDP ratio will soar and inflation will sky rocket—putting further pressure on yields—we will be entrenched in an inflationary death spiral.

I know we have reviewed this but it must be stressed, the three primary factors that determine the interest rate level a nation must pay to service its debt in the long term are the currency, inflation and credit risks of holding the sovereign debt. All three of those factors are very closely interrelated. Even though the central bank can exercise tremendous influence in the short run, the free market ultimately decides whether or not the nation has the ability to adequately finance its obligations and how high interest rates will go. An extremely high debt-to-GDP ratio, which elevates the country's credit risk, inevitably leads to higher interest rates and massive money printing by the central bank. That directly causes the nation's currency to fall while it also increases the rate of inflation.

Europe's southern periphery, along with Ireland, has hit the interest rate wall. International investors have abandoned their faith in those bond markets and the countries have now been placed on the life support of the European Central Bank. Without continuous intervention of the ECB into the bond market, yields will inexorably rise. And regardless of the ECB's intervention, rates will eventually soar once again precisely because of the inflation created by Mr. Draghi.

Banana Ben to the Rescue

I have heard a solution suggested that the Fed could buy all the Treasuries and retire them. OK, let's entertain this thought process for a minute. Let's say that the Fed buys the approximately $11.5 trillion of public debt outstanding and places it on its $3 trillion dollar balance sheet and then retires it. In other words, tells the Treasury they can just forget about paying the central bank back. After, all what's $11.5 trillion between friends. The Fed's balance sheet would go from $3 trillion to $14.5 trillion overnight. Inflation would skyrocket as the Fed counterfeited dollars and exchanged them for Treasuries, pushing $11.5 trillion into the economy that the Fed has promised never to remove. Then the Fed would retire their holdings of U.S. debt (its assets) by taking it off its balance sheet. How would the Fed get the inflation out of the system? Remember, the Fed fights inflation by selling assets on its balance sheet to banks—what do they have left to sell? They have retired their assets—so the increase in liquidity would slosh around creating huge price increases in everything it touches—we would be Zimbabwe! In 48 hours we would go from a World Power to a third world banana republic.

There is an aphorism—you are unable to see the forest through the trees. In this economy, it is easy to get caught up in the trees. It's easy to get in the weeds and focus on the daily or weekly movements of the central banks. Are they going to support Italian bonds? Will the economies of Italy, Portugal, and Spain live to die another day? Will the Fed institute another round of quantatative easing? But if you step back and block out the day to day noise and look at the forest, you realize they have no long term answers. Centuries of economic history leads to the conclusion that this will not work—sure, they can keep it up for a while, maybe longer than you would think. But history has proven eventually they will fail—the laws of economics have been violated. Economies can't exist indefinitely on stifling debt loads and endless money printing—eventually market participants will revolt and we will witness a worldwide depression. Today's central bankers are no different than Diocletian, nearly 2,000 years have elapsed but they haven't learned the economic lessons that centuries of history have established. They can't manage us out of this mess—all they are managing to do is ensure a worldwide depression of an unprecedented magnitude.

Think of this moment in time in the time continuum. If this economic crisis were placed on a time line going back centuries you would see these times aren't so different. The men and women in the Federal Reserve are armed with cutting-edge new technologies but not cutting edge new ideas. Technology has changed—Ben Bernanke is not hulled up at night in the halls of the Federal Reserve whittling down the metal content of the currency—now he can debase currency with a few keystrokes. The U.S. government isn't the first empire to overspend on public welfare and wars. These are new times—but the fundamental laws of economics are centuries old and centuries of information has already predicted the outcome. The United States in on the verge of a major debt crisis—there is no way of avoiding the pain that lies ahead.

We can take our medicine now and start the process of downsizing the empire or we can continue to counterfeit and spend and stave off the debt crisis for a while only to encounter a direr situation ahead.

The Cost of an Empire

I am writing this book during campaign season, and there is one commercial in particular that strikes me—Elizabeth Warren, who is running for the Senate seat in Massachusetts against Scott Brown, has the following ad: Ms. Warren begins the commercial by presenting roads and bridges in disrepair and states, "We've got bridges and roads in need of repair and thousands of people in need of work. Why aren't we rebuilding America?" She then ardently stares into the camera and scolds, "Our competitors are putting people to work, building a future. China invests 9 percent of its GDP in infrastructure. America? We're at just 2.4 percent. We can do better. We can build a foundation for a strong new economy and get people in Massachusetts to work right now. I'm Elizabeth Warren and I approve this message. Let's go to work."

When I first heard this commercial, I thought maybe Ms. Warren fell off that "reservation" she claimed her distant ancestors came from; perhaps she fails to ascertain the federal government is broke and hemorrhaging $1.2 trillion a year—we can't afford to fix roads and bridges. Furthermore, if Ms. Warren read my last chapter containing my commentary on China, she would realize that China built ghost towns, and this misallocation of capital is a huge bubble.

But when you think about it, she makes a point—although not the one she is trying to. I am sure Ms. Warren's ad is a plea for government to do more—tax the productive economy—provide jobs—put people to work to repair our pitiable bridges and tunnels—or the favorite Keynesian elixir of digging ditches and filling them. I have a question for Ms. Warren—why are bridges, roads, and tunnels in disrepair in the first place? Think about it—clear your mind of political rhetoric and think of the things government should provide—items that actually belong in the public sector. Building and maintaining roads and bridges is one of the few things that come to mind.

I am a Libertarian; I believe in small government—but I pay my taxes. When snow falls, I don't expect to strap a plow on my Audi and plow my street. If my house were to catch fire, I don't imagine myself standing with a garden house attempting to put it out. If I came home and found my house burglarized, I don't imagine myself tracking the criminals down in an attempt to redeem my merchandise and avenge my home burglary. And when there is a pothole on the road in front of my house—I don't expect to fix it.

New governments are springing up in Egypt and Libya—the question commentators ask is can they get the water running—can they open the roads to transportation, can they keep the lights on. These are the basics, the essential functions of government that serve the public at large and should be provided by the public sector.

It's obviously not her intention, but what Warren is pointing out is that the United States has gotten too big, too bloated, and too bureaucratic; we have lost sight of what government needs to be at the fundamental level. We have completely blurred the lines between the private and public sector and the traditionally public sector functions are not being performed.

In the 1930s, government took an active role in managing the economy out of a down turn—a decade earlier, the private sector took a year—with government management it took 12. Government also entrenched its authority into areas people historically did for themselves displacing the private sector and the private individual.

The Roosevelt administration, in an attempt to stave off an attack on their left from Huey Long, began to lay the foundations of the American welfare state. The capstone of this new initiative was the launching of Social Security and unemployment compensation. The passage of unemployment compensation and social security marked an important step forward in public assistance. For the first time, such benefits were recognized as rights, not rewards given by employers who need to attract the best talent. Social Security was a revolution that shifted the responsibility for income maintenance from the private to the public sector, from the family to the state, and from voluntary organizations to public bureaucracies.

"a significant, permanent social welfare bureaucracy."[34] Doris Kearns Goodwin writes:

> No longer would government be viewed as merely a bystander and an occasional referee, intervening only in times of crisis. Instead, the government would assume responsibility for continued growth and fairness in the distribution of wealth.[35]

I hear some argue that if Social Security didn't exist, most people wouldn't save for their retirement. I have news for those people—the federal government hasn't been saving that money either. In fact, I think it's safe to say that most American families manage their finances better than the federal government does.

In the 1960s, we witnessed another huge government power grab in the form of welfare, Medicare, and Medicaid. Currently, the government has taken over the health care industry and student loans.

Today, we have a significant amount of the population believing that there is no limit to what government should provide. Now that we have health care, I'm sure dental care will follow—dental care is a human right, not a privilege. And why stop there? Have a pet? Veterinary care should be publicly funded—is it fair that rich people can afford thousands of dollar cancer treatments for their pets, while the poor have to put Fido to sleep?

How do we pay for it? Tax productivity, run-up debt, and counterfeit the currency in order to redistribute wealth and make us all equal. Or better yet—since we are all different why don't we embrace what we are good at and just get paid the same amount. From each according to their abilities, to each according to their needs—that sounds great—that sounds fair! In fact, there was an economic model built on this premise—it was called communism heralded by another great empire—the USSR. In 1989, that empire collapsed under its own economic weight. It appears that when you make everyone equal and ask them to work in order to provide the same lifestyle, people expect somebody else to pick up the slack. And guess what—when the walls of communism came crumbling down, and we took a glimpse behind the iron curtain—we saw the roads to the once glorious St. Petersburg in shambles. Maybe Elizabeth Warren should have her campaign bus travel down those roads; she may rethink her centrally planned utopia.

Historically, we see empires in decline because they spread themselves too thin; they fail to meet society's basic needs. As we debate government's responsibility for providing birth control, potholes don't get filled. While we dispute government's role in retirement benefits, power grids don't get upgraded. While Americans are busy policing the world, we are not sure who is getting through our porous borders. We are all over the world flexing our imperial muscle, and we wish to offer cradle to grave services domestically, but we are failing to meet the essential needs of government to maintain infrastructure.

The Roman Empire found the costs of maintaining an expansive empire unmanageable and spent centuries debasing their currency. By the time the Barbarians came—their empire had already rotted from within. The British Empire spanned the world and fell due to its unmanageable debt.

In America's prime, it was rumored her streets were paved with gold; now, according to Elizabeth Warren, they are plagued with potholes. In the early centuries of the Roman Empire, it was told all roads led to Rome, and in fact that main road (Via Appia) still exists today. If we follow it, we can still see remnants of the coliseum, a reminder of the Imperial Roman Empire that once stood as a cultural center of art and enlightenment. Centuries from now, people will travel to America and see the remnants of the Statue of Liberty—a gift to the United States from France that stands as a beacon of freedom. A century before, immigrants like my grandfather laid eyes on that same statue when they came to America.

When my grandfather pulled into the harbor and observed for the first time America and that statue of freedom—I can only imagine what was going through his mind—hope, fear, excitement, anxiety. When he stepped off the boat, I don't know if he actually expected streets paved with gold as much as he expected a better life, an opportunity for himself and generations that came after—a chance to work hard and to succeed. I can't imagine what he expected, but I do know that he didn't expect a cradle-to-grave welfare system. All he and immigrants like him—going back to the first settlement in Plymouth, Massachusetts—desired was freedom and opportunity.

Those immigrants didn't find gold on the streets of America, they worked hard, and it often took a generation for their dream to be realized. Today, there is a country 90 miles off the shores of Florida—that country provides the cradle to grave welfare system some promote. Yet people risk their lives on homemade floats to travel for the freedoms this country provides—not the other way around.

America still shines bright in the world as that land of hope, opportunity and freedom that my grandfather left everything he held dear in Italy to travel to. Don't get me wrong—a debt crisis still exists and America has tough times ahead. However, it's what we do as we emerge out of this crisis that will determine if America's light of freedom can shine on. We need to recognize that big government is the problem, not the solution. We need to have reverence for centuries of economic wisdom that no nation can borrow and debase their way to prosperity. Every bond market and currency crisis has its genesis in a government that runs up massive obligations and then uses a central bank to monetize the debt. We know where this is headed and how to turn the doomed ship around.

America as an empire may end—but the American dream will live on if we manage our way out of this crisis by downsizing government and get back to what works. American people will soon have to return to saving for their own retirement, funding their own college education, saving on their own for a rainy day. But first we need to elect a government that stops promising Panem et Circenses (bread and circuses)—all paid for with more debt. Then, Americans can return to taking care of themselves and America can get back to what she does best—stand as a beacon to the world of liberty, opportunity, and freedom.

Notes

1. Cassius Dio, *Roman History*, published in Vol. IX of the Loeb Classical Library edition, 1927.
2. Robert L. Schuettinger and Eamonn F. Butler, *Forty Centuries of Wage and Price Controls* (Auburn, AL: Ludwig von Mises Institute, 2009).
3. Peter C. Earle, "Of Krugman and Diocletian," *Mises Daily*, June 8, 2012.
4. Robert L., Scheuttinger, "Price Fixing in Ancient Rome," *Mises Daily*, June 18, 2009.
5. Ibid.
6. Earle, "Of Krugman and Diocletian."
7. Scheuttinger, "Price Fixing in Ancient Rome."

8. Ibid.

9. Ibid.

10. Murray Rothbard, *History of Money and Banking* (Auburn, AL: Ludwig von Mises Institute, January 1, 2002).

11. Scheuttinger, "Price Fixing in Ancient Rome."

12. Rothbard, *History of Money and Banking.*

13. Ibid.

14. Ibid.

15. Jeffrey Tucker, "The Marshall Plan Myth," *The Free Market* 15(9), September 1997.

16. Rothbard, *History of Money and Banking.*

17. Ibid.

18. Ibid.

19. Ibid.

20. David Galland, "The Average Life Expectancy for a Fiat Currency Is 27 Years . . . Every 30 to 40 Years the Reigning Monetary System Fails and Has to Be Retooled," WashingtonsBlog, August 3, 2011.

21. Ibid.

22. Ibid.

23. Ibid.

24. Niall Ferguson, *Colossus: The Price of America's Empire* (New York: Penguin, 2009).

25. Trevor Owen Lloyd, *The British Empire 1558–1995* (Oxford: Oxford University Press, 2009).

26. Rothbard, *History of Money and Banking.*

27. H. A. Scott Trask. "Perpetual Debt: From the British Empire to the American Hegemon," *Mises Daily*, January 2004 (referenced June 24, 2010).

28. Carmen M. Reinhart and Kenneth S. Rogoff, "Too Much Debt Means the Economy Can't Grow," *Bloomberg*, July 14, 2011.

29. Ibid.

30. Ibid.

31. Ibid.

32. Robert Reich, "We Should Not Imitate the Austerity of Europe," Tribune Media Services, May 2012.

33. Bair, Sheila, CNBC, Squawk Box, September 10, 2012 appearance.

34. Michael Tanner, *The End of Welfare: Fighting Poverty in the Civil Society* (Washington, DC: Cato Institute, 1996).

35. Doris Kearns Goodwin, *No Ordinary Time; Franklin and Eleanor Roosevelt: The Home Front in World War II* (New York: Simon & Schuster, 1994), 625.

Chapter 7

Real World Europe

"The trouble with Socialism is that eventually you run out of other people's money."

—*Margaret Thatcher*

I n 1992 producers at MTV created a novel concept—they placed a group of seven strangers with diverse backgrounds in a house to live together for several months as cameras recorded their interpersonal relationships. The idea was to find out "what happens when people stop being polite and start being real." The concept created a media sensation that revolutionized television and introduced "reality TV."

In January 1999, the European Union embarked on a similar novel journey with just as much drama although not as much fanfare. They sought to place 17 countries/regions into the same currency without having a fiscal union; and today we witness the drama that unfolds. To paraphrase the introduction from the *Odd Couple:* "Can 17 countries share the same currency without driving each other crazy?" . . . The world is starting to find out.

The euro, signified by €EUR, is the currency used by 12 members of the European Union, as well as five regions such as Montenegro, Kosovo, Andorra, and others. The euro signifies the most significant monetary reform in Europe since the Roman Empire. The creation of this currency is most obviously a channel through which Europe may perfect a single market (by facilitating free trade between members of the Eurozone). Some view the euro as a means through which Europe may achieve political integration—modeled after the United States.

We could speculate about the drama that would unfold if *The Real World Euro* were a TV show. We can muse about the episode when former Italian Prime Minister Silvio Berlusconi was caught frolicking in the hot tub with a bevy of underage girls. And who can forget the time when the former French Prime Minister Nicolas Sarkozy left his wife for the supermodel Carla Bruni. We can reminisce about the scandal that rocked the house when Dominique Strauss Kahn allegedly chased the chambermaid around exposing himself through his open bath robe while the camera fuzzed over the inappropriate parts. And I am sure numerous episodes would have German Prime Minister Angela Merkel skirting around the house picking up beer cans and cigar butts left by the leaders of Italy, Portugal, and Spain. On numerous occasions she scowls into the camera declaring that she is sick of picking up the mess these other countries leave behind.

Yes, the reality show *Real World Euro* would be fun! Unfortunately, the real world that many Europeans find themselves in today is not. And a careful study of it should provide a stark warning for the U.S. currency and bond market.

The Creation of the Euro

The euro was formally put into circulation on January 1, 2002. However, the idea of a European common currency has been around for decades. The Treaty of Rome was established after WWII as an effort to build a stronger Europe and the European Economic Community (EEC), which later became the European Union (EU), was created with this purpose in mind. It focused overwhelmingly on economic cooperation and a political vision for "an ever closer union" to "eliminate the barriers which divide Europe."[1]

In 1979, the European Monetary System (EMS) was introduced in an effort to stabilize the economy, in doing so it locked exchange rates among participating countries. In 1992, the Economic and Monetary

Union (EMU) was formed, which set the foundation for the creation of a single currency. Seven years later, on January 1, 1999, the euro was born. Participating countries established exchange rates between their own currencies and the euro, creating a monetary union. After three years of transition, where the euro was only used as electric money, the actual euro notes and coins were used. "Now, the 12 euro area member states have a single currency, a common interest rate, and a common central bank (European System of Central Banks). It is the largest monetary replacement the world has ever seen."[2]

Administering the euro is the European System of Central Banks (ESCB), which is comprised of the European Central Bank (ECB) and the Eurozone central banks. The ECB is run out of Frankfurt, Germany, and has the sole authority to set monetary policy; other members of the ESCB participate through printing, minting, and distributing notes and coins. The 12 countries in the European Union that use the euro are Belgium, Germany, Greece, Spain, France, Ireland, Italy, Luxembourg, the Netherlands, Austria, Portugal, and Finland. Territories using the euro are Andorra, Monaco, San Marino, the Vatican, Martinique, Guadalupe (Caribbean), Reunion (Indian Ocean), and Montenegro, Kosovo.

The premise of Europe's sharing a common currency is an acceptable one. It certainly renders traveling throughout Europe a lot less cumbersome and trade among European countries more streamlined. The dilemma with the euro is no different than other fiat currencies because it is subject to the same vulnerabilities of all fiats—the lure to debase, to counterfeit. Stated simply, a fiat currency will always provide rulers with the temptation to monetize fiscal deficits. And markets realized this.

In a free market, banks lend money to people they believe will pay them back. And this is where the euro gets tricky. Let's say you run a local bank and Ed walks in. Ed is a young guy in his 20s—his body is completely tattooed, he has piercings on various body parts. Ed has no legitimate job, no money, and no collateral; but he has a dream of starting a garage band, and he wants your bank to fund his rock-and-roll fantasy. Of course, your answer would be an emphatic no! But just as you are about to show Ed the door, he introduces you to his dad. All cleaned up in a business suit, Ed's dad has a great job and stellar credit and agrees to cosign the loan for Ed. In an instant, Ed has become a lot more creditworthy—despite the fact his only talents are lip syncing and playing air guitar—he is able to leverage off the balance sheet of his dad who is a good credit risk.

What do Ed and his garage band have to do with the crisis in Europe? Well, similar to Ed the "PIIGS" in Europe (an acronym for Portugal, Ireland, Italy, Greece, and Spain), also became more creditworthy the minute they joined currencies with stronger euro partners, most notably Germany. The market perceived an implicit guarantee; they assumed the stronger European Union (EU) members would bail out the weaker members. Herein lies the dilemma that Europeans find themselves in with the common currency—Greece's generous pension plans become Germany's problem just as Ed's rock-and-roll dream became his father's problem.

Unfortunately, the euro was established as a fiat currency like every other one—based on decree, backed by nothing. And as Europe finally finishes its counterfeiting to pay off debt on its excessive welfare system, nothing is what the euro will ultimately be worth. It is clear when the ECB is done with all its debasing, Mario Draghi will be able to wallpaper his Italian Villa in worthless euros.

As in the United States, after the 2008 financial crisis, malinvestments were socialized, and public debts soared in the Eurozone. As economic growth declined, tax revenues collapsed and the governments started to subsidize industrial sectors and unemployment. Even before the crisis emerged, European governments had accumulated malinvestments due to their excessive welfare spending.

One of the defining ideals of Europe since World War II has been its social support system. However, NPR reporter Eleanor Beardsley notes that currently Europeans are questioning the sustainability of such a system largely put in place during the high-growth years following the war. These plans now face both economic and demographic pressures.[3]

Although benefits vary, the European Union's generous social welfare system, as a general rule, provides free health care, long-term unemployment support, liberal vacation time, and extensive maternity and child care benefits.

However, some Europeans speculate their social system just isn't viable anymore, that it survives solely on Europe's ability to keep borrowing to pay for the social programs.[4]

Leaders in Europe and America are realizing that benefits are more easily given than taken away. In fact, France witnessed public outrage and a nationwide strike to protest then President Nicolas Sarkozy's plans to raise the retirement age from 60 to 62. The irony was the majority of the rioters were in their 20s—40 years away from retirement, with obviously no desire to wait another minute. Sweeping reforms to France's money-losing pension system are part of efforts around Europe to cut back on growing public debts.

According to economist Willem Adema, a large percentage of social spending in the European Union goes toward supporting labor market policies such as unemployment benefits and pension systems:

> With the dynamics of an aging population and the increase in life expectancy, and with the financial pressures, raising retirement ages is going on across many different European countries.[5]

Another problem facing the EU is the rigidity of its labor market—it is nearly impossible to fire employees, making it difficult for companies to cut costs during downturns. This has inhibited the economic growth necessary to sustain the welfare state. France was home to the infamous 35-hour workweek that Sarkozy was finally able to abolish. Unfortunately for him, the French abolished his presidency in favor of Socialist Francois Hollande who has pledged 30 billion euros in new taxes to balance the budget.

Part of his plan includes a 75 percent wealth tax on incomes more than one million euros ($1.28 million). Hollande has actually been noted as saying that he does not "like the rich" and plans to pose the biggest hike in three decades.

And in a "touché" of sorts, it appears the rich in France don't like Hollande much either. On September 9, 2012, France's richest man— with an estimated net worth of $25.7 billion, Bernard Arnault, who runs luxury giant LVMH Moët Hennessy Louis Vuitton—confirmed news reports from Belgium that he applied for citizenship there earlier that month. Of course, he claims this move has nothing to do with the new French taxes—perhaps he prefers the weather in Belgium or has developed a preference for Belgian beer over French champagne. I'm sure the timing of this move is mere coincidence. And in a run for the "sortie," famed French actor Gerard Depardieu was right behind him, proudly displaying his newly-minted Russian passport in a recent issue of the *Wall Street Journal*. Ironically receiving tax refuge in the welcoming arms of the former Communist Vladimir Putin, whose country imposes a tax of a mere 13 percent.

The truth is the French are witnessing the effects of the Laffer curve. When onerous taxes are put upon people who have the means of mobility, they mobilize—in other words, they leave. We see this theory play out in the United States; as taxes in California escalate, its rich residents change residency in favor of their ski house in Utah or their beach house in Florida. The rich in Europe are no different, and this is why government solutions for overspending that favor retributory taxing of the wealthy never work. The rich French are trading Vive la France in for Vive la anyplace with a less punitive tax code.

It is evident Europe does not have an income problem—they have a spending problem. Europeans enjoy an unsustainable social welfare system—severe cuts to this system are the only method to curtail their unmanageable debt.

Overspending on social welfare coupled with demographic trends moving in the wrong direction left economically strapped nations such as Greece vulnerable to the lure of increased borrowing that was facilitated by the euro. Philipp Bagus explains in his book *The Tragedy of the Euro* that when several independent governments use one central banking system to finance their deficits it leads to these deficits being partially externalized in the form of higher prices on foreigners:

> Take the following example: The Greek government spends more than it receives in taxes. For the difference, the Greek government prints bonds. The banking system buys these bonds because banks can use them as collateral for new loans from the ECB. When the banks pledge the Greek government bonds as collateral with the ECB, they receive new central-bank money. Banks can then use these new reserves to expand credit. The money supply increases, and prices rise. The deficit is thereby indirectly monetized, and the users of the currency pay.[6]

But this isn't anything new. In fact, it is the tried-and-true recipe for destroying a country's currency and bond market by foolishly attempting to pay off debt through money printing.

And, in fact, this is the other risk—according to the *Wall Street Journal*. In 2010, when the Greek debt crisis first started brewing, German and French banks carried a "combined $119 billion in exposure to Greek borrowers alone and more than $900 billion to Greece and other countries on the euro-zone's vulnerable periphery: Portugal, Ireland and Spain." The article goes on to speculate:

> The fears that French and German banks could fall victim to Greece's debt crisis helps explain why Paris and Berlin have signaled that they would pursue a politically unpopular rescue of Greece—at the same time that they are trying to force Athens to take painful austerity measures.[7]

The easy answer for the euro would be to kick Greece and the other troublemakers out. The problem is Germany and France know that this world cause a major banking crisis for their banks and the banks in the respective PIIGS countries. Think for a moment that you are a successful Greek with euros in the bank. You are well aware if Greece were to return to the drachma that the Greek Central Bank would debase its currency. Your savings would lose a tremendous amount of its purchasing power in days. What do you do? If you were smart, you would transfer your euros into a German bank, if you were really smart you would sell your euros and buy gold—and in fact people have been doing both these things. But for those who are seeking shelter in U.S. dollars, here's a quick reminder: selling your euros to purchase dollars isn't a good idea—just as investing in hydrogen in 1937 or the White Star Line in 1912 didn't go so well, either.

An article in the *Wall Street Journal* notes that the "sharp plunge in yields underscores the haven appeal of German debt." Spain and Italy are increasingly finding themselves in the market's crosshairs over concerns that weak economic activity is impeding their ability to pay off their debt. This reminds us of the "substantial accidental benefits that the German economy is enjoying as a result of the crisis."[8]

As fears of contagion in the Eurozone mount, investors are more interested to just preserve their original investment by parking their funds in German debt with very low nominal yields.

Germany benefits from being in a dwindling group of countries with stable AAA ratings and bond markets that are deep enough to accommodate large flows from investors across the world.

A continued decline in German yields would also suggest a sharp rise in concerns over the fate of Italy and Spain. If Spanish and Italian bond yields were to keep soaring and approach unsustainable levels, that could force policy makers to announce measures to limit tensions or spark wider fears about the fate of the euro, possibly prompting investors to shun Eurozone paper altogether.

Interestingly enough, the European governments considered the possibility of a member nation taking on too much debt. Unfortunately, they weren't inclined to propose the only remedy (a gold standard and 100 reserve banking system to fix it). Instead, they legislated a remedy— the euro was established by the provisions in the 1992 Maastricht Treaty. In order to participate in the currency, member states were told they had to meet strict criteria, such as a budget deficit of less than 3 percent of their gross domestic product (GDP) and a debt ratio of less than 60 percent of GDP. However, right out of the gate, even Germany broke these rules so the provision had a tone of "do as I say, not as I do."

In effect, the euro came with an implicit bailout guarantee from the new ECB, permitting governments to overindulge in debt. Leveraging this implicit guarantee, many governments did not address structural problems such as uncompetitive labor markets or unsustainable welfare systems. They were enabled, for a time, to paper over these problems with government deficits: Philipp Bagus of the Mises Institute notes;

> As the financial crisis hit, government deficits increased sharply due to increasing public spending and falling revenues. Deficits soared, not only in the PIIGS countries (the bailout candidates), but also in the countries that were supposed to pay the costs of bailing out (most prominently Germany).[9]

Without a gold standard, governments become their own judges, until the market becomes the jury and imposes high interest rates as a penalty. Interest rates on the benchmark 10-year note in Greece were under 6 percent for the first half of 2010 until they more than doubled, jumping to over 12 percent by the end of the year. They eventually reached over 39 percent. Rates on the Spanish 10-year averaged below 4 percent and got as high as 7.5 percent in the summer of 2012. When the market decides you can't pay your bills, they are an unforgiving jury. However, for now there is a lull in the action over in Euroland. The ECB has placated the bond vigilantes for the moment. But debt monetization by the ECB can only keep these rates at bay in the short term. Eventually, monetization will lead to rampant inflation in Europe, leaving the ECB in a precarious position of continuing to inflate or owning up to those massive debt loads and default.

Today, government debts in several Eurozone countries are so prohibitive that they will never be repaid. Austerity receives a lot of airtime, but it isn't enough. Much deeper cuts need to be made. Furthermore, these austerity measures often include tax increases that stifle economic growth leading to higher deficits. Austerity should always emphasize spending cuts.

It appears that the leaders of the EU got caught up in the dream of creating the "optimal currency" and failed to set parameters for the possibilities for a structured default, the consequences of a collapse of the euro. The euro is "subject to the limitation of man and not the standard of gold, we have intertwined the behavior of the Greek government with taxpayers in Germany."[10]

Robert Murphy, an adjunct scholar of the Mises Institute, writes:

> Since the world left the last vestiges of the gold standard in 1971, the global economy has been set adrift. The technocrats keep assuring us that they can steer the economy much more efficiently than the "obsolete" gold standard, and yet a continual series of crises suggest otherwise. We can achieve the dream of the euro— an integrated monetary union where people and businesses can plan their activities spanning several countries without fear of exchange-rate risk—without its attendant pitfalls, but only if people go back to using genuine commodity money.[11]

Greece

For years, the Greek government had embarked in reckless spending. This was exacerbated when Greece, by virtue of having entered the

European Economic and Monetary Union, was enabled to pay lower interest rates on government bonds, as we have just discussed.

But the truth is that Greece was living beyond its means even before it joined the euro. After it adopted the single currency, public spending soared. We have recently gotten a glimpse into the lavish retirement benefits the Greeks have been enjoying—policies such as providing people in "hazardous" occupations the chance of an early retirement, at the age of 50. This doesn't sound so preposterous until you understand the liberal method used in determining what qualifies as a hazardous work environment.

It appears that in Greece the seemingly innocuous occupation of hairdresser has a bevy of hidden dangers and is thus relegated as a dangerous occupation. Handling sharp scissors, contact with bleaching chemicals coupled with an inordinate amount of time spent on your feet—it's a wonder a hairdresser even survives to 50. Using this as a barometer of danger, the Greeks have deemed an additional 580 jobs as hazardous enough for the workers to take early retirement, at the age of 55 for men and 50 for women. Including not only the treacherous occupation of hairdressing, but also equally dangerous professions such as television and radio presenters, who are thought to be at risk from bacteria on their microphones, and musicians who use instruments like the "deadly saxophone," leading to a strain on the respiratory system.

> All in all 700,000 members of Greece's work force, or 14 percent, have been promised the boon of early retirement, its national average retirement age is 61, one of the lowest levels in Europe. This 'deal' was born out of lengthy bartering between strong-arm unions and pandering governments, and has certainly added to the problems that plague Greece's financial state, its spending, and inevitably the sovereign debt problem that Europe is currently facing.[12]

Public-sector employees in Greece also received lavish wages and benefits sharply outpacing their private sector counterparts. These groups have been asked to take strong pay cuts from austerity. Worried workers who want the governments to keep their promises have been leading massive protests at the prospect of reduced wages and a later retirement age.

And just like the United States, the specter of unfunded pension liabilities is more of a concern than the vast amounts of money that governments owe to creditors—their official sovereign debt. Research conducted in Washington by noted economist Jagadeesh Gokhale shows that were Greece to "declare their promised pensions on their balance sheet it would show that its debt was actually 875 percent of its GDP."[13] Lest we become too judgmental, if the U.S. public pension plans were put on the balance sheet, our debt-to-GDP ratio would be about 740 percent of GDP.

But Greece is not the only country in the Eurozone to downplay its obligations. France would be at a level close to 549 percent of GDP and in Germany the same calculations lead around 418 percent.[14]

Looking at these inflated figures is a sobering albeit more accurate way of assessing debt in countries with large pension liabilities and demographic shifts showing people approaching the age of retirement. Severe action is necessary to address these issues.

Now, some of these obligations will not be paid out for a number of years, even decades, but most countries are now reaching their saturation points in terms of borrowing; they are rapidly getting to the point where more borrowing will not be possible.

As money flowed out of the government's coffers into lavish social welfare programs, its income was hit by widespread tax evasion. So, after years of overspending, and undercollecting, its budget deficit spiraled out of control.

At its economic height, in the fourth and fifth centuries B.C., ancient Greece was the most advanced economy in the world, yet direct taxation was not well developed. In modern-day Greece, it appears little has changed—despite a countless number of taxes. Greeks appear to view the tax system as optional.

People are more inclined to pay taxes when they believe there's a reasonable chance that dishonesty will be detected and punished. But Greek tax officials are rumored to be notoriously easy to bribe with a fakelaki (small envelope) of cash. Even when the system does track down evaders, it is next to impossible to get them to pay, as tax courts can take as long as 7 to 10 years to resolve a case.[15]

In the United States, we sometimes witness elected officials responsible for writing tax code caught cheating on the very taxes they expect their constituents to pay. This was perhaps on the most vulgar display during the Obama cabinet appointments a few years ago. It should come as no surprise that the Greeks are plagued by similar concerns.

> According to a preliminary investigation, 70 Finance Ministry employees have real estate holdings ranging from €800,000 to €3 million in value. The average real estate holdings for these employees are valued at €1,228,337, while their average declared income is €50,834. The Finance Ministry is launching investigations into all these cases.[16]

While dealing with protests and open riots, the new Greek government is trying to change things. They are attempting to simplify taxes and have done away with some loopholes. Ironically, in a country where few chose to pay taxes, most expect benefits they feel the government is obligated to provide. As Greece is working to bring in tax revenue, it is also rethinking some of its cushy social welfare and pension programs.

When the global financial downturn hit, Greece was ill-prepared to cope. Decades of reckless spending came to the surface. Eventually, debt levels reached the point where the country was no longer able to repay its loans, and were required to request help from the other European members and the International Monetary Fund (IMF) in the form of massive loans.

This is the consequence that arises when the market determines you don't have a sufficient tax base to pay your bills—it is a watershed moment. As mentioned earlier, the Greek 10-year note, which historically averaged around 5 percent, soared to just less than 40 percent by March 2012. If the United States ever had to pay an average interest rate of 40 percent on its debt, the bill just for servicing that debt would be over $4.6 trillion—or 190 percent of all federal revenue! The market had spoken and it determined Greece was a bad credit risk.

At that juncture, Greece had two options: (1) to leave the euro and then print the drachma and to default via inflation—leading to complete economic devestation; and (2) to work within the confines of the European Union and request a bailout and to restructure their debt. An explicit default is always the better option. But that road isn't smooth either.

In May 2010, the European Union and IMF provided 110 billion euros ($140 billion: £88 billion) of bailout loans to Greece to help the government pay its creditors. The package represented the first rescue of a Eurozone member. Opening the door for a bailout in return for extra budget cuts of 30 billion euros ($43 billion) over three years. But the Greeks soon learned that making budget cuts wasn't easy as later that month public sector workers staged a 48-hour nationwide strike. Three people were killed when a bank was set on fire during this protest.[17]

It soon became apparent that the original loan would not be enough, so a second, 130-billion-euro bailout was agreed to in that same year. Global policy makers also installed an emergency safety net worth about $1 trillion to bolster international financial markets and prevent the crisis from damaging the euro.[18]

Greece embarked on a round of austerity measures including raising women's retirement age from 60 to match men at 65. In 2011, Greece unveiled a series of privatizations; part of its goal to raise 50 billion euros by 2015 to reduce its debts. In July 2011, Eurozone leaders agreed on second rescue package of 109 billion euros, plus contribution by private-sector bondholders estimated to total as much as 50 billion euros by mid-2014. But it was far from smooth sailing from there. In October 2011, Greece admitted it would miss a deficit target set just months earlier. The 2012 draft budget approved by cabinet predicted a deficit of 8.5 percent of GDP for 2011, short of target leading Greece to put additional austerity measures in place. The Eurozone leaders reached a deal with private banks and insurers allowing them to accept a 50 percent loss on their Greek government bonds under a plan to lower Greece's debt burden. In November 2011, former European Central Bank vice-president Lucas Papademos was appointed to head a new coalition. He confirmed that Greece would implement the bailout deal before calling elections. In December of that year, unions held a 24-hour general strike to test the resolve of the new national unity government, and violence broke out at protests outside parliament in Athens. Some people were wounded, and 38 people were arrested.

Unemployment in Greece rose to 20.9 percent, a new record, after austerity measures were put in place. In February 2012, Greek lawmakers endorsed a new austerity deal after 10 hours of debate. Protesters fought pitched battles with riot police outside parliament and set buildings on fire.[19]

It's true—spending is the enjoyable part; austerity is no fun. Maybe that's why they call it austerity—derived from the word *austere*, meaning serious, grim, and somber. If it were meant to be fun, they might have called it "spring break," "vacation," or, in an effort to sound European, "holiday." The government might seek to request a holiday from all the social welfare programs in order to provide the public coffers a much needed rest. Citizens would be encouraged to have fun—just not at the government's expense. Riots and protests could be billed as "Europeans gone wild"—just those crazy Europeans letting loose while the government takes a holiday from paying them. Unfortunately, there is no "fun" in austerity—it's the pain the market inflicts on you when it finds you are unable to pay your bills.

Calls to end austerity measures in Europe are moot points, as debt-ridden economies have no choice but to undergo painful belt-tightening measures to right the bloated economies. Greece agreed to hike taxes and lay off public-sector workers in exchange for bailout money under the notion that painful reforms today will lead to a sleeker and more competitive economy tomorrow that can repay rescue lenders.

Yet critics say austerity sends already sky-high unemployment rates even higher and cuts tax revenues, thus exacerbating recession. Either way, once a country runs up as much debts as Greece has, default is inevitable, and there are two ways to handle it—the country can go the traditional way and restructure with creditors. They can tell you, explicitly, "I cannot pay you back. Let's restructure the debt."

The other way a country can default is to continue to borrow and print money and pay its lenders back, although the currency will be seriously debased and worth far less than it was when initially borrowed.

The purchasing power of the money that I have given you will erode so dramatically, it will be the same mathematical equation as if I didn't pay the money back at all.

Restructuring leads to austerity, while hyperinflation that comes with money printing ultimately leads to higher borrowing costs and greater economic pain. Either way, a painful reconciliation is needed. The sooner and more honestly you take the hit, the better off the country will be.

The countries that are insolvent are going to have to choose how to default on their debt. It's not my opinion—it's a fact. If they owe more money than they can possibly pay back, they must default.

Two years into Greece's debt crisis, its citizens are reeling from austerity measures imposed to prevent a government debt default that could cause havoc throughout Europe.

As GDP decreases and unemployment increases, crime, homelessness, emigration, and personal bankruptcies are on the rise.

The most dramatic sign of Greece's pain, however, is a surge in suicides.

Recorded suicides have roughly doubled since before the crisis to about 6 per 100,000 residents annually, according to the Greek health ministry and a charitable organization called Klimaka.[20]

About 40 percent more Greeks killed themselves in the first five months of 2012 than in the same period last year, the health ministry says.[21]

While some countries have higher rates of recorded suicides, including the United States' over 10 per 100,000, mental-health professionals here say Greece's data greatly understate the incidence of suicide because it carries a strong stigma among Greeks. The Greek Orthodox Church forbids funeral services for suicides unless the deceased was mentally ill. Families often mask suicide deaths as accidents.[22]

A suicide help line at Klimaka, the charitable group, used to get 4 to 10 calls a day, but "now there are days when we have up to 100."[23]

The true cost of overspending and debt are unfathomable—the effects run deeper than economic statistics and interest rates—it cuts through the heart of a nation, it sucks the life blood out of its people—it diminishes an individual's desire to live.

Soft tyranny evolves through dependencies born out of promises made by those in government to take responsibility for your well-being. You trade your freedom and self-sufficiency in return for a vote and get a promise to be taken care of. In order to get elected, more promises are made and you become more reliant on empty promises promulgated by those in power. Today, Greece stands as an example of the pain experienced when people begin to realize promises made cannot be kept. Massive debt loads are endured to keep the façade going for just a little while longer. Huge debts put a burden on growth, and tax revenues shrink as the cost of caring for the unemployed surge until the market cries—No More! At that point, interest rates skyrocket—central banks have to endure massive counterfeiting to keep up with the promises made by men and women in power. Riots, bloodshed, and suicides are the human tragedy experienced when citizens mistakenly place their well-being at the mercy of impetuous fools.

Dr. Hayek vs. Dr. Keynes

A morbidly obese gentleman labored into Dr. Hayek's office suffering from severe chest pain. The patient also complained that he was unable to consume his usual 10,000 calorie-per-day diet; in fact, he was feeling so sick that he could barely scarf down 9,000 calories. He pleaded that his love for food remained as strong as ever, but his body just wasn't keeping up with his demands.

After having a thorough look at the patient, the good doctor could not find anything wrong outside of the patient's extreme portliness. After a moment of reflection, he delivered to his patient a troubling diagnosis. He explained that the chest pain stemmed from the strain the patient's 500-pound body was putting on his heart and that the lack of appetite was his body's attempt to protect itself from this imbalance. Dr. Hayek's prescription was simple: the patient had to dramatically reduce his consumption while undertaking a moderate exercise program, with the goal of losing 250 pounds as quickly and safely as possible. Dr. Hayek was aware that it would be a physically painful and emotionally difficult process for the man, but it was the only way to avert a life of suffering—or even a fatal heart attack.

Unfortunately, our patient rebelled against such an austere program. He had grown very fond of his high-calorie and high-fat diet and didn't think that now, when he was already depressed from dealing with all these ailments, was a good time to deny himself the few pleasures he had left. In his opinion, the doc's prescription was just too simplistic. He thought there just had to be a way to have his cake and eat his cookies, too—frequently. So he waddled out of Dr. Hayek's office as fast as he could, shouting over his shoulder: "I'm getting a second opinion!"

The overweight gentleman sauntered across the street, where he found the office of Dr. Keynes. He told the new doctor about his acute chest pain and lack of appetite, and complained about the previous doctor's "heartless" prescription. After a cursory examination, Dr. Keynes rendered his diagnosis: the patient's condition did not stem from the fact that his gigantic frame was causing undue strain on his heart; instead, the doctor concluded, the patient's chest pain was merely caused by a temporary lack of hunger. Furthermore, Dr. Keynes argued, the stress of cutting weight at the present time would certainly prove detrimental to the man's already weak heart. Therefore, his prescription was for the 500-pound man to each as much as possible, as quickly as possible. Anything less might cause the man to suffer a heart attack, he noted. Now the doctor did concede that, at some point in the distant future, it might be a good idea for the man to shed a few pounds. But for the present, the most important thing to do would be to consume as much as he could stomach.

The patient left Dr. Keynes's office with a broad smile. After gorging at an all-you-can-eat restaurant, he momentarily forgot about his chest pain. It looked like he had found his solution—except he keeled over walking back from his 12th visit to the buffet table.

The preceding allegory discusses the dangers of quackery, whether medical or economic. Right now, economic quackery—in the form of Keynesianism—has overtaken Europe and Washington and the world.

Unlike their forbears, modern-day Keynesians do not argue just for mollification in the rate of deleveraging. They seek to significantly increase debt levels in an effort to boost the aggregate demand in the economy. Apparently, only once the mythical recovery takes hold due to government spending, printing, and borrowing does a discussion of deficits become appropriate.

The argument we hear from Keynesians today is that austerity is causing Europe all their grief and that reckless currency debasement in the form of monetizing the debt is the only relief. That's similar to Dr. Keynes arguing that if the gentleman in the previous allegory were to heed Dr. Hayek's advice for a day or two and eat a salad, the salad was the cause of the man's problems.

In 2010, debt-plagued governments in Europe were brought to their knees. Markets decided certain members of the EU did not have the tax base necessary to fulfill their debt obligations. Once the market has decided you are unable to pay your bills, it's a watershed event—the investment community has lost faith in you and there is nothing you can do. The free market's response is to drive interest rates up. The governments, in an effort to soothe the markets, adopted austerity measures that are necessary but are no quick fix.

European countries and those in America are unable to come to the realization that the lifestyle they have been promised by their governments in an effort to procure reelection is unsustainable. Taking a nation off the public-spending spigot is painful, and there is no way around it. A country like Greece only has one viable option—to default. However, the political economic environment is discouraging Greece and the like from doing so. The ECB has come up with the strategy of monetizing debt. Germany was given an option of a euro bond—a bond that would run through the Eurozone—however, they refused, not wanting to assume an average interest rate of southern Europe. So, instead, they have allowed the ECB to employ a path that will eventually destroy the euro. Currently, inflation is not salient enough for them to feel the full effects. However, as more and more people are forced to spend nearly all their income for food and fuel, their citizens could revolt en masse. Unfortunately, the riots in Greece and Spain occurring today could seem quiescent in the near future.

Krugman, in an August 2012 article, chides:

> The euro can't be saved unless Germany is also willing to accept substantially higher inflation over the next few years—and so far I have seen no sign that German officials are even willing to discuss this issue, let alone accept what's necessary. Instead, they're still insisting, despite failure after failure—that everything will be fine if debtors just stick to their austerity programs.[24]

Currently, Germans seem to have acquiesced to the inflation route. However, in small towns all over Germany, you can still find a few who have already experienced the effects of the inflationary diet the ECB has currently placed the Eurozone on. There are some still left in Germany who could tell hyperinflation's painful tale and warn that the fatal consequences that stemmed from this period are forever ingrained on the psyche of the Germans and the world.

Following World War I, the Weimar Republic emerged from the German Revolution in November 1918. Modeled after the Soviets of the Russian Revolution of 1917, the new government of Germany struggled with the onerous requirements brought upon by the Treaty of Versailles. In order to pay the large costs of World War I, Germany had suspended the convertibility of its currency into gold when that war broke out. The German kaiser and Parliament funded the war entirely by borrowing. The Treaty of Versailles served to further accelerate the decline in the value of the mark. By the end of 1919, more than 47 paper marks were required to buy one U.S. dollar.[25]

Knowing the Germans were debasing their currency, war reparations were required to be repaid in hard currency, in lieu of the rapidly depreciating paper mark. To solve the problem, Germany employed a strategy of mass printing bank notes in order to buy foreign currency and then pay reparations, greatly exacerbating inflation rates of the paper mark.[26]

Germany had exited the war with most of its industrial power intact; the destruction from the war hit France and Belgium disproportionately. Germany was arguably in a better position to once again become a dominant force in the European continent. In order to temper Germany's strength, the Allies demanded reparations in gold or foreign currency to be paid in annual installments of 2 billion gold marks plus 26 percent of the value of Germany's exports.[27]

This was the beginning of an increasingly rapid devaluation of the mark, which fell to less than one third of a cent by November 1921 (approximately 330 marks per U.S. dollar). The total reparations demanded was 132 billion gold marks, which was far more than the total German gold and foreign exchange.[28]

Beginning in August 1921, Germany began to buy foreign currency with marks at any price, but that only increased the speed of breakdown in the value of the mark. The lower the mark sank in international markets, the greater the amounts of marks were required to buy the foreign currency demanded by the Reparations Commission.[29]

In January 1923, French and Belgian troops occupied the Ruhr, the industrial region of Germany in the Ruhr Valley to ensure that the reparations were paid in goods, such as coal from the Ruhr and other industrial zones of Germany. Because the mark was practically worthless, it became impossible for Germany to buy foreign exchange or gold using paper marks. Instead, reparations were paid in goods. Inflation was exacerbated when workers in the Ruhr went on a general strike, and the German government printed more money in order to continue paying them for "passively resisting."[30]

The cause of the immense acceleration of prices that occurred during the German hyperinflation of 1922–1923 seemed unclear and unpredictable to those who lived through it, but in retrospect was relatively simple. The Treaty of Versailles imposed a huge debt on Germany that could be paid only in gold or foreign currency. With its gold depleted, the German government attempted to buy foreign currency with German currency, but this caused the German mark to fall rapidly in value, which greatly increased the number of marks needed to buy more foreign currency. This caused German prices of goods to rise rapidly.[31]

Author Adam Fergusson notes,

> This placed the government and banks between two unacceptable alternatives: if they stopped the inflation this would cause immediate bankruptcies, unemployment, strikes, hunger, violence, collapse of civil order, insurrection, and revolution. If they continued the inflation they would default on their foreign debt. The attempts to avoid both unemployment and insolvency ultimately failed when Germany had both.[32]

You see history rhyming in real time today. Europe and America are in the early stages of the same dilemma. If central banks stop printing money, deflation will destroy the economy. Keep on printing, and they'll eventually reach a hyperinflationary default.

Hyperinflation in Germany was even more tragic than storied wheelbarrows of cash to buy a loaf of bread. Most believe that the hyperinflation left Germany vulnerable to the lure of despots like Hitler and was indirectly responsible for the atrocities that came out of the death camps of World War II.

The Weimar Republic isn't the largest example of hyperinflation; it is outpaced by Yugoslavia, where inflation rates were 76 percent from 1971 through 1991, until inflation exploded in 1994 to 313 million percent until Yugoslavia changed to the German mark. Hungary's inflation rate in 1946 was 41.9 quadrillion percent—prices were said to double every 15.3 hours.

And, of course, who can forget Zimbabwe with a 2008 annual inflation rate of 89.7 sextillion percent—you can't make up a number like that. Prices in Zimbabwe doubled every 5 days, although some estimates do show as much as every 24 hours. Bond yields on the one year in Zimbabwe averaged around as 340 percent. This is the market telling you that you can't pay your bills.

You have to imagine there are some in Germany who see amazing parallels between the Weimar Republic and governments of the world today. Putting the war treaty aside, the hyperinflation was created as a result of the mass printing of a fiat currency in order to pay back debts.

The United States has persisted under the flawed Keynesian theory of government spending, borrowing, and printing for close to a century. After all, with interest rates guaranteed to be near zero percent for years on end, what's a government to do except borrow more money? Curiously, the world has yet to fully recognize our precarious condition, even as they provide us with life support. Washington is now entirely dependent on the reserve currency status of the dollar and the continued hibernation of bond vigilantes. Without these supports, the United States would face complete economic arrest. Rather than allowing the American people to get back on our feet, Washington is stuffing us with even more debt. It's almost as if the feds are daring our foreign creditors to pull the plug. As a consequence, I predict that just as Dr. Keynes killed his patient, Keynesian economics will kill our economy.

Dr. Keynes and Dr. Hayek and America's Bout with Hyperinflation

We don't need to locate a little old lady in a small, remote German village to recount the tales of inflation. We've had a small taste of runaway inflation in the United States. I am old enough to recount those days. The double-digit inflationary recession of 1973–1974, followed soon by the even more intense inflationary recessions of 1979–1980 and 1981–1982 were a troubling time in America's history. In fact, it was a time period that left Dr. Keynes without a remedy. If the government was supposed to step on the spending accelerator during recessions, and step on the brakes during booms, what is it going to do if there is a steep recession (with unemployment and bankruptcies) and a sharp inflation at the same time? "Since 1973–74, Keynesianism has been intellectually finished, dead from the neck up."[33] The 1970s inflation left the Keynesians at a dead end fiddling with their Philips Curve, attempting to derive a mathematical formula to get us out of the stagflationary mess they created.

When the United States exited World War II, it was saddled with an enormous federal debt; however, household debt had subsided dramatically after long years of the depression and the war. Americans had sacrificed, and there was pent-up demand—"happy days were here again." Americans had an enormous economic advantage. Europe had been devastated from the bombings and the treacherous war. America was the only intact manufacturing base. In addition to this, as we discussed in the previous chapter, the American taxpayer helped foot the bill through foreign aid to rebuild Europe that greatly benefitted U.S. manufacturers. All of the worldwide economy was tied to the U.S. dollar, and that peg gave the United States a lot of latitude. The American economy had a lot of room for error. Keynesians like to reference this period as the golden years of high growth and try to attribute the high tax rates of the 1950s to prosperity. I would agree—if we raised taxes back to those levels and carpet bombed every industrial nation, we may be able to rekindle those glory years once again.

Despite all the warm memories and favorable economic data that flow from this period, the 1950s economy wasn't as glorious as some remember it. We had two recessions, in 1953–1954 and 1957–1958, and a bout with high inflation. However, this was a period that Keynesians incessantly point to as the good old days. Dr. Keynes was in the driver's seat and, as we are about to see, ready to drive the economy off a cliff.

Taking the economy by the reins, they created additional entitlements in the 1960s—the "war on poverty" in effect created generations bound to poverty via government subsidies that paid them as long as they remained poor. Easy money and government stimulus kept the economy of the 1960s going for a while, but in the 1970s failed Keynesian policies finally caught up with the U.S. economy. Prohibitive tax policies made it unattractive to take risk—high inflation–low growth, a term referred to as *stagflation*, brought about Jimmy Carter's famed misery index. America no longer held the only intact industrialized base—other nations had caught up and surpassed us. I cannot recount firsthand the economies of Diocletian, the Weimar Republic, or the Great Depression. However, I was a child of the 70s—I lived through it and, aside from listening to an occasional Bee Gees song, have no desire to go back.

The decade that began with recession and the abandoning of the gold monetary system saw the emergence of stagflation (economic stagnation plus inflation) and ended with the coining of the aforementioned "misery index" (inflation rate plus unemployment rate). While not recognized in the statistical senses as a decade of depression, and certainly not as a great depression, the decade was nonetheless a period of economic gloom and despair that was compounded by rampant drug abuse and bell-bottomed pants.[34]

The 1970s was a turning point in the wrong direction for the American economy. According to Mark Thorton, a senior fellow at the Mises Institute;

> Gold was abandoned, prices increased, and the dollar rapidly depreciated. Unemployment and underemployment increased, and both the duration of unemployment and the unemployment rate set post-WWII highs in the early 1980s. The federal government abandoned a long standing tradition of balanced budgets for the current regime of ever-increasing deficits and escalating national debt while the personal saving rate of Americans, which had been on an increasing trend, flattened out and began its current declining trend toward a zero savings rate. It was the 1970s when the trade balance first destabilized and then began the trend of escalating trade deficits (naturally when the people are saving less and the government is borrowing more, the new loans have to come from foreigners).[35]

All of these problems were not due to the laziness of the American people—on the contrary, Americans were working harder. Females moved into the workforce in record numbers, and the two-income family was established, mostly to try and maintain their standards of living. Unfortunately, the 1960s and 1970s were two decades when government employment expanded the most, so that much of this increased labor effort produced little of value. Working for the government can even be a net negative for the economy in that government employees can do actual harm to the production of useful goods and services.[36]

In the 1970s, the Keynesian utopia hit a dead-end with no way out. Jimmy Carter, with a melancholy intonation, prepared us for what he thought to be the new norm—Dr. Keynes had run out of medicine; we had to think smaller, we had to want less. Iran held our hostages in an embassy, Japan was kicking our butts in technology and manufacturing—Americans were portrayed as lazy. I was a child of the 1970s' stagflation. It was a decade of despair. When Fed chairman Paul Volcker jacked interest rates close to 20 percent, I was in high school, when Americans were lucky to get a job where they could say, "Welcome to McDonald's, may I take your order?" With unemployment near 11 percent, men and women with families loved to don that yellow and orange uniform.

We endured the pain; the peak of the recession was in November and December 1982, when the nationwide unemployment rate was 10.8 percent, highest since the Great Depression—it is still the highest since the 1930s. There is a saying that it's always darkest before its absolutely black, and that's how the early 1980s felt—dark, drab, absolutely dismal. Then something amazing happened: darkness turned into daylight—it was morning in America! The economy recovered, and not just some run-of-the-mill recovery—it took off.

Paul Volcker gave the economy a dose of Dr. Hayek's medicine and tamed inflation. Ronald Reagan cut taxes and unleashed American exceptionalism—it was always simmering below the surface; it was just stifled by flawed Keynesian policies. Gone was the caricature of the American loser. In came a new acronym, the YUPPY—young upwardly mobile urban professional. They embodied the national sentiment—America felt upwardly mobile. America was back!

When Ronald Reagan left office, America was that shining city on the hill—the beacon of hope and magnet to all who seek freedom.

America took a dose of Dr. Hayek's tough medicine, although it's true we should have taken more. It has to be noted that Reagan did not do enough to reverse government spending. However, his prominent place on the mantle of history and his influence on my life is undisputable. As he so eloquently noted in his final address, his administration and the pioneers of the Reagan revolution didn't just mark time—"they made a difference—not bad . . . not bad at all."[37]

We have gotten a bit off track, but that city on a hill still stands. I want that city to be there, just as vibrant for my children and the next generation as it was for me. But we can't just mark time—we need to elect leaders who will face with honesty the challenges that await us.

The question you have to ask yourself is: where is government borrowing and money printing of the central banks eventually going to lead us? It's just forestalling the inevitable in Europe, Japan and in the United States, as it makes the eventual debt collapse much worse. Dr. Keynes has prescribed an elixir that is easing the pain for the short term, but will cause a lot more pain in the long term.

Inflation and the loss of confidence in the U.S. economy to support outstanding debt will cause an increase in rates that will lead any remaining economic growth to crater. At this point, the Fed will have two choices: they can print even more money in an attempt to usurp control of interest rates from the free market forever, or they can face reality and try to unwind their balance sheet, selling trillions of dollars of U.S. debt and MBSs into the economy, sending rates even higher and the economy (temporarily) into complete destruction. You have to remember the Fed is holding bonds at record low rates—so who would the buyer of an MBS be at 3.5 percent when market rates are 7 percent? The option of indefinite and massive money printing will cause a hyperinflationary depression, and the massive unwinding of the Fed's balance sheet will cause a hyperdeflationary depression. Both options will be devastating—and get more so with each passing day.

Eventually, Dr. Keynes's prescription pad will run dry and we will be forced to swallow Dr. Hayek's difficult pill. But even if we followed the good Dr's prescription right now the consequences will be bleaker than the darkness of the early 1980s. That's because Chairman Volcker's 20 percent Fed Funds rate would quickly expose the nation's $16.5 trillion debt as being insolvent. Back in the relatively halcyon days of the early 1980s, U.S. debt as a percentage of GDP was just 30 percent; not north of 105 percent as it is today. And household debt was just 46 percent, not like the 81 percent of today.

However, if we follow the light of freedom and the free market and shun the seduction of the Keynesian elixir, I am confident a new generation will once again bear witness to the beauty of morning in America.

I'll Take Currency Debasement for $40 Billion . . . a Month

The end of last summer was an important moment in fiat currencies and the central banks that lord over them. In September 2012, central banks embarked on reckless behaviors that will lead fiat currencies and public debt to be flushed down the toilet. It will mark the beginning of the end for money that is not backed by precious metals. The events were perpetuated in a desperate and final attempt to save faltering global GDP, but it will only lead to further economic destruction and intractable inflation.

The excuse being given for the upcoming assault on fiat money is the crumbling economies in Europe, which have taken down emerging market economies as well. For example, China's exports to the EU (17) dropped 16.2 percent in July of 2012, as sales to Italy plunged 26.6 percent from a year earlier.

And now the nucleus of Europe, and Germany, is starting to split. German unemployment increased five straight months in 2012 to reach 2.9 million by August.

And listen up, all you lovers of the Phillips Curve and inflation atheists: Spain's unemployment rate reached another euro-era high of 25.1 percent in July 2012. However, inflation is headed straight up, rising from 1.8 percent in June to 2.7 percent in August. But this is just the beginning of rising unemployment and soaring inflation since the ECB and the Fed launched their attack in September of 2012.

The ECB and Federal Reserve both announced an incredible assault on the euro and the dollar. The European Union said on August 31, 2012, that it proposes to grant the ECB sole authority to grant all banking licenses.

This means the ECB would be allowed to make the European Stabilization Mechanism—just sanctioned by the German courts on September 12—a bank, which would allow them an unfettered and unlimited ability to purchase PIIGS debt. This is exactly what Mario Draghi meant when he said he would do "whatever it takes to save the euro."

In a race to debase, the Bank of Japan (BOJ) announced it would boost the size and duration of a government bond-buying program. As a follow-up from a two-day meeting, the BOJ indicated it would spend an additional 10 trillion yen on short- and long-term government bonds and bills through the end of 2013. That brings the recent total to more than 100 trillion Yen worth of BOJ debt monetization. The government of Japan has now pulled the pin on their debt grenade.

Deflation has ruled their land for 10 out of the last 15 years. And because deflation is the arch enemy of Keynesians, the new Prime Minister (Shinzo Abe) has adopted an inflation target of at least 2 percent. As of now, the Japanese 10-year note yields just 0.75 percent. That's a very poor yield; but since holders of Yen are currently experiencing deflation, they still are provided with a real return on their investment. But if inflation does indeed rise to 2 percent, the yield on the 10-year note would have to rise above 3.3 percent in order to offer the same real yield seen today.

However, the problem is that Japan is already spending nearly 25 percent of its national revenue on debt service payments—despite the fact that interest rates are close to nothing. If the average interest rate on outstanding debt were to increase to more than 2 percent—or anywhere close to offering a real yield on Japanese Government Bonds (JGBs)—the country would be paying well over 50 percent of all government revenue on debt service payments alone. Of course, some will say that yields won't go that high even if inflation creeps higher. But these investors should be reminded that the Japanese 10-year note was 1.8 percent back in May of 2008. Once the Japanese government achieves their inflation goal, it will detonate JGBs. That will cause their currency, bond market, and economy to explode.

Not to be outdone, Fed Chairman Bernanke gave a speech on the same day as the ECB, indicating that an open-ended quantitative easing program will take effect. The Fed would print at least $40 billion per month of newly created money until the unemployment rate and nominal GDP reach internal target levels set by the central bank. And then even after that, the money printing won't end.

Incredibly, Mr. Bernanke has said that previous QEs have provided "meaningful support" for the economic recovery. He has also contradicted himself by saying that the recovery was "tepid" and that the economy was "far from satisfactory." He also said, "The costs of nontraditional policies, when considered carefully, appear manageable, implying that we should not rule out the further use of such policies if economic conditions warrant."

He then said after officially announcing quantitative counterfeiting forever that, ". . . the Federal Reserve will provide additional policy accommodation as needed to promote a stronger economic recovery and sustained improvement in labor-market conditions in a context of price stability."[38] Mr. Bernanke actually believes he has provided the economy with price stability, despite the fact that oil prices have gone from $147 to $33 and back to $100 per barrel in the last four years—all due to Fed manipulations.

Therefore, the Fed believes its attack on the dollar has helped the economic recovery and that it has been conducted with little to no negative consequences. Of course, you first have to ignore the destruction of the middle class. And incredibly, Bernanke also believes the $2 trillion worth of counterfeiting hasn't quite been enough to bring about economic prosperity, so he's going to have to do a lot more.

What the Fed and ECB don't realize is that their infatuation with inflation, low rates that are factitious, and debt monetization has allowed the United States, Europe, and Japan the ability to borrow way too much money. Their debt-to-GDP ratios have increased to the point that these nations now stand on the brink of insolvency.

And now these central banks will embark on an unprecedented money printing spree that will eventually cause investors to eschew their currencies and bonds. Therefore, they have managed to turn what would have been a severe recession in 2008, into the current depression in southern Europe and a U.S. currency and bond market crisis circa 2016.

If an endless amount of money printing is the answer, what do these Counterfeiting Keynesian Kamikaze central banks believe is the question? Let's put the central banks of Europe, Japan, and the United States on *Jeopardy!* and find out.

Final Jeopardy

Alex Trebek: We want to welcome back our central bankers Ben Bernanke, Mario Draghi, and Masaaki Shirakawa for the Final Jeopardy clue:

"An open-ended money-printing policy employed by a central bank to monetize debt."

Thirty seconds on the clock and good luck.

Cue Jeopardy! music as 30 seconds elapse.

Alex Trebek: OK, let's start with Mr. Shirakawa—the question again was:

"An open-ended money-printing policy employed by a central bank to monetize debt."

Shirakawa: What is—how to fight a deflationary depression?

Alex Trebek: Umm, no, I'm sorry, and I see you have wagered Japan's economy on that. No, unfortunately, that's not the correct answer. Let's go to Mr. Draghi—the question again is:

"An open-ended money-printing policy employed by a central bank to monetize debt."

Draghi: What is—how to save the euro?

Alex Trebek: No, that's two for two—that answer is also incorrect. Let's hope Mr. Bernanke can get this right. Again, the question is:

"An open-ended money-printing policy employed by a Central Bank to monetize debt."

Bernanke: What is—getting an employment rate down to 6.5 percent?

Alex Trebek: Ah, Ben, I'm sorry—that answer is not correct. The answer is actually: "What is creating an enormous bubble in the bond market that will lead to a hyperinflationary depression?" and it looks like you wagered the entire worldwide economy on that answer. Apparently, you didn't read Michael Pento's book that explains there is actually a high correlation between high unemployment and rising inflation. And, obviously, none of you have studied any part of history that would have given you the answer that indefinite rounds of money printing in an attempt to pay back debts and keep interest rates low always leads to the destruction of your respective economies. But on a lighter note, we do have some parting gifts! Here are some wheel-barrows full of your worthless currencies as a souvenir.

It is no joke—Bernanke has promised the market no clear end to his counterfeiting—some claim he is stepping in where he believes those in government have failed. I am not claiming he has embarked on this open-ended easing with malicious intent. I am claiming that he is fol-lowing the flawed model that centuries of data tell us will fail. His intentions may be pure but his actions are reckless and destructive. . . . The road to Zimbabwe is paved with good intentions.

The Canary in the Coal Mine

As we glance over the pond at Europe we see the window to our future. They stand as the proverbial canary in the coal mine. But let's stop for a minute and explore what purpose a canary in a coal mine serves.

Early coal mines did not feature ventilation systems, so miners would routinely bring a caged canary into new coal seams. Canaries are especially sensitive to methane and carbon monoxide, which made them ideal for detecting any dangerous gas buildups. As long as the bird kept singing, the miners knew their air supply was safe. A dead canary sig-naled an immediate evacuation.

The canary served as a warning signal for miners to evacuate— change course—to stop what they were doing for fear of death. For some countries in Europe that canary sang her final song in 2010. The free market heard that canary's final gasp in Greece and drove interest rates up. But central banks are refusing to let that canary die. They are doing everything to keep this bird on life support and forcing her to sing. In fact, taking a page from the movie *Weekend at Bernie's*, they have that bird stuffed with a voicebox inserted in its throat and are pulling marionette strings mimicking this bird's song.

But one has to imagine there are some in Germany who recognize that bird's final muzzled cry. This was a song they heard decades before—they understand the pain this bird is warning of. They lived through the recklessness of a central bank who believed they could print their way out of debts. They remember the wheelbarrows of cash to buy a loaf of bread, the death, the starvation that came from reckless monetary policies they had no control over. They want to heed that bird's warning signs to reverse course.

The actual canary had little control over its fate, but it continued to sing anyway. And so we go about our business, some oblivious of the fate that governments and central banks have sealed for us. But we would be smart to heed that bird's silence, and it would be imprudent to ignore the warning signs of Europe and what is to come.

Decades ago, Margaret Thatcher warned that eventually social welfare programs would run out of other people's money. Today, central banks have a disconcerting solution for governments that are going bankrupt—when you run out of other people's money, you just need to print more.

Notes

1. Treaty establishing the European Community, March 25, 1957.
2. "What is the Euro?" GoCurrency.com. August 2012.
3. Eleanor Beardsley, "Can the European Social Welfare State Survive?" NPR, September 27, 2012.
4. Ibid.
5. Ibid.
6. Philipp Bagus, *The Tragedy of the Euro* (Auburn, AL: Ludwig von Mises Institute, 2012).
7. Vanessa Fuhrmans and Sebastian Moffett, "Exposure to Greece Weighs on French, German Banks," *Wall Street Journal*, February 17, 2010.
8. Ibid.
9. Philipp Bagus, The Irish Subjagation, Ludwig Von Mises Institute, November 30, 2010.
10. Robert P. Murphy, "Fiat Money and the Euro Crisis," *Mises Daily*, October 10, 2011.
11. Ibid.
12. "Greek Pensioners Take the 'Old' out of OAP," Wichoffshore.com, March 2010.
13. Ibid.
14. Ibid.
15. Ibid.
16. Stephen Fidler, "Greek Finance Ministry Millionaires," *Wall Street Journal*, May 25, 2010.

17. "Timeline: The Unfolding Eurozone Crisis, BBC News Business, June 13, 2012.
18. Ibid.
19. Ibid.
20. Marcus Walker, "Greek Crisis Extracts the Cruelest Toll," *Wall Street Journal*, September 20, 2011.
21. Ibid.
22. Ibid.
23. Ibid.
24. Paul Krugman, "Crash of the Bumblebee," *The New York Times*, July 29, 2012.
25. Adam Fergusson, *When Money Dies: The Nightmare of Deficit Spending, Devaluation, and Hyperinflation in Weimar Germany*, 1st [U.S.] ed. (New York: PublicAffairs, 2010), 16.
26. Ibid., 36.
27. Ibid.
28. Sally Marks, *The Illusion of Peace* (New York: Palgrave Macmillan, 2003), 53.
29. Fergusson, *When Money Dies*, 40.
30. M. Kishlansky, P. Geary, and P. O'Brien, *Civilization in the West*, 7th ed. (New York: Pearson Longman, October, 2007), 807.
31. Fergusson, *When Money Dies*, 254.
32. Ibid.
33. Murray Rothbard, *Making Economic Sense* (Auburn, AL: Ludwig von Mises Institute, 1995).
34. Ibid.
35. Mark Thornton, "The Economics and the Great Depresssion of the 1970s," *Mises Daily*, May 7, 2004.
36. Ibid.
37. Ronald Reagan's Farewell Address to the Nation, January 11, 1989.
38. Ben Bernanke, Federal Reserve Press Release, August 1, 2012.

Chapter 8

The Debt Crisis

"The obligation of freedom is a willingness to stand on your own feet."

—*J. Bracken Lee, Governor of Utah*

The idea of the U.S. government defaulting on its debt is difficult to fathom. Economies that produce $16 trillion worth of gross domestic product (GDP) just aren't supposed to collapse. It is unprecedented in history, and the ramifications of such an Earth-trembling cataclysm are beyond the comprehension for most. In this chapter we will lay out what a default by the U.S. government could look like. We will do this by reviewing recent economic defaults such as that of Russia—an economy one fifteenth the size of ours.

But before we get into that, let's take a brief look at how we got into over $16 trillion in debt in the first place.

From Pioneer to Penurious . . .

On November 9, 1620, the 102 passengers on the *Mayflower* spotted land. They had endured miserable conditions for 65 days, but they were soon to find out the voyage was worth it. Their search of a better and easier place of living and quest for freedom had been found. The group settled and established what would be referred to as Plymouth Plantation. Years later, Daniel Webster would refer to this group as pilgrims.

The pilgrims were superseded by "the revolutionary"—leaders in this new country who were prepared to take a new step—uncouple themselves from British rule and establish a new government. They sought to expand on the original concept of freedom and add to it self-governance. A nation was established that was unique to the world whereby rights were established at birth at the hands of your creator, not sanctioned by the hand of government. They fought to create a democracy ruled by its people, not by birthright. The American revolutionaries led by the founding fathers were about to embark on the American experiment that would change the course of history.

The freedom of America was heard of around the world. No longer did you have to be born and die in the confines of your birthright—in America you had freedom and opportunity. This concept drew immigrants from Europe and American pilgrims and revolutionaries were soon joined by eager immigrants. Imagine a place where the marketplace for ideas was free to be dreamed and realized. A place where markets ruled and not despots. A place where individuals and their "invisible hands" could freely and equally express what they wanted to consume and produce without the steering hand of government.

All these people wove the fabric of this nation, referred to as the *American melting pot*. A convergence of backgrounds and ideas coupled with men and women who took risks to fulfill their dreams is the cornerstone of what is referred to as American exceptionalism. As people from all over the world sought to make America their home, Americans traveled west and developed the new frontier. They were called the pioneers. America was to embark on a journey like no other, following the road laid out by the wisdom of those great men who founded this nation—that road map was the Constitution and it begins aptly with the words "We the people." Although America still holds the basic values of our founding fathers' vision, we have veered off course of their vision of a weak central government as stated in the 10th Amendment.

The Sixteenth Amendment . . . The Beginning of the Slippery Slope

Thus, the immunities of property, body, and mind have been undermined by the Sixteenth Amendment. The freedoms won by Americans in 1776 were lost in the revolution of 1913.

—*Richard E. Byrd, speaker of the Virginia House of Delegate*

. . . a hand from Washington will be stretched out and placed upon every man's business. . . . Heavy fines imposed by distant and unfamiliar tribunals will constantly menace the taxpayer. An army of Federal officials, spies and detectives will descend upon the state. . . .

—*Richard E. Byrd*

America's road to a centralized government can be traced back to 1913 and was seeded in the Sixteenth Amendment. Over one century ago, Americans embarked on a new journey, the lure of freedom was slowing being replaced by the seduction of state.

Voters in the presidential election of 1912 had no choice; it was contested among three advocates of an income tax. The winner, Woodrow Wilson, proceeded to pass an income tax of 1 percent on incomes above $3,000 and applied surcharges between 2 percent and 7 percent on income from $20,000 to $500,000. Now if you remember, 1913 was a year where all kinds of "progress" was made; it is no coincidence this was also the year the Federal Reserve was established.

Wilson was "an ardent prophet of the state, the state indeed as it was known to European scholars and statesmen. . . . He preached it. . . . From him supremely comes the politicization, the centralization, and the commitment to bureaucracy of American society during the past" 100 years.[1]

Suffice to say Woodrow Wilson trampled on the Constitution during his presidency. The income tax was "the product of an unholy combine between statist intellectuals with visions of state-sponsored utopias, envious demagogues and the desire by established, wealthy interests to prevent any competition to their place and to offload business costs to an expanding regulatory welfare state."[2] A tax that started at 7 percent at the high end soon ballooned to 67 percent in 1917 and 77 percent in 1918. In the 1920s the rates fell to a low of 24 percent but never again got as low as the pre-war rate of 7 percent. As Chief Justice John Marshall remarked, truly "the power to tax involves the power to destroy."[3]

America had been established under the concept of federalism, the belief that states should be united but also allowed to act as their own small government laboratories. The Tenth Amendment states the Constitution's principle of federalism by providing that powers not granted to the federal government by the Constitution are reserved to the States or the people. With the Sixteenth Amendment, the federal government now had the power to confiscate your earnings. And with this enormous new source of income, power was centralized into the hands of a small group of people.

The early American was inherently wary of government that appeared so far out of his reach. Americans had just rid themselves of British rule—a far-away political establishment. They recognized the need for government, to keep order, to protect him in the exercise of his rights. But they desired for the powers of government to be clearly defined and limited. The Founding Fathers put very specific restraints on the federal government into the Constitution. According to J. Bracken Lee

> The state governments likewise lost more and more of their autonomy the United States was completely centralized a nation as any that went before it; the very kind of establishment the Founding Fathers abhorred was set up by this simple change in the tax laws.[4]

The Sixteenth Amendment opened Pandora's Box—we were about to embark down the slippery slope of large centralized government.

In 1935, when FDR signed the Social Security Act, opponents decried the proposal as socialism. In a Senate Finance Committee hearing, one senator asked Secretary of Labor Frances Perkins, "Isn't this socialism?" She said that it was not, but he continued, "Isn't this a teeny-weeny bit of socialism?"[5]

Despite its current popularity, Social Security paved a new path for America. America opened the door a teeny bit to socialism—the federal government was now playing an active role in retirement savings and the loss of employment. The Sixteenth Amendment had given congress the authority to siphon your wage. Now the government stepped in for what had been an individual's responsibility and placed that responsibility on the state.

We didn't know in 1935 that Social Security, which began as a small program, would one day claim 62 million people as dependents, with an additional 5.7 million new dependents added every year.

The wages garnished from Social Security were never segregated; it was set up similar to a Ponzi scheme, reliant on new participants to pay for retired participants. Currently, the system is in huge financial stress because there are simply fewer younger workers than in years past. The promise made in 1935, with different demographics, will put a huge burden on the next generation that will have 15 million fewer workers to support the 80 million Baby Boomers who will soon be retiring over the coming years. Any good Ponzi scheme needs to attract more participants in order to keep up the façade. According to CNBC, the ratio of workers to retiring will eventually plunge from 16-to-1 to 2-to-1. At that point, every worker will in effect adopt half a senior they are required to take care of.[6]

Seniors correctly view this as their savings and not a handout. Unfortunately, the savings doesn't exist; the surplus some boast of is in actuality a big IOU from the federal government. According to the Trustee's Report, Social Security's

> . . . expenditures exceeded non-interest income in 2010 and 2011, the first such occurrences since 1983, and the Trustees estimate that these expenditures will remain greater than non-interest income throughout the 75-year projection period. The deficit of non-interest income relative to expenditures was about $49 billion in 2010 and $45 billion in 2011, and the Trustees project that it will average about $66 billion between 2012 and 2018 before rising steeply. After 2020, Treasury will redeem trust fund assets in amounts that exceed interest earnings until exhaustion of trust fund reserves in 2033, three years earlier than projected last year. Thereafter, tax income would be sufficient to pay only about three-quarters of scheduled benefits through 2086.[7]

Of course, we all should be fully aware that every dollar in the trust funds of all such government repositories is simply another dollar the U.S. Treasury must borrow right from the start.

Today's seniors rely heavily on this program. A study done by the Center on Budget and Policy Priorities shows that for two thirds of Americans over age 65, Social Security provided half or more of retirement income. As for the remaining third, it provided 90 percent or more! With a large voting bloc relying on this, any proposed reductions in benefits will face an impenetrable line of defense from AARP and other lobbying groups that represent retirees—a voting bloc with increasing numbers and influence. When you factor in the wealth decline from the Dow Jones Industrial Average, the decline in home prices, the decline in influence of most private pension plans, and negative interest rates, you understand that the reliance on entitlement programs is increasing substantially.

Nobody in 1935 thought that there may come a day when the government can't pay their bills, when they can't make good on their promises. But those in power saw this opportunity to garner a group of votes in exchange for government transfer payments.

An empowered centralized government left the door open for another president's dream of a Great Society and war on poverty. This war on poverty would actually throw more into poverty and dependency, leading to nearly 45.8 million people today who are reliant on food stamps or welfare. This war on poverty also led to the creation of Medicare, already in a cash flow–negative situation. Medicare Part A turned cash flow negative in 2008, as payments exceeded revenue by $21 billion. According to the Trustee's Report:

> Social Security and Medicare are the two largest federal programs, accounting for 36 percent of federal expenditures in fiscal year 2011. Both programs will experience cost growth substantially in excess of GDP growth in the coming decades. The drawdown of Social Security and HI trust fund reserves and the general revenue transfers into SMI will result in mounting pressure on the Federal budget. In fact, pressure is already evident. For the sixth consecutive year, the Social Security Act requires that the Trustees issue a "Medicare funding warning"

because projected non-dedicated sources of revenues—primarily general revenues—are expected to continue to account for more than 45 percent of Medicare's outlays, a threshold breached for the first time in fiscal year 2010.[8]

In 1913, when America started down the slippery slope to a large centralized government that did away with individual responsibility and the freedom of markets, they didn't realize that in the name of "saving the free market," another U.S. president would use taxpayer money to bail out banks, throw government-sponsored enterprises (GSEs) into conservatorship, enacting the largest bailout in the history of the United States.

This government takeover of the GSEs served the purpose of continuing their operation rather than putting them into receivership, which would seek to sell off their assets and shut down future business, giving way to the central government's owning or guaranteeing 95 percent of all new mortgages issued in this country and allowing the Federal Housing Administration (FHA) to provide mortgages once again for next to nothing down and backed explicitly by the government.

My Libertarian heart sank when I witnessed Republicans and Democrats slap each other on the back as they congratulated themselves from saving us from the natural workings of the free market. And we have come to a day where neither party represents capitalism and the free markets. The Republicans reek of hypocrisy, claiming the bailout of Fannie Mae and Freddie Mac (FNM and FRE) was necessary for the health of the real estate market and the economy. I guess government intervention in the free market is only mandatory if you're a bank, insurance company, foreign government, or a pension fund that owns GSE debt.

When asked in a CNBC interview how much his bailout plan will cost taxpayers, Hank Paulson responded that he "did not use a calculator" in putting together this scheme. He did not care what the bill to taxpayers would be. And even if every penny is eventually paid back, it will not result in a reduction in the Fed's phony funds used to make those loans in the first place.

Is this the government that Washington and Jefferson had in mind? Hank Paulson made the case for allowing Treasury the unlimited power to purchase the GSEs' debt and equity. His reasoning was, if the bad guys know you have a bazooka on your hip, you are unlikely to be called into a gunfight. The bad news for Americans is that his bazooka will be used to destroy the U.S. Constitution. Article One, Section Ten of the document, which he definitely doesn't comprehend, says that money should consist of only gold and silver. Our Founding Fathers wanted to place a yoke upon the states and those in power in order to prevent them from usurping the purchasing power of the Republic's currency. How wise they were. They knew that once in control of government, those in power would do anything they could to maintain it. Even those who espouse free-market capitalism will try to abrogate the system for personal gain. And now these Republicans want to extend the powers of the Fed and Treasury, giving them a blank check to purchase even the equity portion of these failing companies. Be it stimulus checks, GSE bailouts, FDIC reimbursements, or artificially low interest rates, the purpose is always the same—to buy votes.

When America started down this slippery slope in 1913—they didn't realize by allowing the federal government to leverage the earnings of the American taxpayer, the U.S. government would one day run up a more than $16 trillion dollar debt. That another U.S. president would habitually spend an excess of $1.2 trillion, 40 percent of total tax revenue collected, in yearly deficits. That total U.S. government spending at all levels would reach as much as 40 percent of GDP.[9] That unfunded liabilities of the federal government would total $61.6 trillion ($534,000 per household).[10] These liabilities include "federal debt of ($9.4 trillion) and obligations for Medicare ($24.8 trillion), Social Security ($21.4 trillion), military retirement and disability benefits ($3.6 trillion), federal employee retirement benefits ($2 trillion), as well as state and local government obligations ($5.2 trillion)."[11] That the only answer to sustain this insanity would be to print money, thus destroying the purchasing power of the poor and middle class. They would never have been able to fathom the amount of debt our federal government would exceed 100 percent of the nation's output—an amount that will never be able to be repaid. And that this will lead to a set of circum-stances possibly worse than the ones any generation has ever endured.

Where I stand today, it is hard to see where the free market in this country is. For some, the American spirit is still just as alive today as it was for the pilgrims, the revolutionaries, and the pioneers; but the federal government has their hands in everything—they are stifling that spirit. Real estate, education, college loans, retirement savings, health care, food, and basic necessities—there is no limit to what the centralized government believes they should control. In 1913, when the Sixteenth Amendment was passed and Pandora opened her box, many Americans didn't know— they didn't realize the destruction that would be caused in the name of "progress." Over $16 trillion in debt doesn't seem like progress to me.

During the 2012 presidential campaign, an Obama political campaign staffer thought it would be smart to introduce Americans to a fictional character called "Julia," who represented the cradle-to-grave welfare system Americans had now become dependent on. They quickly swept that campaign under the rug because they realized Americans didn't want to look in the mirror and see Julia. Americans didn't want to look in the mirror and realize how dependent on government they had become.

Americans still wanted to look at themselves as the pioneers; the men and women who conquered the West; or the immigrant, the one who left all they knew to come here for opportunity. They wanted to view themselves as the revolutionary, the people who created a new government based on individual freedoms. Americans didn't want to see they were now a nation dependent on government with a government addicted to debt.

Americans didn't realize in 1913, when the government siphoned that first paycheck, or in 1935, when Ida May Fuller cashed the first Social Security check, what would happen—they were lured, they were tempted. America had been settled, plains in the Midwest had been pioneered, gold in California had been mined. America had set course on a new journey; America had found a new frontier—in statism. In 1776, America declared its independence; in 1913, we veered off course; and a century later, we didn't want to be reminded how dependent we were.

Mexican Debt Crisis

Those who lived through the 1970s know firsthand that oil prices were high. Countries in Latin America, in particular Mexico, who produced oil, benefitted from the high prices Americans suffered at the pump. By 1981, Mexico had become the fourth-largest producer of oil in the world, its production having tripled between 1976 and 1982.[12] As production in Mexico increased, the price per barrel of crude oil soared. Foreign banks and the international lending agencies began to view Mexico as a secure investment due to its abundant energy resources, and flooded the country with loans that kept the peso overvalued. Money flowed into this region leading the Mexican government to take on enormous amounts of debt. This new money fueled a level of inflation never before seen in modern Mexico; the inflation rate eventually surpassed 100 percent annually.[13] The Mexican government chose to ignore warning signs of inflation and opted instead to increase spending.

The severe recession of the early 1980s coupled with the increase in interest rates drove down demand for oil and drove up debt service costs. In July 1981, the government announced it needed to borrow $1.2 billion dollars to compensate for lost oil revenue. The month before, Pemex had reduced its sales price for crude oil on the international market by $4 per barrel. The high levels of imports coupled with the drop in oil exports had boosted Mexico's current account deficit to $10 billion dollars. This uncertain situation—high external debt, stagnant exports, and a devalued currency as of February 1982—prompted investors to pull their money out of Mexico and seek safer havens abroad. In turn, the Mexican government felt it necessary to nationalize the banks in September 1982. Most of Mexico's debt was in dollars and tied into the U.S. debt markets. When interest rates skyrocketed in 1979 and the early 1980s in the United States and in Europe, debt payments also increased, making it impossible for these borrowing Latin American countries to pay back their debts.

A dangerous accumulation of foreign debt had amassed over years, with expectations that oil prices would always remain high. Some warned of the potential implications of the accumulation of this debt by the United States and world financial systems. The *Wall Street Journal* noted in 1981:

> It doesn't show on any maps, but there's a new mountain on the planet. A towering $500 Billion of debt run up by the developing countries, nearly all of it within a decade . . . to some

analysts the situation looks starkly ominous, threatening a chain reaction of country defaults, bank failures and general depression matching that of the 1930s.[14]

Eventually, the ominous warnings came true and international capital markets became aware that Mexico would not be able to pay back its loans. Interest rates increased—an instinctive reaction by markets determining you can't pay your debts. In August 1982, Mexico's finance minister, Jesus Silva-Herzog, declared that Mexico would no longer be able to service its debt. Mexico was unable to meet its payment due dates and announced unilaterally a moratorium of 90 days; it also requested a renegotiation of payment periods and new loans in order to fulfill its prior obligations.[15] When Mexico announced it would default on its predominantly U.S.-denominated $80 billion in debt, it spread throughout Latin America, and by October 1983, 27 countries owing $239 billion had rescheduled their debts; others would soon follow. Sixteen of the nations were from Latin America, and the four largest— Mexico, Brazil, Venezuela, and Argentina—owed various commercial banks $176 billion dollars; $37 billion was owed to the eight largest U.S. banks. As a consequence, several of the world's largest banks faced the prospect of failure.[16] It would take as much as a decade before these loans were written off the books of banks such as Citibank that were deeply affected.

Commercial banks significantly reduced or halted new lending to Mexico and Latin America. Most Latin American loans were short term; a crisis ensued when their refinancing was refused. Billions of dollars of loans that previously would have been refinanced were now due immediately.

The debt crisis of 1982 was the most serious of Latin America's history. Debtor countries had to agree to impose very strict economic programs on their countries in order to reschedule their debts. The governments in turn, limited their costs by slashing social spending— education, health, and social services. As with all countries that suffer a recession and depression, the poorest of the poor are most affected. Poor, women, children, and other groups suffered disproportionately. As Latin America's economies stagnated, per-capita income plummeted, and poverty increased and widened the already wide gap between the rich and the poor. The debt crisis seriously eroded whatever gains had been made in reducing poverty through improved social welfare measures over the preceding three decades. A deep recession ensued, migration to the United States increased and a permanent rise in the unemployment rate manifested. Still today in much of Latin America, poverty and malnutrition are significant; "children are increasingly recruited into the drug trade and prostitution; long-term unemployment and its adverse social effects are increasing; the weakening of local communities and networks of mutual support are being destroyed; and the growth of crime and an epidemic of homicides, are but a few of the many dilemmas that this debt crisis has caused." In fact, in the 10 years after 1980, real wages in urban areas actually dropped between 20 and 40 percent.[17]

Unlike the debt crisis in Latin America, the debt crisis in East Asia stemmed from inappropriate borrowing by the private sector. Due to high rates of economic growth and a booming economy, private firms and corporations looked to finance speculative investment projects. However, firms overstretched themselves and a combination of factors caused depreciation in the exchange rate as they struggled to meet the payments.

The Asian Contagion

The crisis that started in Thailand spread like wildfire all throughout Asia, with Indonesia and South Korea also becoming deeply affected. From 1985 to 1996, Thailand's economy grew at an average of over 9 percent per year, the highest economic growth rate of any country at the time. It is believed for a number of reasons a lot of "hot" money flowed into this region. During this time, inflation was at bay and the Thai kept the baht pegged at 25 to the U.S. dollar. Foreign debt-to-GDP ratios rose from 100 percent to 167 percent in the four large Association of Southeast Asian Nations (ASEAN) economies in 1993–1996, then shot up beyond 180 percent during the worst of the crisis.[18]

In May 1997, the Thai baht was hit by massive speculative attacks. The markets believed that Prime Minister Chavalit Yongchaiyudh failed to defend the baht, which was pegged to the basket of currencies in which the U.S. dollar was the main component against international speculators.[19]

Like all economies before them that became saddled with debt that they could never repay, eventually Thailand's booming economy came to a sudden halt. Massive layoffs in finance, real estate, and construction resulted in huge numbers of workers returning to their villages in the countryside. The baht lost more than half of its value and reached its lowest point of 56 units to the U.S. dollar in January 1998. The Thai stock market dropped 75 percent. While a devalued baht was able to levitate asset prices during the mid-1980s, in 1997 devaluation led to the collapse of the financial system and a regional meltdown. The financial collapse in 1997 was largely caused by private-sector failure in managing loans and a lack of investment confidence that propelled the entire economy into a severe credit crunch. "The initial capital flight triggered currency depreciation, domestic credit shortages, widespread corporate financial difficulties and severe contractions in demand and output. The second round of contagion effects led to falling export demand (through a fall in other currencies), which further dragged down income and output levels. This led to more drops in employment and wages. Lower output led to lower government revenues, which in turn negatively affected government budgets, including social sector programs."[20] Imprudent lenders and investors were the hardest hit by the Asian crisis. In Korea, many merchant banks suspended operations, commercial banks were required to be recapitalized and restructured. In Indonesia, 16 insolvent banks were closed, in Thailand 56 of 91 finance companies had to be liquidated. Investors in equity markets, incurred losses because of the financial crisis, foreign investors in Asian equities (excluding those in Japan) lost an estimated $700 billion—including $30 billion by Americans.[21]

In August 1997, the International Monetary Fund (IMF) unveiled a rescue package for Thailand of more than $17 billion, subject to conditions such as passing laws relating to bankruptcy (reorganizing and restructuring) procedures and establishing strong regulation frameworks for banks and other financial institutions. In August 1997, the IMF approved another bailout package of $3.9 billion.

By 2001, Thailand's economy had recovered. The increasing tax revenues allowed the country to balance its budget and repay its debts to the IMF in 2003, four years ahead of schedule. The Thai baht continued to appreciate to 29 baht to the dollar in October 2010.[22]

Unlike the experience of Latin America, Asian economies were better equipped to bounce back from their crisis. One reason was that many Asian economies rely more heavily on the free market and private enterprise, which rebounded after malinvestments were allowed to be liquidated instead of being deemed too big to fail. An important lesson of the Mexican crisis is that domestic savings matter greatly. They help finance the accumulation of capital and facilitate growth. High domestic savings are associated with lower current-account deficits. "Latin America, however, has traditionally had very low saving rates. In 1980 the region saved on average only 19 percent of its GDP, by 1994 this ratio was basically unaltered. This contrasts sharply with fast growing regions of the world that save 35 percent or more of GDP."[23] It is interesting to note that China has the largest savings rate in the world at 35 percent, due primarily to the fact there is no social safety net.

No sooner had the Asian crisis subsided than a new crisis emerged in Russia. This crisis would not only take down the Russian economy but also a large hedge fund with big bets placed on the direction of interest rates.

In 1998, Long Term Capital Management (LTCM) lost $4.6 billion in less than four months following the Russian financial crisis, requiring financial intervention by the Federal Reserve and a bailout from 14 financial firms, many of whom they did business with. Long Term's crisis sent shock waves through the U.S. financial system and in what would later be a twist of "karma," the one holdout in LTCM's bail out, Bear Stearns, would be requiring its own bailout a decade later.

Russian Debt Crisis

In the 1990s, the Russian economy was in transition. Struggling to rid itself of the strains of communism and embrace free market principals was an appealing concept; however getting there would prove to be much more painful. In an attempt to ease the pain and aide in the transition Russia took on an enormous amount of debt, most facilitated by the IMF. By December 31, 1995, the Russian central government had borrowed over $10 billion through the IMF. On March 26, 1996, the IMF and Russian central government reached an agreement on a new loan of $10.2 billion—the second-largest loan ever made to any borrower by the IMF.[24]

Due to the contraction of the Russian economy, revenue streams were declining. The IMF used the loans as a means to induce Russia to reduce its budget deficit to stipulated targets: 4 percent of GDP in 1996, 3 percent in 1997, and 2 percent in 1998. These goals were never reached and the Russian government continued to borrow, rising debt service costs only added to the strain on the budget.[25]

Speculators chased stratospheric investment returns as the Russian stock market became the world's leading developing country stock market. Unfortunately, momentum was exceptionally short lived; it would not even last the year. By the fall of 1997, the trends were again all negative.[26]

Russia's energy exports were hit with continued low gas and oil prices. Remnants of communism led to the lack of productivity improvement in the private sector. Debts and liabilities significantly outweighed assets for many Russian businesses. Back wages rose to more than $4.4 billion by the end of 1997, and reached as high as $5.6 billion by July 1998.[27]

Soviet-era laws and regulations rendered many Russian firms unable to earn enough to pay taxes. The government's revenues were falling as much as 50 percent below budgeted tax receipts. All of these factors coupled with the heavy reliance on borrowing to finance budget shortfalls caused investors to demand a large premium to hold Russian debt. In order to attract investors, the government offered ever-higher interest rates—at its height approaching 250 percent. Even with what most would consider very attractive returns, the market wasn't biting. Russia's rapidly inflating short-term debt was unsustainable and an important factor in the August 1998 collapse. In a last ditch effort to smooth out budget shortfall, the Russian government turned to short-term borrowing through ruble-denominated government bonds, known by their Russian acronym GKOs. The GKOs only delayed and intensified what was to be the final reckoning.[28]

The markets turned on Russia—they were running out of time. Their failure to develop a market economy and the concomitant poor investment climate led the government to pay investors a steep premium to sell them the GKO risk. Interest rates, which had averaged 26 percent in 1997, reached triple digits in July only solidifying the government's inability to meet its obligations. "The GKO pyramid was by then a full-blown Ponzi scheme, with new bonds being issued to pay the interest on old bonds."[29] GKO debt exploded during the spring and summer of 1998 and by then some 30 percent of Russian budgetary outlays was devoted to debt service.

Russian and foreign investors earned enormous returns in the so-called GKO casino but were eager to convert their ruble profits into dollars and other stable currencies. These conversions exerted even more downward pressure on the already battered ruble. In fact, a considerable portion of the IMF's $4.8 billion July 1998 rescue package was spent to prop up the ruble in the days before the collapse. The IMF was persuaded to issue new credits, but there was no containing this force of nature. The Russian economy was inevitably going to collapse.[30]

It soon became clear that the economic situation in Russia was deteriorating too rapidly. Even a large-scale international financial package could not stave off the Russian free fall. As you can imagine, this led to unrest, and angry miners began demonstrating in Moscow to protest wages that sat in arrears. The interest rates on Russian debt were soaring. The Russian treasury market was on the verge of collapse: despite sky-high interest rates, a Russian Treasury bill auction failed to attract enough interested investors.[31]

On July 16, 1998, the Russian government and the IMF, joined by the World Bank and Japan, agreed to one of the largest-ever infusions of cash into the central government of Russia: $17.1 billion. On top of this, Russia anticipated another $5.5 billion in international lending from prior agreements, for a grand total of $22.6 billion.[32]

For a fleeting moment the reaction to the IMF loan agreement was euphoric. The Russian stock market, after months of free fall, recorded a 17 percent rise. Unfortunately, this boost was short lived, and by the end of July, the market resumed its plunge.

Instead of rewarding the Russian government for its temporarily cash-rich position, the market understood that Russia was now deeply mired in debt, with no discernible means of repayment.[33]

Demand for Russia's debt declined dramatically, despite yields that soared above 200 percent. Russian banks were broke and began calling on each other for loans. Some banks went as far as not allowing panicked Russians and foreigners to buy dollars with rubles.[34]

On Monday, August 17, 1998, the Russian government saw no way out—they cried "uncle." They announced a devaluation of the ruble and a 90-day moratorium on repayment of $40 billion in corporate and bank debt to foreign creditors—coupled with unilateral "restructuring" of domestic debt scheduled to mature in 1999. The *Wall Street Journal* reported the next day, "Facing a choice between two economic evils to fight its financial woes, Russia chose both."[35]

The Debt Crisis Fallout

In August of 1998, the Russian government announced that it would no longer be able to pay its official debts. At the same time, they devalued the ruble. The default and devaluation led to Russia's total economic collapse—a cataclysm worse than America's depression of 1929.

In just 24 hours, the free-falling ruble forced retailers to raise prices by more than 30 percent and led shopkeepers to raise prices daily, even hourly. "People are in a state of shock," one Russian woman told the *New York Times*. In the first week of September, prices rose by 36 percent.[36]

Dozens of Russian banks became insolvent and disappeared. Savings accounts were frozen, and ATM and debit cards ceased to work. Millions who had deposited their money in Russian banks lost everything. "Within days, individual deposits in Russia—which before August 17 had totaled some $27 billion—fell in value to less than $12 billion."[37]

Millions of senior citizens, whose pension income had been delayed for months, were cut off completely. Those who were fortunate enough to have jobs often found their wages suspended. When wages were finally paid, the average Russian saw his or her wages drop by two thirds, from $160 to $55 per month. The number of people living below the official poverty line rose to nearly 40 percent. The standard of living for the average Russian, which was already a lot lower than America, plummeted by 30 percent.[38]

Urban areas that couldn't make their own food were the hardest hit. As in Soviet times, Russians were waiting in lines for the necessities and hoarding what they could find. Staples such as flour, butter, rice and sugar were purchased as soon as they appeared on shelves. The devastation of Russia's economy wreaked the kind of human misery that America experienced in the Great Depression. Within six months after the 1998 crash, Russia's economy, measured in dollars, had fallen by more than two thirds. From $422 billion in 1997, Russia's gross domestic product fell to only $132 billion by the end of 1998. The Russian stock market lost 90 percent of its value in 1998 alone. When the dust finally settled in March 1999, the ruble had lost fully 75 percent of its value.[39]

Retail stores closed repeatedly throughout the day, just to figure out how much to charge. Russians were forced to do without Western products, as the price of imports soared beyond their reach.

The collapse of international trade created scarcities and high prices for Russian-made goods with foreign components. Foreign providers refused to let Russian firms buy on credit because of fear of nonpayment. Foreign suppliers demanded payment in hard currency, not wanting the depreciating ruble.

With a lack of a reliable currency, much of Russia was reduced to a barter economy. Citizens were often paid with whatever goods were currently available. Farmers were devastated by the 1998 economic collapse. Grain harvests fell 30 percent below 1997 levels. Shortages of food were so severe that humanitarian food aid from the West, which had not been necessary since the collapse of Communism, was resumed on an emergency basis.

In addition to the unemployment, lost wages and pensions, and financial hardship, there has been an attendant social crisis. Russia's medical system suffered a run on medicine that quickly reduced supplies in hospitals and pharmacies to Soviet-era levels. The collapse of the ruble's value, the widespread unemployment, and the freeze on savings, wages, and pensions left millions of patients unable to pay for medical services.[40]

Hospitals suffered from lack of adequate medication. Drugs became even more difficult to come by—particularly those that had to be imported. Nurses and doctors were forced to ration drugs to patients.

Illegal drug use and addiction in Russia skyrocketed, fueled by growth in organized crime and widespread economic depression. Russia's widespread joblessness and poverty led to an increase in crime, homelessness, and school dropout rates.

That, my dear readers, is the real Fiscal Cliff. The United States desperately needs to avoid a collapse of our currency and bond markets while we still have the chance.

What Would It Look Like Here?

A debt crisis is devastating; the market deals a heavy blow when they determine that you can't pay your bills. The standard of living that Americans feel entitled to will greatly lessen. The Russian economy recovered fairly quickly thanks in part to the high price of oil. Economies can rebound, and despite the pain, the depression works to correct imbalances. An economy needs to rid itself of imbalances and malinvestments in order to heal. By the year 2008, it was painfully obvious that the American consumer was allowed to take on too much debt. The natural process an economy needs to go through is recession and depression to cleanse itself of misallocation of capital. A period of time is necessary where asset prices fall, debt levels are reduced, and money supply shrinks. This would have been a very painful process and fortunes would have vanished—many have already. But the government intervened with the economy's purging process with a series of bailouts that has ultimately made the situation much worse.

I see this with my kids. My son will fall down and cut his knee— I clean it up and then it starts to heal. The healing process in nature isn't always a pretty one—scabs can be pretty ugly. And there is always a temptation to pick. Underneath this brown and yellow crusty blob is new pink skin—it's tempting to rush it.

From 2008 through today, the federal government and the Federal Reserve have picked the scab on the U.S. economy. They refused to let the economy purge the bad and go through the normal healing process. Bailouts of banks, failed stimulus packages, increase in welfare programs, and mass rounds of counterfeiting and enormous debts have only made this worse. I said at the time that the real estate market—much like water that seeks its own level—will eventually reach a point that reconciles the imbalance between household income and price. Once that level has been achieved, the financial industry can stabilize and the economy should regain its footing. In the meantime, we can only hope that those in the administration and at the Federal Reserve realize that in the end there is no such thing as a bailout. Merely placing distressed assets on the taxpayer's balance sheet is no panacea. In the long term, markets will always prevail and the sooner we let them work the quicker we will find a resolution to this crisis. Clearly, those in Washington have yet to listen because they have done everything I warned against up to this point.

Currently, the Federal Reserve is pumping $85 billion dollars a month in MBSs and Treasuries in an attempt to reflate the housing bubble. Now, rising prices occur every time the central bank prints money in excess of what is necessary to address population and productivity increases—the Fed knows this. Inflation is often defined as too much money chasing too few goods. The Fed wants the "too much money" they are pumping into the economy to start chasing real estate in order to reflate the bubble. The American homeowner has just seen this movie—do they believe we are that easily fooled? Apparently, they do. Too much money didn't rechase Internet stock in the 1990s, and it's not going to rechase housing now—it chased housing already and got burned. Perhaps Mr. Bernanke thinks millions of Americans will hit their respective heads and develop amnesia.

Even if Americans had the desire to reflate that bubble, too many Americans are under water in their house, too many are saturated in debt and cannot continue to borrow. The only bubble that is getting inflated is the bubble in the Treasury. The only entity with the means to borrow in reckless amounts is the U.S. government.

By the way, the housing market is far from clear sailing. The government now represents 95 percent of all new mortgages created and around 40 percent of those are explicitly guaranteed by Uncle Sam's Federal Housing Administration with only a 3.5 percent down payment—see how much we've learned! Just wait until the upcoming interest rate shock hits. The overburdened taxpayer and insolvent government will once again have to bail out the housing market.

When evaluating Bernanke's latest round of counterfeiting, pundits like to speculate on the effect lower rates will have on the economy.

But few ever consider the effects higher rates will have. Interest rates returning to more normalized levels would have a huge negative effect on the economy. What will the end of the 30-year bull market in Treasury prices and the beginning of a secular bear market in bonds values have on the economy? Higher rates would preclude millions of mortgage refinances that have been a perpetual source of dollars in consumers' pockets. Higher rates will have a negative effect on real estate, home prices will plummet as people consider the additional mortgage payment that will be needed to obtain a house at current prices. Higher rates would also have a negative effect on car loans, student loans and credit card interest. How many less cars will be sold when dealers can no longer offer zero percent interest rates?

The Fed has been counterfeiting in a futile attempt to revive the economy, they haven't accomplished that, but they have prevented the economy from experiencing the pain of a deflationary depression. Some view this as a positive, but by preventing a true contraction they have also failed to allow the economy to heal and thus grow on solid ground. In a 2010 commentary, as others were reviewing data and predicting a "V" shaped economic recovery was at hand, I said that the healing has not been built on the back of healthy and viable growth. It has been the result of making available for loan a virtually unlimited amount of money for free and by increasing our borrowing by trillions of dollars. That is not the kind of growth that can be sustained by the free market. It is instead exactly the type of unbalanced, inflationary and debt induced growth that brought our economy down in the first place. That recovery never happened, and the American economy has been in stagnation ever since. Why? It was never allowed to purge the mal-investments and excess rung up in the previous years. Government and the Federal Reserve felt the need to pick the scab and they have been picking it ever since.

The American economy is in a state of limbo. The consumer is slowly going through a very slow deleveraging process as the government is picking up more and more debt. So much so that the total of federal debt, state debt, and consumer debts are at all-time highs, and the Federal Reserve is attempting to keep all of this in balance by manipulating interest rates. With the enormous amount of debt the government has already taken on and the enormous amounts of unfunded liabilities that still exist, if interest rates were at the disposal of the free markets, rates would have to be much higher. But the Fed is monetizing debt to keep rates artificially low. How long can this last? Not long at all because sooner rather than later, the free market always supersedes government intervention.

If the U.S. institutes austerity measures, this day of reckoning can be delayed and ameliorated to some degree. Cuts in spending should be the preferred method. This would displace many people who have come to rely on the government. However, more than likely the political forces will lead to a vain attempt to raise taxes as well. A VAT tax, a tax on 401(k)s and individual retirement accounts (IRAs), and a wealth tax are all areas the federal government may tap to garner additional revenues. Similar to Europe, if the United States were to institute large tax increases, we would see a slowdown in growth and tax revenues that would exacerbate the budget deficits and increase debt-to-GDP ratios.

If this fails to settle the markets, the federal government will be unable to service its debt; printing money will only exacerbate the situation. Remember, we are already defaulting through monetization. The markets will demand we stop our currency devaluation. The U.S. dollar has retained its status as the world's reserve currency due to perceived confidence in the Federal Reserve's ability to maintain the dollar's value. When international markets lose confidence in the Fed's abilities, the dollar will become greatly devalued; foreign market participants will demand to be paid in another form. This will lead to a currency crisis and cause the U.S. dollar to plummet. The United States currently runs huge trade deficits, so the price of imports will skyrocket. Think for a moment what the price of a gallon of gasoline will be when the Saudis demand payment in gold instead of dollars. U.S. market participants will be forced to take their depreciating dollar and exchange it for an increasing sum of gold to buy a barrel of oil. The high price of imports will further stifle economic growth and send inflation soaring. Intractable inflation coupled with negative growth will render the United States unable to continue down this path. The United States would have no other option but to default on trillions of dollars of debt.

What would a default of the United States look like? I can speculate by looking at prior debt crises. First, you have to remember that Russia's economy was $442 billion prior to collapse; we have a $16 trillion economy, which is an enormous difference. The Russian debt crisis blew up the hedge fund Long Term Capital Management. How many hedge funds across the globe lie in the wake of a U.S. debt default?

America will soon come to a tipping point where the markets will doubt the ability of the American taxpayer to make good on their debt. At some point inflation will rise and the Fed will no longer be able to monetize the debt. Currently, markets are greeting endless rounds of quantitative counterfeiting favorably. The stock market rises in anticipation of the inflation Bernanke is creating. However, the time will come when foreign investors will pull money out of the American economy due to loss of confidence in the stability of our bonds and the dollar. Please be aware that about half of all U.S. publicly traded debt is held by foreigners. And U.S. dollars represent 62 percent of all foreign exchange reserves. Talk about an overowned, overpriced, and oversupplied asset! When foreigners reach the epiphany that the United States can't pay its debts, there will be an earth-shaking stampede through the narrow exit to sell Treasuries and get out of dollars.

As foreigners run for the exit, and the U.S. dollar loses its reserve status, the market will be flooded with dollars—many of them from the Fed. The U.S. stock market may rise initially due to the enormous inflation this event will cause. But eventually markets will plummet as foreign investors seek to repatriate dollars into their respective currencies. At this point the United States will be in the throes of a hyperinflationary depression and a currency collapse. Due to the rapid insolvency of banks, credit markets will freeze, enterprises will fail and unemployment will soar. Imports will plummet due to high exchange rates, energy prices will skyrocket and the world will be thrust into a depression second only to the fall of the Roman Empire. Looking at history, we will have to be prepared for price controls that will lead to a shortage of staple goods. Interest rates will skyrocket, as the only buyer of debt will be the man with the printing press and America will become insolvent—unable to pay their debt and forced to default.

The dominoes can fall fairly quickly when an actual default arrives. Just think about the reverberations of the Russia crisis taking out LTCM and the bailout that ensued—and that number was only in the billions of dollars. The U.S. economy is enormous compared with that of Russia,

Mexico, and Thailand—IMF loans in the billions would then have to be in the trillions. And considering the United States is the majority of the IMF it is clear that the IMF will not be able to bail the United States out. Any intervention by the Fed will be viewed negatively, as they will have lost the confidence of domestic and foreign market participants.

If the United States explicitly defaults on its debt, most banks will become insolvent—many banks would fail due to rising interest rates and the repricing of deposits. Banks' assets would be paying far less than what they would now be forced to borrow. The U.S. dollar may have completely collapsed, and Americans may be using gold or barter as the preferred medium of exchange.

It's hard to tell if there are any winners in this scenario—Europe and Japan are already fragile economies—they will surely decline along with the United States. China's economy is still very reliant on exports. It is clear we would be entrenched in a worldwide depression far greater than the worldwide depression of the 1930s.

In Russia, retail prices skyrocketed. When the market loses faith in the U.S. dollar, people will want to exchange dollars for hard assets, which cannot be increased by government decree. Energy-related investments will also increase significantly in price in relation to the U.S. dollar. In Russia, people attempted to exchange their rubles for dollars; unfortunately, most in the political class were allowed to do this and the common man was left holding their rapidly devaluating ruble. In the United States, people will want to exchange their dollars for gold or commodities they could trade later on. Remember, the Russian ruble was never the world's reserve currency—a crisis in the U.S. dollar will be a lot more significant to worldwide markets. The worldwide economy holds dollars and when the world seeks to exit the dollar the currency crisis will be on the scale of no other.

If such a crisis does occur, you have to be prepared for the government to do something unexpected and unconstitutional. You can't expect the U.S. Constitution to act as a barrier—it hasn't in the past. In the 2008 crisis it was rumored that Hank Paulson strong-armed Ken Lewis into buying Merrill Lynch. Many things were done in an attempt to "save the free market" that one would have never imagined could happen. This wouldn't be the first administration to trample on the Constitution in the name of patriotism.

Lincoln, along with declaring martial law, ordered the suspension of the constitutionally protected right to writs of habeas corpus in 1861, shortly after the start of the American Civil War. Woodrow Wilson, during the First World War, expanded the laws around espionage and made speaking out against the war a felony that could lead to imprisonment. In 1942, FDR imprisoned approximately 110,000 Japanese Americans and Japanese who lived along the Pacific coast of the United States. They were taken by force into camps called "War Relocation Camps." And perhaps the most relevant was in 1933, when Roosevelt signed an Executive Order "forbidding the Hoarding of Gold Coin, Gold Bullion, and Gold Certificates within the continental United States." The order criminalized the possession of monetary gold by any individual, partnership, association or corporation. Leaders in the face of crisis tend to dismiss the Constitution at the very time they should look to it for guidance.

But more than our constitutional freedoms are at stake. Banks in Russia failed, and people lost all their money. Now you may be thinking to yourself that your deposits are insured—so you are guaranteed to get your money back as long as it doesn't reach the $250,000 limit per account. Before you wipe that sweat off your brow, I would like to remind you of something. The FDIC collects what amounts to insurance premiums from banks. They keep a cash balance on hand somewhere around $15 to $20 billion. The rest they invest—not in gold and silver, but in you guessed it—the U.S. Treasury. Now if the United States wasn't paying its bills, then how will it pay back the FDIC? Now, the Fed could just print money in order to make good on those insured accounts—but what will these newly counterfeited Fed dollars be worth?

Large banks are sitting on a tremendous number of Treasuries— since the U.S. consumer is overextended, they have been lending to the federal government instead of the private sector. In Chapter 1, we reminded you that with the fractional reserve banking system, banks don't actually have your money safely deposited in that huge vault. They have actually lent that money out. Did you ever wonder why there is a bank in every strip mall? I think this is to lure people into a false security that their money is safe. It is a comfort mechanism; it's as if those banks are saying, "see your money is right here—not so far from the mattress—you can get it anytime you want." Just don't everyone try to take it out at once because it's really not here here." In Russia we see 66-year-old Yevgeny Ushakov, who had spread his life savings of $4,000 among three different banks to diversify his risk. "I didn't think all three would fail," he said.[41]

In Russia, government retirement pensions were not paid. Remember, the United States had to borrow over $1 trillion each of the last four years just to pay its bills—will social security remain that sacred cow when the U.S. government is unable to borrow? Furthermore, you have to question the solvency of the states during this time. Public employee pension plans are already greatly underfunded. We would have to imagine state bankruptcies would be coupled with the fear of insolvency of the federal government.

Unemployment will surge to levels higher than that of the Great Depression. At the beginning of the Great Depression the United States had nowhere near the debt it has today. It is true that after the depression and fighting WWII, our national debt was near today's levels—but the United States began this period in much better shape. Household debt was virtually nonexistent by comparison to today. We would also have to imagine that worldwide unemployment will surge in the face of a U.S. debt crisis.

Russians fell into poverty and those who were unable to grow their own food went hungry. Americans already have more people coming on its social welfare programs—we have to imagine, unfortunately, there will be tremendous suffering, starvation and violence during this period.

So where does this ugly period lead? Nature renews itself—new life replaces old—this is commonly referred to as the circle of life. Economies can also rebuild—the economies of Asia and Russia rebounded quickly. Even forest fires have a cleaning effect, they burn through brush; to clear out "fuel" that would otherwise accumulate and create the potential for dramatic forest infernos. When forest fires have been suppressed for many years, they create a tinderbox of logs, limbs, and brush in nearby forests. One lightning bolt or match could set off a massive fire-in-waiting. Sometimes it's better to allow the small fires to happen—when you try to prevent what should happen naturally, fires can rage out of control and become much worse.

Prior recessions should have been able to run their course. Economic imbalances should have been able to clear. Recessions and depressions are an economy's cleansing mechanism. Imbalances in an economy are created that need to be corrected—a recession and depression are the natural way to allow this to occur. The Federal Reserve, in an attempt to subdue the little fires, has allowed a tinderbox of economic imbalances to accumulate. Forest fires like depressions are extremely damaging, but they have a cleaning effect. There are trees in nature that rely on fire to germinate—out of the ashes comes new life inspired by the free market.

Fortunes will be lost, millions who rely on government will be displaced, and Americans will have to adjust to a new standard of living—but the economy can recover. If we embrace the principals this country was founded on, and harness the exceptionalism of America's people, the United States can rise from the ashes and rebuild. If we rebuild our economy with a sound currency, savings, and investment, we will emerge stronger. If we shun the forces of statism and embrace the Constitution; if we follow the lead our Founding Fathers set, we can once again be that shining city on a hill.

It Can't Happen Here?

When I am sparring with pundits, I often use the debt crisis of Zimbabwe as an example of how high rates can go when an economy monetizes debt. I was scolded one time by a host who stated that the United States is not Zimbabwe; and he was right. Zimbabwe would never be able to accumulate over $16 trillion in debt; the markets would have cut that credit line long ago. But the truth is the American economy is like no other—we are not Zimbabwe or Greece—the American economy is like no other economy in the world. But don't use that as a crutch to believe that it can't happen here. It can, and it almost did.

In this book, we have gone all the way back to the Roman Empire—so you may be thinking: "Pento—why are you going to recount some obscure time in history where the United States was on the verge of collapse?" Actually, we don't have to travel too far to recount a time where the U.S. economy was brought to its knees. We just have to travel back in time to the year 2008—let's take a short walk down memory lane to consider how close the U.S. economy came to cataclysm:

- *January 24:* The National Association of Realtors (NAR) announces 2007 saw the largest drop in existing home sales in 25 years and the first price decline in going back to the Great Depression.[42]
- *March 10:* The Dow Jones Industrial Average (DJIA) fell more than 20 percent from its peak just five months prior.
- *March 16:* In a twist of fate, Bear Stearns, who refused to bail out LTCM, is itself in need of a bailout and Jamie Dimon of JPMorgan Chase comes to the rescue and acquires them for $2 a share—what is considered a fire sale in order to avoid bankruptcy. The deal is backed by the Federal Reserve, providing up to $30 billion to cover possible Bear Stearns losses.
- *July 11:* IndyMac Bank, is placed into the receivership of the FDIC—it represents the fourth-largest bank failure in United States history at the time and stood as the seventh-largest mortgage originator in the United States.[43]
- *July 17:* Major banks and financial institutions are reported to have lost approximately $435 billion in mortgage-backed securities.
- *September 7:* Just as Barney Frank was wrapping up his "All's good with Fannie and Freddie tour," Fannie Mae and Freddie Mac, which at that point owned or guaranteed about half of the United States' $12 trillion mortgage market, are placed in conservatorship. Investors worldwide owned $5.2 trillion of debt securities backed by them.[44]
- *September 14:* Lehman Brothers collapses, and Hank Paulson demands that Ken Lewis buy Merrill Lynch—so it is sold to Bank of America amidst fears of a liquidity crisis.
- *September 15:* Lehman Brothers files for bankruptcy protection.
- *September 16:* Finally waking up from a daze—Moody's and Standard and Poor's realize AIG exposure to the banking industry and downgrade AIG on concerns over continuing losses to mortgage-backed securities, sending the company into insolvency. Also on that day, Reserve Primary Fund "breaks the buck," leading to a run on the money market funds. Over $140 billion is withdrawn versus

$7 billion the week prior. This creates huge fallout in the commercial paper market, a key source of funding for corporations, funds dry up and much higher interest rates are required.[45]

- *September 17:* American International Group (AIG) requests and is granted an $85 billion loan from the Federal Reserve in order to avoid bankruptcy.
- *September 18:* Treasury Secretary Henry Paulson and Fed Chairman Ben Bernanke meet with key legislators to propose a $700 billion emergency bailout through the purchase of toxic assets. This will later be referred to as the Troubled Asset Relief Program (TARP). Obviously cool in the face of economic collapse, Bernanke tells them: "If we don't do this, we may not have an economy on Monday."[46]
- *September 25:* Washington Mutual is seized by the FDIC, and once again Jamie Dimon comes to the rescue as its banking assets are sold to JPMorgan Chase for $1.9 billion.
- *September 29:* Sheila Bair is busy wheeling and dealing, and the FDIC announces that Citigroup Inc. will acquire banking operations of Wachovia.
- *September 30:* In order to sweeten the pot for supposedly solvent banks, the U.S. Treasury changes tax law to allow a bank acquiring another to write off all of the acquired bank's losses for tax purposes.
- *October 1:* Europe catches the American flu.
- *October 3:* President George W. Bush abandons free-market principles in order to save the free market and signs the Emergency Economic Stabilization Act, creating a $700 billion Troubled Assets Relief Program to purchase failing bank assets. In addition to providing a taxpayer-funded bailout, it also contains a decision by the Securities and Exchange Commission to ease mark-to-market accounting rules.
- *October 3:* Wells makes a higher offer for Wachovia, stealing it from Citigroup.
- *October 6–10:* The Dow Jones loses 22.1 percent, its worst week on record.[47]
- *October 6:* The Fed, being so generous with the people's money, announces that it will provide $900 billion in short-term cash loans to banks.

- *October 7:* The Fed makes emergency move to lend around $1.3 trillion directly to companies outside the financial sector.[48]
- *October 8:* Central banks in the United States (Fed), England, China, Canada, Sweden, and Switzerland and the European Central Bank cut rates in a coordinated effort to aid world economy. The Fed also reduces its emergency lending rate to banks by half a percentage point, to 1.75 percent.
- *October 11:* The DJIA caps its worst week ever with its highest volatility day ever recorded in its 112-year history. Over the past eight trading days, the DJIA has dropped 22 percent amid worries of worsening credit crisis and global recession. Paper losses now on U.S. stocks now total $8.4 trillion from the market highs of the previous year.[49] The bumbling bureaucrats from the G7, a group of central bankers and finance ministers from the Group of Seven leading economies, meet in Washington and agree to urgent and exceptional coordinated action to prevent the credit crisis from throwing the world into depression, and, of course, accomplish nothing.
- *October 14:* The United States taps into the $700 billion available from the Emergency Economic Stabilization Act and announces the injection of $250 billion of public money into the U.S. banking system. The form of the rescue will include the U.S. government's taking an equity position in banks that choose to participate in the program in exchange for certain restrictions such as executive compensation. In Soviet style, Paulson gathers representatives from nine banks in a room and forces this money down their respective throats—they "agree" to participate in the program and receive half of the total funds: (1) Bank of America, (2) JPMorgan Chase, (3) Wells Fargo, (4) Citigroup, (5) Merrill Lynch, (6) Goldman Sachs, (7) Morgan Stanley, (8) Bank of New York Mellon, and (9) State Street. Other U.S. financial institutions eligible for the plan have until November 14 to agree to the terms.[50]
- *October 21:* "The U.S. Federal Reserve announces that it will spend $540 billion to purchase short-term debt from money market mutual funds. The large amount of redemption requests during the

credit crisis have caused the money market funds to scale back lending to banks contributing to the credit freeze on inter-bank lending markets. This government is hoping the injection will help unfreeze the credit markets making it easier for businesses and banks to obtain loans. The structure of the plan involves the Fed setting up four special purpose vehicles that will purchase the assets."[51]

- *November 12:* Treasury Secretary Paulson abandons plans elected officials had voted on under the $700 billion TARP. Mr. Paulson decides to do his own things—stating the remaining $410 billion in the fund would be better spent on recapitalizing financial companies.[52]
- *November 24:* The U.S. government (or should we say U.S. tax-payer) comes to the rescue of Citigroup after an attack by investors causes the stock price to plummet 60 percent over the past week under a detailed plan that included injecting another $20 billion of capital into Citigroup, bringing the total infusion to $45 billion.[53]
- *November 25:* "The U.S. Federal Reserve pledges $800 billion more to help revive the financial system. $600 billion will be used to buy mortgage bonds issued or guaranteed by Fannie Mae, Freddie Mac, and the Federal Home Loan Banks."[54]

Ben warned, "If we don't do this, we may not have an economy on Monday." He didn't see this coming and he doesn't see what is coming now. Think of all the federal government and the Federal Reserve had to do to keep this economy temporarily afloat in 2008. The dam was ready to break and they used all the might of the federal government and Federal Reserve to block this dam. The problem is that they are still blocking the dam and the water that almost took down the economy hasn't receded. In fact, more water has been added—$6 trillion dollars more and over $1 trillion more every year from now on. The dam will break—there is no way of avoiding it. The economy will get flooded by the malinvestments, imbalances, and debt and counterfeiting propagated by this small group of men and women.

But you don't have to drown in their bad decisions. You can still protect yourself.

I Don't Want to Be Right

Following is a transcript of a conversation I had with a financial news anchor in 2010:

Pento: How can the Fed create demand? The consumer is still in full deleverage mode, the savings rate should go much, much higher. Companies are hoarding cash because the money markets got completely frozen in 2008. That's why they are hoarding cash and they are doing it because they believe they see another credit crisis down the road.

Anchor: That's irrational.

Pento: It's very rational because the next credit crisis will be a sovereign credit crisis and will be about three to five years away.

Anchor: I am not sure it is rational.

Pento: OK, 30 to 50 percent of all federal tax revenue will go to pay interest on the debt in 2018. China is slowing, Europe is slowing; they have embraced austerity, thank God. The United States has yet to embrace austerity that's coming too down the road.

Anchor: What is in the long-term interest of those companies?

Pento: You want them to spend money, hire people, buy capital goods when there is no final demand? Nominal household debt now stands at 92 percent of GDP. Households have a lot of deleveraging ahead of them, so they are not going to spend money if there is no final demand.

Anchor: Do you not think the consumer will have turned tail in a year's time?

Pento: No.

Anchor: That's a very serious judgment.

Pento: Household debt will turn when they sell assets and pay down debt. That takes years.

Anchor: Are you writing off the American economy for years?

Pento: I am.

Anchor: That's a huge thing to say.

Pento: We have bailed out the private sector by seriously endangering the public sector.

Anchor: I think you are wrong. The AAA rating will always stay in this country.

Pento: The AAA rating held for Enron, too, and CDOs, but they still collapsed.

Anchor: But the American government can always tax people more. It can always pay its bills.

Pento: If you can raise taxes to 100 percent does that mean you are going to raise revenue?

Anchor: Nonsense. That's a political view. America will always be able to pay its bills.

Pento: How do you know that? Because the bond vigilantes will always be sleeping?

Anchor: You are just peddling the power of nightmares.

Pento: That's what people told me in 2006 about the housing market. The housing market can never decline. . . . But it brought down the entire global economy.

After this exchange, Mark Haines came to my defense and noted over the years he has known me, my opinion had been remarkably prescient. I really appreciated that, as I had great respect for his opinion as well, and although I didn't say this to him at the time and now unfortunately will never get the chance to—I would like to note that he was cunningly intelligent, brutally honest, and could smell a shill from a mile away. He was a great man. I miss him very much.

But the truth is that the American consumer never "turned tail"; America lost its AAA rating, and the American economy has stagnated since my interview. In the prior chapters, I laid out the economics that shaped my predictions. I have referred to this as *Pentonomics*. This economic philosophy led me to anticipate a huge sell-off in housing years before the 2008 economic collapse, a prediction many disputed until it was right in front of them.

The following is a commentary I wrote in October 2006:

The Federal Reserve's pause in its rate hiking campaign has dovetailed with the decline in energy prices and interest rates sending the Dow Jones to record territory. It is now universally accepted by the market that the slowdown in housing and the economy will result in a soft landing, one that keeps the Fed on hold and G.D.P. at trend growth or slightly below. These market cheerleaders have embraced this perfect scenario and the recidivism to their behavior prior to the equity collapse of 2000 may be to the downfall of investors. What is being overlooked by most pundits is that the unraveling of the housing bubble will be much longer lasting and more damaging to the consumer than anticipated.

During 2007, approximately $1 trillion of the $9 trillion in outstanding mortgages will reset. The increase in these adjustable rates will send consumers' monthly payments hundreds of dollars higher and cause many more foreclosure homes to enter into this already saturated market. According to the Indymac bank of California (the 7th largest mortgage originator in the nation), up to 4 percent of home owners might lose their home in the next few months. That's four times the average rate of borrowers who normally default on their loan!

Remember the axiom that as goes the housing market, so goes the economy. One has to look beyond home equity extraction which has reached a total of $600 billion per year. When you account for the durable goods, commodities and labor that are supported by the housing market you begin to realize the expanse of the spectrum related to this part of the economy. What is difficult to factor into the equation is consumer's response to flat or declining home values. It is reasonable to assume that their current negative savings rate (it was negative for only two other years 1932–1933) will again turn positive as consumption declines.

A key point that must be stressed again is that home builders are still expanding supply well beyond the intrinsic demand. Home construction is running at 1.7 million units while actual demand is about 1.15 million units. This could add another .55 million units to an already near record 4 million unsold homes. In order for the market to achieve balance, home construction must drop below population growth and price to income ratios must fall. Neither of those situations is occurring. Sellers have been trying to avoid lowering their asking prices; this has kept year-over-year declines muted and hence caused prognosticators to claim the bottom has been reached and the worst is over for real estate.

Through real estate, many banks are exceeding federal guidelines regarding concentrated loan exposure. According to Fed Reserve data, ten states have over 50 percent of total banks in violation of guidelines for real estate loans, meaning the dangers of a banking debacle similar to the S&L crisis are elevated. New Jersey–based home builder Kara Homes, for example, filed for chapter 11 bankruptcy protection after defaulting on nearly $300 million in debt. But the stock market is too busy rejoicing over better than expected pro-forma earnings reports to worry about financial disruptions like bank failures or home builder bankruptcies.

What appears evident is that the economy is slowly weakening due to housing and the decrease in money supply and credit (inflation). Since the Fed mistakenly measures inflation as growth, we can predict that G.D.P. rates will be declining for at least the next two quarters. And the equity markets are not pricing in the shortfall in earnings which should accompany the slowing economy. Keep an eye out for an unusually weak Durable goods number on Thursday or G.D.P. number on Friday; any crack in the soft landing mantra would prove damaging for stocks, especially after this huge rally. This leads me to present the best play in the market today: invest in the stocks of balloon companies — you know, the ones you tie "For Sale" signs onto.

I didn't write this commentary with the hopes of giving homeowners around the country nightmares. If one person backed out of the McMansion they were prepared to buy. Or if one person decided to short IndyMac—which, in case you were unaware, was placed into conservatorship by the FDIC on July 11, 2008. Even if you sold your IndyMac and Freddie Mac stock and didn't suffer a huge loss. If anyone changed their financial behavior by listening to me—my job is done.

I could easily run a long-only mutual fund and go on CNBC and lie through my teeth. I could say trite and banal things like, "the economy is showing signs of improvement, Bernanke's doing God's work, everything is going to be great—have happy dreams—don't worry about the bubble in the bond market!" This may endear me to certain TV anchors, but that's not going to enable you to make the best investment decisions. Throughout my career I have always prided myself in telling the truth.

Keeping this in mind, in 2009 I predicted a debt crisis and asked who is going to TARP America?

It should be noted at this time that the continued belief in the existence of any government trust fund (including FDIC insurance) is tantamount to a belief in the tooth fairy, because the special-issue bonds will need to be redeemed just as would any ordinary Treasury obligation. Therefore the only date of importance is the date at which expenditures exceed revenues, which in the case of Social Security, has been moved up one year to 2016. The report also bumped up the amount needed over the next 75 years to fulfill its benefit obligations by $5.3 trillion.[55]

So back to the original question: Who will bail out the USA? Up until now it has been foreign Central Banks. For instance, the Chinese now have $1.9 trillion in currency reserves of which $740 billion are in U.S. Treasuries. The notion that they will continue to provide the United States with an unlimited supply of Treasury demand is specious in nature. Premier Wen Jiabao has already expressed his concern over his country's concentrated dollar position. Additionally, the Chinese have a waning trade surplus and their own stimulus program to fund. This means that they may not have the desire or the means to fund our ballooning debt.

Increasing taxes have been proposed by some to close the gap. In reality, imposing new taxes or increasing existing tax rates does not necessarily equate to increased revenue. In fact, an increased tax burden imposed on this already fragile economy may prove to have the opposite effect on government income.

A partial solution is to grow the economy as much as possible. But the truth is that the antithesis of growth is what is being deployed. Higher taxes, inflation and debt are the antidotes to growth and will only exacerbate our funding issues.

That leaves the Federal Reserve in charge of bailing out the entire country. TARPer in Chief Banana Ben Bernanke—who has unlimited counterfeit funds to deploy—will be looked to once again to provide relief by leaving interest well below inflation and keeping the monetary base incredibly high. The worst fear of all is that he will be the buyer of last resort and purchase an ever increasing quantity of U.S. Treasury debt. Any relief experienced by his prodigal efforts will be fleeting. Unfortunately, we will have to learn the hard way that inflation solves nothing and seeking a panacea through the printing press leads to perdition.

And just as I predicted, Bernanke is seeking a panacea through a printing press to no avail. When the Fed launched QE1, I predicted QE2, critics scorned, "Pento, you are nuts—QE is going to save us and grow this economy by leaps and bounds—we won't need QE2." With QE2, I predicted QE3. Now with QE3 in the rear view mirror, I then stated Bernanke would launch QE4. I wrote this commentary last fall:

Stock markets around the world continue to levitate despite the fact that the fundamentals behind the global economy continue to deteriorate.

The simple reason behind the ebullient stock market during last quarter was the Fed's persistent threat to soon launch a massive amount of debt monetization. Mr. Bernanke followed through on that threat by announcing an open-ended counterfeiting scheme on September 13th 2012.

The United States is headed over the fiscal cliff and into another recession but who cares? Investors can't sit in cash while the Fed is destroying the purchasing power of the dollar. Europe is in recession and its Southern nations are flirting with a depression; but it just doesn't seem to matter. You can't hold bonds when the ECB is rapidly inflating the Euro and is pushing bond real yields further into negative territory in real terms. China's growth rate is plunging and a substantial portion of their economy has been in recession for almost a year. However, it isn't enough to stop shares from turning higher. You can't hoard Renminbi if the PBOC is flooding the banking system with new money at a record pace.

Adding to the money printing mayhem was Chicago Fed President Charles Evans. He is the architect behind QE III, a voting member of the FOMC in 2013 and Bernanke's right-hand man. Mr. Evans hinted on Monday that QE IV is just around the corner—even though the echoes of QE III are still reverberating from Bernanke's lips. QE3's plan is to buy $40 billion of mortgage-backed securities every month and until the unemployment rate magically declines.

But Evans now says that the Fed should continue buying at least $45 billion more of long-term Treasuries and MBS, even after Operation Twist ends in January. However, he did not indicate that these new and additional purchases, which will start in January, would be sterilized.

The $40 billion each month of MBS purchases (QE III) is not sterilized, but the $45 billion in Operation Twist is sterilized. The Fed is currently buying long-term Treasuries and selling government paper that matures in less than 3 years to offset the $45 billion. But the reason why Evans didn't say that these new purchases would be sterilized is because they will not.

The truth is the Fed doesn't have many short-term Treasuries left to sell. Evans said the $45 billion a month should last at least a year. That's $540 billion worth of new central bank purchases of longer-dated Treasuries. However, the Fed cannot sterilize that $540 billion when the Fed's balance sheet shows that they are almost out of short-term Treasuries. So if the plans for QE IV go into effect; it would be an unsterilized, open-ended, double-down version of QE3.

Bernanke is forcing investors out of cash and bonds. Of course, the move into commodities and equities is being done out of desperation. It is simply an effort to keep ahead of inflation; and in no way represents the hope that real growth will resume anytime soon. In fact, these counterfeiting efforts do serious damage to the economy.

But investors should never fight a central bank that has pledged to do everything in their power to prop up asset prices. A firm commitment from those that control the currency to systematically destroy its value renders investors with no choice but to plow money into precious metals, energy and agriculture.

Of course, QE IV was officially launched January 1, 2013. Lately, many more have started to recognize the bubble in the bond market and the severity of the coming debt crisis. Some in the mainstream have started to catch up with where I was years ago. In fact, in the summer of 2012, I was on CNBC with Bill Gross. I was expecting Bill would take the other side of the argument. However, when I finished my point he took me off guard by saying he agreed with everything I just said. Therefore, I wasn't surprised when I read his letter to shareholders:

Gross starts by noting the obvious—the current budget deficit is running at more than $1.2 trillion while the total national debt is more than $16 trillion and there is a fiscal gap of 11 percent of gross domestic product, which is currently $15.6 trillion.

Gross goes on to say:

Unless we begin to close this gap, then the inevitable result will be that our debt/GDP ratio will continue to rise, the Fed would print money to pay for the deficiency, inflation would follow and the dollar would inevitably decline. . . . Bonds would be burned to a crisp and stocks would certainly be singed; only gold and real assets would thrive within the 'Ring of Fire.' Should that happen, the results both for investors and the U.S. economy would be catastrophic.

If the fiscal gap isn't closed even ever so gradually over the next few years, then rating services, dollar reserve holding nations and bond managers embarrassed into being reborn as vigilantes may together force a resolution that ends in tears.

It would be a scenario for the storybooks, that's for sure, but one which in this instance, investors would want to forget. The damage would likely be beyond repair.[56]

The man who runs the largest bond fund and should be a shill for bonds is telling you to buy gold.

The CBO itself wrote in its highlights:

Recently, the federal government has been recording budget deficits that are the largest as a share of the economy since 1945. Consequently, the amount of federal debt held by the public has surged. At the end of 2008, that debt equaled 40 percent of the nation's annual economic output (a little above the 40-year average of 37 percent). Since then, the figure has shot upward: By the end of this year, the Congressional Budget Office (CBO) projects, federal debt will reach roughly 70 percent of gross domestic product (GDP)—the highest percentage since shortly after World War II.[57]

The CBO doesn't include debt owed to intragovernmental agencies; if they did they would see the situation is even direr.

In a recent *Wall Street Journal* article, George Schultz, Michael Boskin, John Cogan, Alan Meltzer, and John Taylor all warned, "Treasury now has a preponderance of debt issued in very short term durations. . . . Treasury must raise $4 trillion in this year alone. So the debt burden will explode when interest rates go up". They continue by noting "three-quarters of the deficit has been financed by the Federal Reserve." They conclude by stating. "We cannot count on problems elsewhere in the world to make Treasury Securities a safe haven forever. We risk eventually losing the privilege and great benefit of lower interest rates from the dollar's role as a reserve currency. In short, we risk passing an economic, fiscal and financial point of no return." These men remind us that it was our nation's ability to issue debt that allowed us to "preserve the union in the 1860s and defeat a totalitarian government in the 1940s." "Today, government officials are issuing debt to finance pet projects and payoffs to interest groups."[58]

The truth is I don't want to bet against the U.S. economy—I am not trying to peddle the power of nightmares. I believe in this country and I want to bet on it—but I must be honest. Americans don't save enough, and we borrow and spend too much. It's only through sound currency and savings that our economy can have real investments and grow in a healthy way.

I didn't embark on this journey to make you upset, although some of the things that we discussed are upsetting—to me as well. I wrote this book so you would be informed and prepared. Nobody likes to get on a plane and think about its crashing; however, we know that those who make note of exit signs and safety procedures are more likely to survive a crash. Nobody likes to think that the United States government will have a debt crisis—but it is important to prepare and understand.

In the next two chapters I lay out what the government can do and what you should be doing to protect yourself and all you have worked hard for.

Conclusion

In 1913, the federal government centralized power; decisions that should have been made by the American people were placed in the hands of a handful of elected officials who let it be about them—their quest for power, their next election, their legacy. American exceptionalism has never been about a few elected officials, the power of America has always resided in its people—the pilgrim, the revolutionary, the pioneer, the inventor, the entrepreneur. Americans have always had the ability to fend for themselves, but the federal government put its hand into our earnings and declared they could do it better. Now with over $16 trillion in debt and $1.2 trillion yearly deficits, it's clear they cannot. They have not been honorable stewards of our earnings; they have not been noble guardians of our future.

In 2008, the curtain came down and we witnessed the little people that hide behind a large government—scared men and women scurrying around trying to clean up the mess they made of the economy. It is also a mess that we helped inflict on ourselves.

Those in charge for the past century have tried to garner our vote by promising us things. And shame on us that they were able to delude the private sector into believing the country would be better off if we abandoned the principles of sound money and free markets.

The truth is that all we needed was born that fateful day in July with the words—*We hold these truths to be self-evident, that all men are created equal, that they are endowed by their Creator with certain unalienable Rights, that among these are Life, Liberty and the pursuit of Happiness.*

In 1776, our Founding Fathers set us on a momentous course of freedom. Now more than ever we need to follow that path.

Notes

1. Joseph R. Stromberg, "Remembering with Astonishment Woodrow Wilson's Reign of Terror in Defense of "Freedom," LewRockwell.com, September 18, 2001.
2. Adam Young, "The Origin of the Income Tax," *Mises Daily*, September 7, 2004.
3. Young, "The Origin of the Income Tax.
4. Lee J. Bracken, "The Income Tax Is Really Evil," *Mises Daily*, September 16, 2009.
5. Nancy J. Altman, "President Barack Obama could learn from Franklin D. Roosevelt," *Los Angeles Times*, August 14, 2009.
6. Rob Reuteman, "Will Baby Boomers Bankrupt Social Security?" CNBC. com, February 8, 2001.
7. Social Security Trustee Report, April 25, 2012.
8. Ibid.
9. Ron Hera, "A Final and Total Catastrophe?" Hera Research LLC, September 18, 2012.
10. Ibid.
11. Ibid.
12. "Mexico Recovery and Relapse 1976–1982," Mongabay.com, June 1996.
13. Ibid.
14. *Wall Street Journal*, January 23, 1981, pp. 25–28. www.plawlotic.com. Cited January 2013.
15. Bernal García and Cristina Manuela, "Iberoamérica: Evolución de una Economía Dependiente." In Luís Navarro García (Coord.), *Historia de las Américas*, vol. IV (Madrid/Sevilla: Alhambra Longman/Universidad de Sevilla, 1991), 565–619.
16. Ibid.
17. Greggory Ruggiero, "Latin American Debt Crisis: What Were Its Causes and Is It Over?" *Independent Study*, March 15, 1999.
18. www.adb.org/Documents/Books/Key_Indicators/2003/pdf/rt29.pdf.   September 2012.
19. G.Kaufman, The Asian Financial Crisis, Kluwer Academic Publishers, Norwell, MA: pp. 193–198.
20. Sauwalak Kittiprapas, "Social Impacts of Thai Economic Crisis." In *Social Impacts of Asian Economic Crisis: Thailand, Indonesia, Malaysia and Philippines* (Bangkok: Thailand Development Research Institute, 1999).

21. Ibid.
22. Haider A. Khan, *Global Markets and Financial Crises in Asia* Palgrave Mcmillian Ltd, New York, NY(University of Denver, 2004).
23. Ruggiero, "Latin American Debt Crisis."
24. Christopher Cox, Ben Gilman, Porter Goss, et al., "Russia's Road to Corruption: How the Clinton Administration Exported Government Instead of Free Enterprise and Failed the Russian People." Members of the Speaker's Advisory Group on Russia United States House of Representatives 106th Congress, September 2000.
25. Ibid.
26. Ibid.
27. Ibid.
28. Ibid.
29. Ibid.
30. Ibid.
31. Ibid.
32. Ibid.
33. Ibid.
34. Ibid.
35. Ibid.
36. Ibid.
37. Ibid.
38. Ibid.
39. Ibid.
40. Ibid.
41. Ibid.
42. Denise Lones, "2008: The Year in Review," *Realty Times*, February 19, 2009.
43. Vern McKinley and Gary Gegenheimer, "Bright Lines and Bailouts to Bail or Not To Bail, That Is the Question," *Policy Analysis*, April 21, 2009.
44. Tom Raum, "US Rescue of Fannie, Freddie poses taxpayer risks," Associated Press, January 20, 2009.
45. "Bailout of Money Funds Seems to Stanch Outflow," Wall Street Journal Online, September 20, 2008.
46. Andrew Ross Sorkin, Diana B. Henriques, Edmund L. Andrews, and Joe Nocera, "As Credit Crisis Spiraled, Alarm Led to Action," *New York Times*, October 1, 2008.
47. J. Cox "Credit Crisis Timeline," University of Iowa Center for International Finance and Development E-Book.
48. "Fed officials said they would buy as much of the debt as necessary to get the market functioning again but refused to say how much that might be. They noted that around $1.3 trillion worth of commercial paper would qualify. "Fed, in emergency move, will lend to companies". Bernanke, Ben,

Speech to the National Association of Business Economics, Associated Press, October 7, 2008.

49. Tim Paradis, "Stocks End Worst Week Mixed after Wild Session," Associated Press, October 10, 2008.

50. Cox, "Credit Crisis Timeline."

51. Ibid.

52. Ibid.

53. Ibid.

54. Ibid.

55. Social Security Trustee Report. April 25, 2012.

56. William H. Gross, "Damages," *PIMCO Investment Outlook*, October 2012.

57. CBO's 2011 Long-Term Budget Outlook, June 22, 2011.

58. George Schultz, Michael Boskin, John Cogan, et al., "The Magnitude of the Mess We're In," *Wall Street Journal*, September 17, 2012.

Chapter 9

What Can the Government Do to Mollify the Debt Collapse?

Government big enough to supply everything you need is big enough to take everything you have . . . The course of history shows that as a government grows, liberty decreases.

—*Thomas Jefferson*

Accxording to the Bible, after crossing the Red Sea and leading the Israelites towards the desert, Moses was summoned by God to Mount Sinai, where he had previously spoken to the burning bush, and later produced water by striking the rock with his staff. Moses remained on the mountain for 40 days and nights and received the Ten Commandments directly from God. Moses delivered those commandments to God's people and also laid the foundation for what would be called a tithe. Moses, who had direct dealings with God, believed the God who had turned his staff to a serpent, delivered 10 plagues to the Egyptians, and parted the Red Sea should henceforth receive a tenth part of their seed crops and fruit trees plus every tenth animal and this should be delivered to the treasury in the newly erected Tabernacle.

One has to wonder—if the God that has saved His people from slavery, delivered 10 plagues, and parted the Red Sea sought only 10 percent—why should our federal government require any more?

In this chapter we will explore how much of our earnings the federal government should garnish and what the federal government should do now to preclude a debt crisis.

The Principles of a Free Market

"If a businessman makes a mistake, he suffers the consequences.
If a bureaucrat makes a mistake, you suffer the consequences."

—*Ayn Rand*

Before we begin with my eight recommendations for government, I want to review the principles of a free market. There is a program on the Discovery channel called *American Pickers*. If you have never seen the show, you can substitute its premise with a garage sale. In this show, the two real-life characters, Frank and Mike, drive around America looking for articles to "pick." This is how it works: They pull up to an old farmhouse with assorted junk and relics sprinkled on the front lawn and ask the owners if they would be willing to sell some of their cherished possessions. If the two parties agree there is interest, Mike and Frank rummage through the items to ascertain if there is anything they would like to buy with the intention of reselling in their antique store in Iowa.

When they find an item of interest, they make an offer, the seller makes a counteroffer, and the two parties haggle back and forth until they determine a price one is willing to sell at and the other is willing to buy. This in economics is called *price discovery*. Now, they run into all types on their travels—some are sophisticated "pickers" with a keen idea of the appropriate price, others have less of an idea of value, and some just may need the money. Often, background stories are shared about the parties' willingness to part with the item and Mike and Frank's desire to own the item. Regardless, this in its simplest form illustrates the fundamental principles of free market—two or more parties coming together in their own self-interest, developing a market, determining price, and completing a transaction. Now it would be silly to think that Mike and Frank and the other party needed a thousand pages of regulations and a government panel to determine the price of these items. Market participants operating freely and in their own self-interest are the best determinants of price. And just as Mike and Frank encounter all sorts in their travels, the market is filled with all types of people who have different ideas and different motivations.

Mike and Frank and the other party haggle and arrive at a price, but what would happen if we threw a few million other buyers and sellers on that front lawn? Would markets and price discovery be hampered by an increase in participants? On the contrary, price discovery is optimized by free-market competition—many market participants operating unencumbered by outside forces deciding on price. Noting this, free-market capitalism is an economic system where the prices for goods and services are set freely by the forces of supply and demand and are allowed to reach their point of equilibrium without intervention by government policy.

An essential element in a free market is competition. And to illustrate this I will refer to another market we all participate in—the super market. In this market, grocers provide a good and buyers purchase the good for their own use. Prices aren't haggled individually between a buyer and a seller; prices are offered by the grocer and a customer accepts by taking possession of and paying for those items. Even so, both participants still play a role in price discovery. The grocer sets the price of an item at what he feels he needs to make a profit, the buyer makes a determination to purchase the item based on what they ascertain is reasonably priced in relation to the marketplace. Therefore, if the grocer were to charge $10 for a gallon of milk, when milk was selling for $4 in other stores, the grocer would not sell much milk. Prices are set low enough to be competitive and high enough to make a profit and consumers insure this by having many options, competition allows consumers the freedom to shop where they want. It also provides them with a lot of selection. When I go to the grocery store and purchase milk, this purchase sends a signal to the seller that there is demand for milk and he calls his supplier to restock, if a lot of people purchase that milk he will buy more, if I am the only one, he may make the decision not to carry milk. But market participants are the best at determining the supply and demand equilibrium with milk, just as they are in making decisions about education, health care, the cost of money, just to name a few. Free-market competition places millions in the market place voting with their wallets to create the optimum price and production levels. Basically, the free market is allowing every individual the freedom to decide what they want to consume and what they desire to have produced on a continuous basis. In this model, consumers drive up production of items they desire; for example a cell phone in lieu of items they find obsolete, such as a beeper.

Through the free market, consumers ultimately garner the best price and selection choices. At the grocery store it is the obligation of the buyer to know what a reasonable price is for milk. You wouldn't imagine a federal bailout precipitated from a bad milk purchase. If Stop and Shop decides to charge an additional dollar for milk and a group of consumers fail to ascertain the optimum market price offered, it is the consumer's responsibility to "shop around." We would reject government interference in setting the price for a ubiquitous item such as milk. Therefore, we must more strongly reject government's interference with a more thoughtful decision such as home ownership, for example.

Yet ironically, we were reminded recently that the federal government does interfere with the supply/demand equilibrium of milk as in 2013 we almost fell off the "milk cliff." It seems there is a price support program guaranteeing to milk producers a minimum price for milk. So as we will see, government through tax policy, legislation, encouragement of additional market participants and, most importantly, attempting to control the cost and quantity of money has a large influence over the free market's ability to ascertain supply and demand in many other areas of the economy; even milk.

Often, governments try their best to get in between a buyer and seller in the free market. From mayors of large cities outlawing the sale of 32-ounce sodas to Congress passing thousands of pages of legislation on the banking and insurance industries—government seems determined to stand between the buyer and seller in the marketplace. They do so in all cases under the guise of "working in our interest," but more than likely, they are working in their own. Many in government believe it is their responsibility to protect us from ourselves and other market participants; therefore, they pass thousands of pages of legislation to protect us from the evils of the marketplace. However, those in government are often tainted by their own self-interest and their own reelection. Therefore, they skew the marketplace by putting their thumb on the scale in an attempt to pick winners and losers. Those winners and losers often reflect those who supported their campaigns with contributions. Free markets are optimized when government is a bystander, ready to uphold legal obligations but not influence outcomes. Still, government has done a good job in making us believe that their motives are pure and our fellow market participants are evil. That while their actions are untainted by outside influence, it is only the marketplace that works in their self-interest and are motivated by greed. I have no better argument to this statement than to quote Milton Friedman's response when Phil Donahue posed that very question:

Donahue: When you see around the globe the maldistribution of wealth, the desperate plight of millions of people in underdeveloped countries, when you see so few haves and so many have-nots, when you see the greed and the concentration of power, did you ever have a moment of doubt about capitalism and whether greed's a good idea to run on?

Friedman: Well, first of all, tell me is there some society you know that doesn't run on greed? You think Russia doesn't run on greed? You think China doesn't run on greed? What is greed? Of course, none of us are greedy; it's only the other fellow who's greedy.

The world runs on individuals pursuing their separate interests. The great achievements of civilization have not come from government bureaus. Einstein didn't construct his theory under order from a bureaucrat. Henry Ford didn't revolutionize the automobile industry that way. In the only cases in which the masses have escaped from the kind of grinding poverty you're talking about, the only cases in recorded history are where they have had capitalism and largely free trade. If you want to know where the masses are worst off, it's exactly in the kinds of societies that depart from that. So that the record of history is absolutely crystal clear: that there is no alternative way so far discovered of improving the lot of the ordinary people that can hold a candle to the productive activities that are unleashed by a free enterprise system.

Donahue: But it seems to reward not virtue as much as ability to manipulate the system.

Friedman: And what does reward virtue? You think the communist commissar rewards virtue? You think a Hitler rewards virtue? You think—excuse me, if you will pardon me—do you think American presidents reward virtue? Do they choose their appointees on the basis of the virtue of the people appointed or on the basis of their political clout? Is it really true that political self-interest is nobler somehow than economic self-interest? You know I think you are taking a lot of things for granted. Just tell me where in the world you find these angels who are going to organize society for us? Well, I don't even trust you to do that.[1]

It is important to remember that in a free society and a free market, participants need to take personal responsibility for their actions. The government should step in only if one participant doesn't hold up their end of the negotiated bargain. And, in fact, we see when the government does interfere with the markets ability to set price, to offer competition and ascertain supply and demand equilibrium imbalances occur. We see examples of this today in higher education, health insurance, and real estate—just to name a few.

There is the risk an entrepreneur takes under free market capitalism—he enjoys the fruits of success as well as the repercussions of failure. In turn, there is the risk you take as a consumer—you have the responsibility to understand the market place too. I know when I mention the free market to some people, they give me a litany of gripes they have about the stock market. The stock market is one example of a free market; it is made up of mostly sophisticated buyers and sellers, and it is easy to understand how the individual investor can feel slighted when they enter casually into a market comprised of seasoned professionals. However, the beauty of the free market is your freedom not to participate in it. It's not government's role to moderate the risks of any market just because you have decided to participate in a market you don't fully understand. Government has a function in making sure transactions between market participants are carried out as stated, but government should not interfere in mollifying the risks.

Now, unfortunately, there are always unscrupulous people in this world. Sociopaths such as Bernie Madoff exist in all areas of society. But when somebody's house gets robbed, we don't suggest this is the outcome of having personal possessions and seek to institute new regulations on owning things. We view it for what it is—a crime—and use the laws currently in effect to prosecute the individual who perpetuated the crime. And as I stated before, there is a role for government in the free market to punish those who deceive and to right those who have entered into a contract in good faith. Free market capitalism isn't the Wild West, it isn't anarchy—it only functions in an environment in which market participants understand that a limited number of rules will be enforced and contracts upheld. Certain rules are necessary to ensure a market functions appropriately. For example, athletes compete in games and the winning team should be the one that performs the best on any given day. Rules prohibiting steroid use are adopted to ensure that all athletes have the chance to compete on a level playing field. A juiced-up team with knives might win a game; however, no one could argue that the opportunities were equal.

To quote fellow Libertarian James Ostrowski:

> When government intervenes into some aspect of life, domestic or foreign, where it doesn't belong, it screws it up good, creates problems that would not otherwise exist, and then uses its powerful propaganda machine to disguise the true cause of the problem and convince people that even more government action is required. To paraphrase Ludwig von Mises, government creates its own demand.[2]

As we work through my eight solutions—it is important to keep the free market in mind, it is my belief an economy works the best when it is able to get the closest it can to these free market principles.

Solution 1: Allow the Deleveraging Process to Happen

In 2008 we witnessed the popping of the real estate bubble. Many homeowners realized their houses were worth less and often a lot less than they had originally paid. Holders of mortgage-backed securities saw the value of their holdings plummet. Price discovery can be a painful process, but it is essential in order for markets to clear and rebound.

In a truly free-market banking system, banks lend money to those they deem capable of paying it back. Unfortunately, when markets become influenced by government attempts to increase home owner-ship and regulations are passed in an effort to evade the market's ability to assess the adequacy of borrowers. When the supply and cost of money is taken out of the hands of the free market and manipulated by 12 bureaucrats at the Federal Reserve, imbalances occur. Thus, the markets need to correct those imbalances. To recover, the market needs to clear. Yes, markets can temporarily misprice assets because markets represent the desires of individuals and people aren't perfect; but they must be allowed to also freely rectify that mistake.

Economist David Ricardo more fully developed this principle. According to Ricardo, the market equilibrium for goods is constant. This simply means that markets, "when left alone by government planners or other fraudulent actors, inexorably tend toward an 'equi-librium price,' which eventually balances supply and demand for any particular good . . . Supply and demand in the aggregate are thus not merely equal, but they are identical, since every commodity may be looked upon either as supply of its own kind or as demand for other things. But this doctrine is subject to the great qualification that the proportions must be right; that there must be equilibrium."[3] Thus, markets will naturally clear themselves of any surpluses or shortages in the form of excess supply and demand.

This view contrasts with the current stance of those in government that the problem of overproduction and under consumption can be "solved" by the injection of "purchasing power" into the hands of individuals via government transfer payments. This viewpoint operates on the notion that government should redistribute money in order to enable workers to buy back the products they created, that production and consumption are two unequal and unrelated activities, and that "the purpose of consumption (or "spending") is to clear the shelves of the goods that workers made so that the workers can be employed making more of them."[4]

Instead, you need to ask why there no longer is demand for certain things, and to the larger issue of how the proportions involving the factors of production have been disturbed or distorted.[5]

The corollary that markets clear is critical to understanding the moribund U.S. housing market. In housing, perhaps more than any other good, we see the terrible consequences of government and central bank interference with market forces. Houses were built in excess of the markets ability to support them, mortgages were written in excess of the consumer's ability to pay and consumers in aggregate took on debt in excess of their ability to afford it.

At the time the real estate bubble burst, household debt as a percentage of gross domestic product (GDP) was at historic highs (100 percent). The real estate market needed to correct to the point where the free market could support supply versus demand. The consumer needed to deleverage, foreclosures needed to occur, banks that made bad decisions needed to go out of business. The economy needed to flush out imbalances and malinvestments in order to heal in a real way. This process was never allowed to occur. Too-big-to-fail banks have gotten bigger, the real estate market has been artificially propped up by even lower interest rates, enhanced regulations on foreclosures, and government guaranteeing 95 percent of all new mortgages. The government has now artificially put a floor in home prices that is made of 1/100 inch balsa wood. It will crack as soon as the debt bubble bursts. .

Fannie Mae, Freddie Mac, and the Federal Housing Authority put taxpayers on the hook for millions of mortgages that never should have met prudent market underwriting criteria. Government-controlled Fannie Mae and Freddie Mac need to be wound down. Currently, the federal government is taking the risk of loss on the majority of the real estate market. They need to stop any new purchases, securitizations and guarantees and then as the mortgages mature they would be retired. The government can make good on any guarantees until the government-sponsored enterprises (GSEs) are closed down for good.

It is my belief that deleveraging has to occur before a true recovery can begin. In order for deleveraging to occur, you must abrogate all government attempts to hold up the market and all the rules and regulations that prevents deleveraging from occurring in order to allow the market to clear and to work. The purpose is to allow market prices to fall to a level that can be supported by the free market. Instead of being artificially levitated by government. As the consumer is deleveraging, demand will fall, deflation will occur and a recession will ensue that will clear these imbalances.

I agree with former Congressman Ron Paul, who said at the time:

> Never in American history have we needed to adopt a policy of laissez faire more desperately; never has government seemed more determined to artificially prop up an industry. But only by allowing the housing market to clear can we hope to rebuild our shattered economy from a stable foundation. Clearly, there will be pain in the short term, but we owe it to younger Americans and future generations to allow the reemergence of a rational housing market.[6]

Unfortunately, we live in a consumption-based economy—those in power of the economy favor consumption over savings and debt reduction. Those in Washington and the Federal Reserve are doing everything in their power to allow us to continue debt accumulation. As they are abetting our debt and consumption they are accumulating debt of their own as well as creating a huge bubble in the bond market. For a true recovery to take hold markets have to clear and consumers have to deleverage.

Solution 2: Strengthen and Stabilize the U.S. Dollar

The best way to ensure a strong and stable dollar is for the Fed to disband as an institution. I am sure that this book will be a must-read for Bernanke and those at the Fed. And upon reading this, I am certain they will have an epiphany and realize that their interference with the cost and supply of money has been the source of the problem, not the solution. They will heed my advice and voluntarily relinquish their authority and disband. Just in case they aren't willing to go that easily, I would suggest Bernanke take a break from dictating—take a vacation, get some rest, and let the markets do the work. The Fed should return to a gold standard; or at least act as if they are on a gold standard. And by that I mean they should steer the increase in the money supply to equal productivity growth plus the increase in labor force.

We have reviewed this several times, but perhaps it bears repeating—no man or woman should have the power to dictate the money supply.

No group of bureaucrats should sit at a table and stare into their crystal ball and pretend to know how much money an economy needs and what cost it should carry.

It's important to remember when the Federal Reserve prints money in excess of productivity plus the increase in labor force, the value of the dollar decreases in relation to hard assets. Market participants who understand that the Federal Reserve has devalued the dollar convert dollar assets into commodities, driving up the price of oil and gold, to name a few.

With wages remaining stagnant and the costs of commodities increasing, we have a condition referred to as stagflation. This inflation created by the Fed benefits asset holders at the expense of low wage earners and consumers living on fixed incomes. So as stock portfolios and assets rise, people of moderate income have less disposable income. The Fed is the most pernicious redistributor of wealth—stealing the purchasing power from the poor and redistributing it to the rich. Perhaps that should be the real message of the Occupy Wall Street movement.

Keynesians encourage a weak or debased dollar because they believe it drives consumption. As consumers perceive the loss of purchasing power, they buy things. However, these policies thwart savings and it is only through savings that an economy can grow in a healthy way. It also ignores a key economic principle—that consumption can occur only as a result of productivity that comes first. It is our productivity that allows consumption and never the other way around. A government and central bank can't force consumption to encourage production or most of what you'll end up with is inflation.

Printing money to monetize the Federal deficit is done under the guise of encouraging economic recovery. But the truth is, monetizing your debt is the last option countries have before they enter into an explicit default. Countries saddled with enormous debts will always default implicitly through monetization before they default explicitly.

A strong dollar encourages savings and investment. It leads to the stability of interest rates and inflation. It preserves the middle class, as it locks in their purchasing power. It allows manufacturers to increase profit margins by lowering the costs of raw materials purchased abroad. And it encourages investment from abroad. So my hope is the members of the Fed resign and allow the free markets to determine the cost of money. And we will have no more Fed-induced bubbles and even better, we will never have to labor through another one of Ben Bernanke's press conferences where he fails to realize that gold is money, it has been money for thousands of years and will continue to be long after he steps down.

Solution 3: Allow Interest Rates to Rise to the Supply of Savings versus the Demand for Money

As we have discussed, when government interferes with the free market's ability to set price through subsidies and price fixing, imbalances in the economy occur. Thinking back on my previous example of the free market and *American Pickers*, I argued that the free market through price discovery sets the most efficient price and through free-market competition we achieve the optimal price and supply/demand equilibrium. In simple terms, a bank is a money retailer—you lend them your savings and they provide you with a return, they lend your money out and charge interest to the borrower. In an environment where the free market sets interest rates, when there is high demand for money, banks attract savings by offering higher rates. However, when there is a surplus of savings and low demand for borrowing, interest rates decrease. This is how the free market would discover the rate of interest on money. Doesn't that make more sense than offering free money forever, which is now the rule at the Fed? We need to ask ourselves how we got here and if having a central bank is really worth the inevitable bankruptcy of the nation.

Just as you get the best price at the grocer with competition, the same applies with money and banking. And just like it seemed ridiculous that a 12-person panel or a 435 person congress would dictate the price of milk, it is equally ridiculous that any bureaucratic group should dictate and influence the cost of money.

But instead of allowing free-market forces to determine interest rates based on the market's supply and demand of savings, the Fed has interjected itself in this process by dictating the over-night interbank lending rate, artificially and massively increasing the base money supply and interfering in the demand of debt instruments. Instead of millions of market participants determining the cost of money, the rate is artificially manipulated by 12 unelected bureaucrats at the Federal Reserve. Now, I don't want the Fed to control the price and supply of milk. But let's say they directly manipulated the milk market—I could always substitute cow's milk for soy milk or almond milk. With milk I have choices, but by law, the U.S. dollar has no competition in the United States. Yes, sophisticated market participants can engage in commodities and foreign exchange markets, but for the average person the U.S. dollar has no competition.

We went over how the Fed controls the supply and demand for money in Chapter 1, and although in the long run free markets do eventually prevail in setting the rates, when the government steps into any market people tend to follow their lead—the U.S. Treasury is no exception. Let's say the government announces it will buy shares of IBM. The Federal Reserve is going to print money and the government is going to buy IBM shares. What would you do? If you were smart you would buy shares of IBM, anticipating with the power of Bernanke's printing press shares of IBM are bound to rise. This is what is happening in the U.S. Treasury today, the Fed has informed the market they will be a significant buyer of Treasuries for an indefinite period of time, so naturally the market is going along with the Fed—they are riding Ben's wave. Now, let's imagine the Fed has to stop its endless quantitative easing (QE), even worse let's envision the Fed has to increase rates and start selling bonds. What will the market do? They will also reverse course leading to a huge sell off in Treasury prices and a large increase in rates. This is one of the two scenarios (the other being a failed auction resulting from excess supply and inflation) that can trigger a bursting of the enormous asset bubble the Fed has created in U.S. Treasury debt.

Since its inception in 1913, the Fed has been an instigator of asset bubbles. And as we stand today it is facilitating the largest bubble in its history in the U.S. Treasury. When this bubble bursts, interest rates will skyrocket and the United States will not be able to manage their debt obligations.

The cost of money should be the supply of savings versus demand for money, the more I want to borrow and the less I have to lend, the higher the cost—that is the market—that is the way the market should determine interest rates. Factitiously low interest rates caused by the central bank encourage more money consumption and creation—the rocket fuel for bubbles. Zero percent interest rates, which will be in effect for at least six years, will go a long way in ensuring this bond bubble will be epic in scale.

Market forces should never be thwarted by 12 angry men influencing the cost of money. The Fed needs to get out of the way and put the free market in control.

Solution 4: Balance the Budget

"Most bad government has grown out of too much government."
—*Thomas Jefferson*

Those in charge of Washington promise they will go through the budget line by line—with a scalpel or a hatchet or a chain saw they will attack each budget line and cut spending to the bone. All sorts of lofty promises are made during elections that politicians will work together and take initiative to get our fiscal house in order. Unfortunately, after the election is over and the politician is left only to focus on the next election, when the budget line is examined the scalpel is left on the operating table, the hatchet is dull, the chain saw is out of juice and nothing of significance can be cut. Washington grandstands in Big Bird suits and finds it impossible to give an inch; they can't even give the large androgynous yellow bird the pink slip. Some may say that Washington will agree on a budget deal and entitlement reform when hell freezes over—I say it will happen when Nancy Pelosi falls in love with Grover Norquist.

As I write, those in Washington are concocting or delaying the concocting of another "Grand Bargain." And although I must be honest that the time between now and this books publishing date I will not be able to speak of the bargain specifically, something tells me it will be far from "grand." I am imagining, now that we have another four years of Obama, that there will be a somewhat grand combination of growth-killing tax increases that will reduce GDP and bring in less money than planned, and a perfunctory attempt to reduce spending—which is the real problem with our fiscal imbalances. This half-hearted attempt at spending restraint will sound grand—"one trillion over 10 years," but will actually boil down to less than one tenth of the decade's overspending.

I would like to see an amendment to the constitution that the annual deficit could never be greater than 3 percent of GDP. In other words, I would like to hold government accountable to balancing the budget, or at least come very close to doing so. Keep in mind that balancing the budget should lie heavily on spending restraint rather than tax hikes—especially given that our tithe would limit government's take to just 10 percent of our income.

Consider an American family managing their finances like the federal government. First, instead of locking into a 30-year fixed rate mortgage, they finance their McMansion with primarily short-term paper. They save for their kids' college and their retirement by writing themselves an IOU. They make $100,000 a year and spend $150,000. When the husband expresses his concern that maybe they should make some reductions to their monthly expenditures, his lovely wife suggests he should get another credit card. They have an onslaught of expenditures coming on the horizon, yet they have convinced themselves their drawer full of IOUs will cover it. Their idea of getting serious about their overspending consists of their agreement not to go further over budget next year. With the full faith and credit of the U.S. taxpayer and a printing press, the federal government can sustain itself under these circumstances better than one American family. However, eventually market forces will demand for government to live within its means. You only have to look to France or California to realize that you can't just "tax the rich" your way to a balanced budget. Money moves where it is treated best. Just ask Gerard Depardieu and Phil Mickelson. Real cuts will have to be made.

This is a more sobering look at what it would take to balance the budget. An entire book can be dedicated to a line-by-line reduction of our federal spending. In an attempt to not bore you and myself, I have outlined some general cuts that need to be on the table for a bargain to really be grand—this is just an overview.

1. Research—The federal government spends money on research—energy, health care, and forestry and fishing to name a few. People like to point to fanciful studies conducted on cow feces, to make the point that this research is pointless. But for the moment, I will imagine that this research is fantastic, and I am not taking anything

away from the wonderful work being done. However, similar work is done in the private sector, private health care and energy companies also do research and usually more effectively. This could save as much as $50 billion dollars a year.

2. I understand that farmers have bad years; however, there is private insurance that can be purchased to protect farmers from unfavorable weather. If there's not, there soon will be when government eliminates the farm subsidies. This could reduce the deficit by as much as $16 billion a year.

3. Defense—Being the police force to the world is a noble task—but when you are borrowing money from China to police the world, it stops making sense. We have to reduce military expenditures to what is necessary to take care of our nation's defense, and stop placing an enormous debt burden on ourselves and future generations by policing the world. After all, we have enough nuclear weapons to destroy the globe many times over, so what are we so afraid of? Our International presence has to be reevaluated and scaled back to only what is needed to keep America safe. If a nation would like to continue with our services, they can pay for our presence. With a near $700 billion defense budget, even if we could eliminate one third of the spending we would be closer to a balanced budget and still remain safe.

4. Stop blurring the lines between federal and state spending. Push down education and welfare to the state level. At the state level, welfare will need to be limited to people who are truly unable to take care of themselves. Federal departments that deal with education and welfare will be eliminated. This would greatly reduce the budget. Yes we would most likely pay more at the state level—but government works best when it's local and you have more control over it.

5. I live in New Jersey, the toll capital of the world, and like all New Jersians, I hate them. However, the most efficient way to pay for the repair of roads and bridges is by directly charging the people who drive on them. Having tax payers in New Jersey pay for a bridge in Kansas makes no sense. Therefore, I am eliminating federal roads out of the budget for an estimated $35 billion.

Ok, now we are on a roll.

6. Foreign aid—If I paid somebody to be my friend and they housed my biggest enemy and set my embassies on fire, I wouldn't think I was getting my money's worth—it seems like they would hate us for free—this $46 billion needs to be cut.

7. Refinance short-term debt to longer term maturities. This may buy some time to make cuts before higher rates are bearing down on us. However, this would increase the deficit in the short-term.

8. And of course, the most important budget item to address is Entitlement reforms.

The sad truth is there are no easy answers for our nation's unfunded liabilities—a promise that government made to workers to aid in their retirement. The outlook for Social Security's trust fund has deteriorated to an astonishing degree according to the Congressional Budget Office (CBO). The nonpartisan budget scorekeeper expects the trust fund to peak in 2018 and decline to $2.7 trillion in 2022—a full $1 trillion less than Social Security's own actuaries predicted last year.[7]

Remember, the trust fund is just a drawer full of IOUs from the government, so it doesn't mean much for the government's ability to afford benefits—Social Security's assets are offset by Treasury's equal debt. But it does give the program the legal authority to pay all promised benefits until its special Treasuries are spent.[8]

Under current law, once the trust fund is gone, Social Security could only pay 78 percent of benefits. Older retirees and the disabled would be protected, leaving new retirees to face much deeper cuts.[9]

Furthermore, President Obama will have to address a near-term crisis in Social Security's disability insurance program that CBO expects to hit in 2016. This has been a refuge in this economy for people who have exhausted their 99 weeks of unemployment. It's not surprising that its funds are dwindling fast as the separate trust fund for the working-age disabled is nearly depleted. As current law is written, resources can't be shared between the two trust funds.[10]

Social Security already is cash flow negative, taking less in revenue than it pays out in current benefits. CBO sees the program's $48 billion cash gap in 2011 rising above $100 billion by 2019.[11]

As bad as Social Security looks, Medicare looks worse and will probably feel more strain from the upcoming Obama care legislation that is tantamount to a government takeover of the health care industry.

And as if all this wasn't sobering enough, in a recent article in the *Wall Street Journal*, Chris Cox and Bill Archer evaluate the unfunded liabilities of Social Security and Medicare as if they were accounted for as a private enterprise. They note if "the accrued expense of the governments entitlement programs are counted, it becomes clear that to collect enough revenue would require $8 trillion a year in tax collections." To put this number in perspective, "Individuals filing tax returns in America last year earning more than $66,193 per year have a total AGI of $5.1 trillion, all corporations had income for tax purposes of $1.6 trillion"—it's clear that even with a 100 percent tax, it wouldn't be enough.[12]

So what can be done?

One solution is to means test these programs. Unfortunately, you only gain traction in means testing when you start to phase out benefits beginning at incomes over $55,000. Taking Social Security benefits away from millionaires politically is easy and should be done—but sadly it won't be enough to save this program from insolvency. In the end, our government has to be honest with the American people and simply admit it doesn't have anywhere close to the $120 trillion needed to fulfill its entitlement promises and these programs will have to be cut dramatically.

The demographics aren't working in favor of Social Security and Medicare, as Baby Boomers retire there are less people working to pick up the slack. Therefore, another solution would be to attract workers, preferably high-income wage earners from abroad. Attaching a green card to every college diploma is an idea floated by both sides of the aisle and should be done.

Abolishing the Fed—I know you're thinking, "Pento that's your answer to everything." But you have to admit nobody suffers more under Bernanke's monopolistic dictatorship then our seniors who live on fixed incomes. A stronger dollar would help seniors have more purchasing power and would slow down the growth of benefits in a way that wouldn't affect the beneficiary's standard of living.

Any conversation about bending the health care cost curve downward would have to include tort reform. Reducing malpractice insurance and unnecessary testing and diagnostics would go a long way in making healthcare more affordable.

The last is economic growth—a rising tide lifts all boats. We need to grow this economy and get the unemployed back into the work force so they can stop collecting from government and start contributing to the deficit and paying into these programs. Unfortunately, with the growth-killing agenda laid out by the Obama administration, I am not sure how much growth we will have over the next four years. Embracing the free-market principles laid out in this chapter would increase GDP, reduce unemployment, and help fund these programs. We should also explore our energy resources—a huge untapped area of growth lies beneath the surface—we have to seize it and make it work for us. This would not only increase growth but reduce our trade imbalance.

Just as you think we are making progress—remember, FEMA is in the red, FHA needs a bailout, Obamacare is underfunded, and the Post Office is bankrupt—and we are back to the cutting room.

These cuts sound drastic—but not a drastic as Obama's budget that predicts $1 trillion deficits for the next decade and beyond. And remember—Obama's budget forecasts a rosy economic environment with robust growth, subdued interest rates and low inflation, which will certainly not be manifested out of his high tax/overregulatory statist agenda. The truth is, these are some of the grand initiatives that congress will have to be willing to discuss for a true balanced budget to be achieved. I think a plan such as Simpson Bowles can be a good starting point—however, I would like the cuts to be deeper and the tax hikes to be minimal.

Washington is always worried about the next election, that's why they find it hard to strike a grand deal. I would like to have the president and Congress serve just two years and then be out—pulled from a pool of ordinary citizens, sort of like jury duty. The pool of eligibility would be optional (unlike jury duty), and individuals would have to be over 40 years old and born in the United States. The president would be chosen from the 535 who serve. A law must be passed to make it as illegal to pay someone serving in this new people's Congress as it would be to pay a juror to influence his verdict. This would eliminate government going to the highest bidder and being controlled by lobbyists. It would also get rid of Political Action Committees and the millions of dollars spent on election campaigning. Middle-class citizens could have much greater control over this country's destiny; with the motivation of knowing they only have two years to do the best thing for the nation. Just imagine: no longer would we be subject to career politicians and political dynasties like the Kennedys and Bushes.

Our problems are steep and escalating, with millions more enrolling in Social Security and the enormous debt looming, that will one day have to be serviced at higher rates, dire problems lie ahead. There is an image I have in my head of Indiana Jones attempting to outrun an enormous boulder barreling down behind him, you can substitute the bolder for our $16.5 trillion debt and our unfunded liabilities, you can substitute Harrison Ford for Barack Obama and Harry Reid and John Boehner. There is a saying on Wall Street: "Sell when you can, not when you have to." I would give similar advice to those in Washington—cut when you can, because when the bond vigilantes reemerge and the market says that you have run out of time, those higher rates will be barreling down like a boulder behind you—and then it will be too late.

Solution 5: Aggressively Reduce the Amount Of Regulatory Burden

"Were we directed from Washington when to sow and when to reap, we should soon want bread."

—*Thomas Jefferson*

"In every administration, the tools of inflation, borrowing, taxation, and regulation are used to transfer wealth from the people to the government and its cronies."

—*Llewellyn H. Rockwell Jr.*

There is a humorous adage, "If something moves, tax it; if it continues to move, regulate it; and if it stops moving, subsidize it." Regulation is another way those in government attempt to get in the way of buyers and sellers in the free market. We are led to imagine that regulation is there to help us navigate the malevolent and treacherous market place. Government regulations are imposed to protect consumers from the evils of business. And furthermore we are made to believe that Big business, in particular, hates regulation; they spend millions in Washington lobbying congress to eliminate regulation so they can take advantage of an uninformed consumer. Without regulation we would see the reinstatement of evils in the workplace, and companies would pollute freely and indiscreetly dirty our air and water. Our children would sit shackled in sweatshops, forced to sweep chimneys. We would certainly all die of salmonella poisoning from the toxic food that would undoubtedly populate grocer's unrefrigerated cases. The government has many convinced that the market is filled with greedy and unscrupulous characters waiting to deceive us. As Elizabeth Warren frantically screamed at the Democratic Convention: "The system is rigged against you!" And so those in government are doing the noble task of reining in the evil market participants and regulating the system in your favor.

Okay, so now for the truth: big business most often drives regulation. Shocking, but true! When business can't adequately compete in the marketplace, they lobby Congress to place legislative obstacles in the way of their usually smaller competitors. Big food producers, such as Monsanto, lobby Congress in an attempt to throw additional regulatory burdens on the local farmers under the cover of safety for the consumer. But the truth is that Monsanto isn't concerned with safety; they don't want competition from the smaller farms. The Food and Drug Administration (FDA) actually ran a sting operation followed by "guns-drawn raids usually reserved for terrorists and drug lords" as part of a crackdown on unpasteurized milk. I can imagine the look on the cows' faces as they were milked at gunpoint to seize their harmful supply. At the same time, the FDA let the highly consolidated industrial meat and factory farm industry off the hook despite growing problems.[13] Libertarian Llewellyn H. Rockwell Jr. notes:

> Just one clause in the Federal Register can mean billions for a favored firm or industry, and disaster for its competitors, which is why lobbyists cluster around the Capitol like flies around a garbage can."[14]

Founded by Richard Nixon, the Occupational Safety and Health Administration (OSHA) is an anti-entrepreneur agency. OSHA affects small and medium-sized businesses disproportionately, as its regulatory cases are easily handled by Exxon's squad of lawyers, while they can bankrupt a small firm.[15]

The Consumer Product Safety Commission, also a gift from Nixon, issues regulations drawn up in open consultation with big business—ironically, often issuing regulations that often conform exactly to what those firms are already doing. Small businesses, however, must spend heavily to comply.

And perhaps the Nixon administration's crowned jewel is the creation of the Environmental Protection Agency, whose budget is larded with the influence of politically connected businesses, and whose regulations buttress established industries and discriminate against entrepreneurs.[16]

Mr. Nixon was a Republican who also endorsed wage and price controls. He and others like George W. Bush and Mitt Romney are perfect examples as to why I believe America needs a third party that adheres to the Constitution and believes in balanced budgets, a strong currency, low taxes, fewer regulations, market-based interest rates, and stable prices.

The Department of Housing and Urban Development was founded by Lyndon B. Johnson, but its roots stretch all the way back to the New Deal, and whose purpose was to subsidize builders of rental and single-family housing.[17]

The Securities and Exchange Commission (SEC) was also established by Franklin D. Roosevelt, with its legislation written by corporate lawyers to cartelize the market for big Wall Street firms. Over the years, the SEC has stopped many new stock issues by smaller companies, who might grow and compete with the industrial and commercial giants aligned with the big Wall Street firms. Sarbanes Oxley inhibits smaller companies from going public as it saddles them with regulations they can't handle. Nobody understands all the implications of Dodd-Frank, but since former creators now have cushy jobs at some major banks, we can only assume that it will favor the too-big-to-fail over the community banks.[18]

The Department of Agriculture runs America's farming on behalf of large producers, keeping prices high, profits up, imports out, and new products off the shelves.[19]

The Federal Trade Commission—"as shown by the fascist-deco statue in front of its headquarters—claims to "tame" the "wild horse of the market" on behalf of the public. Since its founding in 1914, however, it has restrained new participants in the market in favor of established firms.[20]

Economist Ludwig Von Mises pointed out that "as business becomes more heavily regulated, business decisions are based more and more on compliance with governmental edicts than on profit-making." And because of this, we see American labor unions also call for more regulation of business because, "in order for them to survive, they must convince workers—and society—that "the company is the enemy." They claim workers need to be protected from the "enemy," or their employer, by labor unions.[21]

However, the substitution of bureaucratic compliance for profit-making decisions reduces profitability, usually with little or no benefit to anyone from the regulations being complied with. The end result is once again a reduction in the profitability of investment, and subsequently less investment takes place.

We need to become much more competitive internationally and therefore have to eliminate agencies that only service certain businesses and slow down productivity and growth. And greatly reduce our regulatory burden.

Solution 6: Simplify the Tax Code

"The democracy will cease to exist when you take away from those who are willing to work and give to those who would not."
—*Thomas Jefferson*

"Lower rates of taxation will stimulate economic activity and so raise the levels of personal and corporate income as to yield within a few years an increased—not a reduced—flow of revenues to the federal government."
—*John F. Kennedy, January 17, 1963, annual budget message to the Congress, fiscal year 1964*

Economist Stephen Moore often says that efficient tax policy should be aimed at making the poor rich and not the rich poor. Every so often a politician parades the tax code around in an attempt to show how overly convoluted and cumbersome our tax code has become. Of course, nothing ever gets done about it—but it is often a talking point of conservatives such as Steve Forbes and also espoused by liberals such as Jerry Brown (in one of his political iterations). Government uses this cumbersome tax code in an attempt to influence the market—and inasmuch as they are putting their thumb on the scale—our thousand-page tax code is one fat thumb.

Therefore, tax policy works best when it is simple and government steps aside from the business of picking winners and losers. Even I agree there is a function the federal government should perform, and those few functions do need to be funded by the collection of revenue. But ask yourself, does it serve the average citizen to make the tax code so complicated? Let's examine the prized deduction of the tax code—the cherished mortgage deduction. It is a deduction no homeowner feels they could live without. However, what if they eliminated the deduction and reduced the rate, leaving your tax liability the same or lower. Why should the average homeowner have a problem with this? Who loses in that scenario? Mention this in Washington and you soon realize, the home mortgage deduction has less to do with the home-owner and more to do with the home seller. The powerful Realtor and Mortgage Broker lobbies persuade government through campaign contributions to tip the scales in favor of home ownership and mort-gages. They are the ones that need that deduction, because it sways market forces in their favor.

Personally, I would prefer to eliminate the federal income tax altogether and replace it with a small consumption tax that would exclude food and clothing. Let me make myself clear, this tax would not be in addition to any federal taxes—it would replace them. And it would also eliminate taxes on income and capital gains. A tax on consumption would encourage savings and investment—something our current income tax code punishes. In addition, it would also eliminate the need for all those loopholes, deductions and exemptions that allow the Federal government to pick who the winners and losers are, as they try to steer the market's free hand.

The tax would only be imposed on discretionary and luxury items—items not needed to survive such as food, clothing, and shelter (investment homes excluded) would not be taxed. Since most low-income wages earners spend most of their money for items that are necessities they would pay little to no tax—in this way it is progressive. What is a luxury item? I don't think you need thousands of pages to define it. Just as Justice Potter Stewart tried in 1964 to explain what is obscene, by saying, "I know it when I see it." I will make the same statement for the definition of a discretionary or luxury item.

The Obama administration clings to the belief that all the deficit problems can be solved if we just "tax the rich." As a matter of fact, he proposes we raise taxes on the rich to not only close the deficit, but to make new "investments"—code word for more spending. Now, he may think there is an unlimited number of rich people to tap in order to achieve his government largess. The sad truth is that even if placing an onerous tax on productivity was effective, there are not enough rich people to close the deficit and entertain all the new spending.

First, the income of the top 2 percent of taxpayers is typically more volatile than that of taxpayers lower down the income scale. Many of these top income earners rely more heavily on economic growth, so when the economy sours, so often do those high-end income streams. When the economy declines incomes at the upper end decline as well. That means less revenue than expected will flow into federal coffers.

But perhaps more importantly, there just aren't enough rich people to generate the kind of revenue needed to substantially reduce deficits.

To illustrate this, consider some recent calculations by the Congressional Budget Office. Raising all six income tax rates by 1 percentage point would yield an additional $480 billion over 10 years. By contrast, raising the top two rates by 1 percentage point would yield just $115 billion.[22]

The president has proposed letting the top two income tax rates revert to 39.6 percent and 36 percent, up from 35 percent and 33 percent today. He also called for an increase in the capital gains and dividend rates to 20 percent that high-income households pay, up from 15 percent today. And he would reduce the value of their itemized deductions and personal exemptions.[23]

All told, those proposals—which would affect individuals making at least $200,000 and couples making $250,000 and up—would reduce deficits by just under $1 trillion over 10 years. So even if they were to collect the additional one trillion over ten years, which by the way I question, as the economy would slow due to these increases and we would never collect that much. But let's assume you can—that would give you about $100 billion in revenue toward a $1 trillion dollar deficit—it's just not enough.

And more recently in the "fiscal cliff" bargain, taxes were raised on every American who brings home a paycheck and tax breaks were simultaneously handed out to politically favored groups such as wind farms and movie studios. The net effect was an increase to the federal deficit and a "redistribution of wealth" from every American who collects a paycheck to political apparatchiks. I am not in favor of raising taxes to reduce the deficit, but it makes even less sense to raise taxes and increase the deficit in order to hand out political favors.

Of course, according to Democrats, the tax debate is far from over, after all—rates can be raised even higher. Let's go back to the 90 percent rates of the 1940s! Happy days are here again! But remember, higher tax rates are going to negatively affect economic behavior by increasing tax avoidance and discouraging otherwise growth-spurring investments. And that, in turn, can reduce the revenue raised.

We only have to look to California and France to see that money is fungible—it goes to where it will be treated best. We can't balance the budget and reduce our debt solely on the backs of our wealthy. We need a simple tax plan such as a Federal consumption tax and the government has to shrink to accommodate what it brings in.

Solution 7: Fair Trade and a Free Trade

"Peace, commerce, and honest friendship with all nations— entangling alliances with none."

—*Thomas Jefferson*

When the American Pickers go town to town, state to state, and negotiate to purchase people's cherished possessions sprinkled across their lawn—they don't have to search through a 1,000-page rule book to explain the intricate rules of picking in each jurisdiction. Buying junk off a person's lawn is free trade. It's free-market capitalism at its purest, unencumbered by outside forces—negotiated between the picker and the pickee and that's as it should be. So why when dealing with foreign countries do we need thousands of pages of trade agreements. Trade agreements that span thousands of pages are unnecessary and are government's way of picking winners and losers. Free trade should be just that—free of government tipping the scales.

England did this in the mid-nineteenth century, Hong Kong in the mid-twentieth century. In 1789, the Constitution of the United States needed a mere 54 words to establish free trade among the states. NAFTA (North American Free Trade Agreement), the "free" trade agreement between Canada, Mexico, and the United States has 2,000 pages, not surprisingly 900 of which are tariff rates.[24]

According to Jeffrey Tucker, the executive editor of Laissez Faire books:

> Trade agreements are filled with "exceptions." A favor is protection from foreign competition for those who wield political influence through vested interests, typically the producers of essential items. Rather than free trade these agreements create a regime of managed trade and, not least lots of expensive useless wealth-consuming jobs for bureaucrats.[25]

Trade agreements have other detrimental implications. They discriminate against lower-cost imports from countries that are not part of the treaty. Trade is diverted away from them to more expensive tax-exempt suppliers, in countries that signed that Free Trade Agreement (FTA). Now, the importers of these higher-cost goods need more foreign currency to pay for them. And as a bonus, part of the tax revenue the government gave up with the tariff exemption winds up as income of the pocket of the favored supplier.[26]

Free trade should be free from government influence.

And believe it or not fair trade should apply to individuals as well. Our immigration policy needs to flood this country with doctors, engineers, scientists and mathematicians who have come here to obtain an advanced degree. They should be compelled to stay in America after graduating from our colleges. We can send graduates with a degree in Keynesianism, loafers and the cast from the Jersey Shore abroad in exchange.

Solution 8: Overhaul Education

Our education system has been the establishment for so long, most people equate schooling with tax-funded, government-run schools.[27]

It's hard to think outside the box and take a new approach toward education; however, it's about time we did. Severely underprepared college freshman, declining test scores, poor analytical skills, and students who cannot demonstrate basic literacy, the United States rank 17th in science and 25th in math, this is a disgrace. At least people in the former Soviet Union had the freedom to shop at the best government stores; people in every town in America don't have freedom if they are forced to utilize that one specified provider of education.

The problem with the public schools is the lack of competition and the Teachers Union. Our education system needs an overhaul, therefore I would like to see the department of education abolished and replaced by a voucher system. I agree that everyone should be allowed an opportunity to a good education regardless of the ability to pay. However, what we have now is the pervasive failure of public schools— especially in poorer neighborhoods. Freeing up the educational system by giving people a choice would elevate the entire system. Especially in our inner cities.

The money in education should stop being poured into dysfunctional schools and follow the child and parent to allow them to make the proper education decision. Schools will be established through the free market and forced to compete for the tax dollars. Good schools will get enrollment and bad schools will go out of business.

The wholesale failure of the K–12 public school system to adequately educate children, no matter how much money is spent per pupil, is universally acknowledged by all outside the teachers union that has a stronghold on congress and the White House. I believe the best reform proposal is to give parents a choice where they want to send their children to school. This would entail an educational voucher that parents can redeem at a private school. This would bring some much-needed competition into the education industry. "Genuine competition is the only true reform catalyst.[28]

Conclusion

"Government has laid its hand on health, housing, farming, industry, commerce, education, and to an ever-increasing degree interferes with the people's right to know. Government tends to grow, government programs take on weight and momentum as public servants say, always with the best of intentions. But the truth is that outside of its legitimate function, government does nothing as well or economically as the private sector of the economy."

—Ronald Reagan

While writing this book, I bore witness to what in my mind, were two contradictory events. The first is the presidential election. Now, just for the record, I supported the Libertarian candidate Gary Johnson, and it's safe to say that although I am proud I voted my conscience, I didn't expect to win. But before you say that I threw away my vote, remember New Jersey was never in danger of going red in the first place. I also want to maintain that I am a person who values ideas and philosophies— this presidential election was never about race or "the war on women." I strongly believe in free-market ideals and sought a candidate who I believed had the strength to steer this economy through a downturn, allow the economy to deleverage and the markets to clear. Sadly, I didn't see this in either Romney or Obama.

However, inasmuch as the presidential race was a referendum on the free market vs. a centrally planned Keynesian utopia; and a preference to tax the productive economy in favor of redistribution and government transfer payments. To the extent this election was at all about a move toward a stronger dollar as opposed to spending and printing. I would say all the economic principles I honestly believe work best, not just for Michael Pento, but for all Americans, was lost to a centrally planned government that espouses a tax, spend, borrow and print philosophy.

The night of the election my area was suffering through the aftermath of hurricane Sandy. My house lost power and cable for close to two weeks. Living so close to New Jersey's shore towns and even not so far from Staten Island, New York, I was emotionally drained by the devastation felt all around me. Driving around the neighboring towns, I was deeply saddened by the loss of life and property. The look of despair on people's faces as they worked to salvage what was left of their battered homes and save some of their possessions that were poured out on the front lawn—it was hard not to share in their hopelessness. And on election night, sitting in my house powered by a generator, I processed the election results and needless to say I felt depressed and demoralized. In a democracy, you get the amount of government you vote for, and the results seemed to reflect an electorate seeking more—tax, regulation, printing, borrowing, and spending. My heart was heavy with all I saw around me, and I felt this country moving away from free-market capitalism and toward statism. In fact, a quote from Thomas Paine rang through my head: "These are the times that try men's souls." And in many ways, I felt broken; my soul was tried.

Now I mentioned that I felt contradictory feelings during the election and let me explain. As I bore witness to what appeared to be an electorate reaching out for more government, I saw through the tragedy of hurricane Sandy, the government falling down and the American people rising up. In Jersey shore towns decimated by the hurricane, neighbors didn't wait for FEMA to arrive before they reached out to help fellow neighbors.

In Staten Island, New York, an area that was initially ignored by those in government, fellow Islanders stepped up and became the first responders. In New Dorp Beach on Staten Island, new parents of a six-week-old were trying to wait out the storm in their house when their neighbor, Peter Tacopino, ran over to warn them of a massive wave about to barrel down the block. Wrestling chest-deep waters, Tacopino, placed their new baby atop his shoulder, then waded to his three-story house, straining not to fall.[29]

When many in Long Island were flooded and left in the dark by government controlled Long Island Power and Lighting, the people in Long Island worked together and helped each other with warm shelter and necessities. And when FEMA closed their doors on Staten Islanders due to a nor'easter, fellow Staten Islanders opened their doors to family, neighbors, and friends.

Local businesses such as DeMarcos, a family owned Italian deli near my town, rose to the occasion to service the community, as they always do. Eugene DeMarco suffered a loss with hurricane Irene, but this time he was prepared and acquired a generator to power his store. DeMarco's was able to open for business the day after the hurricane. But they didn't use this advantage as one of the few open businesses to price gouge, on the contrary, he used his business to aide in the relief effort. When he found out a nursing home in Keyport was washed away in the storm and seniors had been displaced, he was the first to offer them a hot meal. His wife, Doreen loaded up her truck and handed out hundreds of sandwiches and coffee to relief workers. I'm sure there was a "DeMarco's" in every town and in fact I know there were. Now I can't lie and say that I didn't hear of a few looters taking advantage of those in need—but those were few and far between. Americans rose to the occasion and helped.

Makeshift relief centers were established by everyday citizens in churches, synagogues and storefronts. I saw on TV a truck from New Orleans filled with supplies intended for those who had suffered on Staten Island. Upon hearing this news the Staten Island woman responded with tears in her eyes, "People are good." And that's how I felt—people are good. Through the destruction and debris, it was an uplifting sight to see—neighbor helping neighbor, town helping town, state helping state and America helping Americans.

And as I reflected on these events and the humanity I witnessed I couldn't help but think—these are the people who make up the free market. To quote a *Sesame Street* song, "They are the people in your neighborhood, the people that you meet each day." This is the market. The free market is all of us coming together, voting with our wallets, deciding what should be produced and what is consumed. The government has done a good job telling us these are the people we should be scared of, that the system is rigged against us and these are the people we need them to protect us from. They have many convinced that businesses like DeMarco's don't exist, that they won't do the right thing unless government made them. But I have more faith in my fellow human being to discover price and determine supply and demand than I do in 12 unelected officials huddled together in secret in the Federal Reserve or 435 members of congress or the 100 members of the Senate, or in the president. I believe in people and I have faith in the market—the economy operates best when it is unencumbered by political forces working in their self-interest and put in the hands of the people, average everyday people, who come together in their self-interest and form the market.

If you can't trust millions of individuals, who posses only limited and balkanized power, then how can you trust those same individuals when you hand over to them the keys of the kingdom?

As Milton Friedman asked—who are these angels who will run our government, and during the aftermath of this crisis I have yet to see those angels in government—I have only seen government politicians who exploit this opportunity for a photo op. But on the devastated beaches of New Jersey, and through the rubble of Midland Beach and South Beach of Staten Island, throughout the burned down houses in Breezy point—I have looked into the face of my fellow man and have seen those angels.

Now don't get me wrong—I don't think Angels run the free market. I don't want to overplay my hand here, so let's agree for the moment with the woman from Staten Island who simply said, "People are good." For if people are by their nature nefarious how does that condition change once you grant them more power? And let's assume that for the most part people in the market and government are good. If we assume that most people are acting in good faith then it really all boils down to who is in a better position to make a more informed decision about price, supply and demand in the marketplace. I would still argue that people who participate in the market are. So, even if I were to take a less cynical view of government, that still doesn't put them in a superior position to make better informed decisions than millions of market participants who vote with their own money for what they want every day.

So where do we go from here? I think we need to stop believing in government and start believing in ourselves. We need to put our faith in people, wary that there are always bad actors, but that most people are well intended and trust free markets to work. We need to recognize our fault in creating an environment where politicians vie for votes by providing handouts whether they be transfer payments or favored deductions. We need to stop asking Washington for things and start demanding they live within their means. We need to stop throwing away money on schools that don't work and open it up to free market competition. We need to greatly reduce the regulatory burden. We need to trade freely with our foreign friends. We need to demand a stable dollar and we need to allow markets to decide the cost of money.

I fear that in the coming years the American standard of living will decrease dramatically, a very tough road lies ahead. But I am enlightened by the humanity I see in my fellow citizen and pray we can get through these tough times together. As the East Coast weathered its hurricane and promised to emerge stronger, so too can this great nation weather its storm and arise stronger as people and stronger as a nation.

After the bond bubble bursts there will a huge economic mess for Americans to clean up. It is our strength, character, and love of freedom that will hasten that process.

Notes

1. Milton Friedman on greed, *Phil Donahue Show*, 1979.
2. James Ostrowski, "Republicans and Big Government," *Mises Daily*, February 19, 2002.
3. Ron Paul, "Let the Housing Market Clear," Congressman Ron Paul, 14th district web site, October 2012.
4. William L. Anderson, "Sinking the QE2 and False Monetary Policy—Fiscal Policy Divide," *Krugman-In-Wonderland*, October 28, 2010.
5. Paul, Ron, "Let the Housing Market Clear."
6. AARP, "Social Security Trust Fund Outlook Takes $1 Trill Dive," February 3, 2012.
7. Ibid.
8. Ibid.
9. Ibid.
10. Ibid.
11. Ibid.
12. Chris Cox and Bill Archer, "Why $16 Trillion Only Hints at the True U.S. debt," *Wall Street Journal*, November 27, 2012.
13. Sowj, "Michael Taylor, Monsanto and the FDA's Armed Raids on Small Dairy Farms," *Food Justice*, September 8, 2011.
14. Llewellyn Rockwell Jr., "Regulatory Industrial Complex", *Mises Daily*, February 29, 2012.
15. Ibid.
16. Ibid.
17. Ibid.
18. Ibid.
19. Ibid.
20. Ibid.
21. Thomas DiLorenzo, "Markets, Not Unions, Gave Us leisure,"*Mises Daily*, August 23, 2004.
22. Jeanne Sahadi, "Tax the Rich! OK, but Then What, Mr. President?" *Money*, April 13, 2011.
23. Ibid.
24. Jeffrey Tucker, "Free Traders, Free Trade Agreements," *Mises Daily*, March 10, 2010.
25. Ibid.

26. Ibid.

27. Lawrence M. Vance, "Vouchers: Another Central Plan," *Mises Daily*, December 23, 2003.

28. Ibid.

29. Alicia Dennis, "Became Heroes in Extraordinary Circumstances," *People*, November, 7, 2012.

Chapter 10

How to Invest Your Money Before and After the Bond Bubble Bursts

I founded a money management firm in November of 2011 for the primary purpose of preparing clients' investments for this upcoming debt crisis. I realized a few years ago that the United States faced an entirely new paradigm—namely, that onerous debt levels had reached the point where the central bank would be forced into a difficult decision; either to massively monetize the nation's debt or allow a deflationary depression to wipe out the economy.

To prove this point we first have to understand why the macro investment climate has changed so dramatically.

In this current economic environment, our government is compelled to seek a condition of perpetual inflation in order to maintain the illusion of prosperity and solvency. However, once inflation causes asset bubbles to increase to such a degree that even a Fed chairman can see them, the central bank shuts off the monetary spigot and deflation then returns with a vengeance.

The problem with the addiction to money printing is that once a central bank starts, it can't stop without dire, albeit in the long-term healthy, economic consequences. And the longer an economy stays addicted to inflation, the more severe the eventual debt deflation will become. As a result, our central bank is now walking the economy on a very thin tightrope between inflation and deflation.

After the credit crisis and Great Recession set in and the healing aspects of deflation began to take hold, the Fed began to rapidly expand the supply of base money in an effort to quickly erode the purchasing power of the dollar and bring real estate prices higher once again.

However, a healthy and cathartic period of deflation was needed, where asset prices fall, money supply shrinks and debt levels are reduced to a level that can be supported by the free market. This is the only viable answer for a nation struggling to maintain solvency.

The return journey from rampant inflation and asset bubbles, to deflation and depression always carries insolvency and defaults along for the ride. Defaulting on debt is deflationary in nature and restructuring your liabilities is the only choice when you owe more money than you can pay back.

The prevalent idea among our government and central bank is that we can borrow and print even more money in order to eliminate the problems caused by too much debt and inflation. But more inflation can never be the cure for rising prices, and piling on more debt can't solve a condition of insolvency.

Investors are now being violently whipsawed by the decisions of the Fed and D.C., as they switch between inflationary and deflationary policies. The choice government now faces is to allow a deflationary depression to finally purge the economy of its imbalances or try to levitate real estate, equities, and bond prices by printing massive quantities of dollars.

It is vitally important for your financial well-being to be able to determine which path our central bank is currently pursuing. The point here is to understand where we are in the cycle between inflation and deflation and then to invest accordingly.

Therefore, leading up to what I believe will be the eventual collapse of the U.S. bond market and currency, a different tactic would have to be deployed when making your investment decisions instead of simply buying and holding a diversified basket of bonds and stocks. Or to just own commodities and non-dollar investments until hyperinflation eventually kicks into high gear.

Investors can no longer deploy a Modern Portfolio Theory of investing and hope to provide themselves with a positive, after-tax return on investments on a consistent basis. Nor can they claim the U.S. dollar will always be in a downtrend and then simply purchase a basket of anti-dollar investments (including precious metals) and then just go to sleep on their portfolios.

Adhering to any one single investment strategy no longer works in this new age of investing. The problem investors face is that most asset classes have now become highly correlated.

During deflationary cycles, most asset classes decline in price with the exception of bonds. However, during inflationary cycles bond prices fall while most other market rise in price, with risk assets taking the vanguard.

Having a diversified portfolio that is about 70 percent stocks and 30 percent bonds won't help you very much during deflationary cycles because even though 70 percent of your equities are diversified among various asset classes, they all tend to drop in value together.

That same strategy of 70-30 stocks to bonds would do better during times of inflation. But the bond portion of your allocation will get pummeled. That means you will greatly underperform the rate of inflation. And, if you don't switch over your portfolio to hedge against a deflation once the cycle has changed, your investments will get crushed.

So let's briefly look back to Great Recession starting in December 2007 and see how adhering to any one investment strategy played out.

Say you wanted to buy and hold a basket of commodities and Chinese stocks to hedge against inflation. I'll use oil prices as a proxy for commodity prices and the Shanghai stock exchange for anti-dollar investments.

The West Texas Intermediate (WTI) crude oil price started to soar in the middle of the last decade. It began its epic rise from $40 in 2005, and eventually shot up to $147 by the summer of 2008. All well and good if you were hedged against inflation. However, if one were to just hold this inflation hedge in their portfolio, things didn't turn out so well. WTI crude fell all the way back to $33 per barrel by the start of

2009 as a result of a significant decline in the growth rate of money supply and inflation.

Of course, the Fed at that time had already embarked on its quest to eventually print $2 trillion more (and counting) to fight deflation, and the government stepped up their borrowing significantly as well. Both of those attempts to reignite inflation helped send oil back to $114 per barrel by 2011. Most other commodity prices acted in similar fashion. They enjoyed a tremendous increase in price during inflation cycles and suffered severe value destruction during cycles where the money supply growth rate contracted.

In similar fashion, the Shanghai Stock Market soared to 5,500 by the start of 2008. However, the global recession hit Chinese shares very hard—especially since the U.S. dollar maintained its world reserve currency status and soared in value during the Great Recession. Shanghai shares plummeted to 1,700 by October of that same year and are still trading at just above 2,000 four years later.

So how should you strategize your investments to profit from this volatility? When the Fed's balance sheet is expanding and commercial banks are buying government debt, your portfolio should be hedged toward risk assets that include; precious metals, agriculture, base metals, energy and non-dollar-denominated international assets. I prefer to invest in Vietnam and Thailand for foreign, non-dollar exposure. Fertilizer stocks work best to profit from the growing global middle class. Gold exchange-traded funds (ETFs) work fine, but I far prefer individual mid-tier miners that are profitable and own mines in less volatile countries. There is a platinum ETF that should also be included in your portfolio. Exploration and production companies will give you the best return when oil prices are rising, and I would avoid heavy exposure to refiners. For base metal exposure I like copper producers that provide a maximum return on the concept of a growing global economy.

However, when the monetary base is static or shrinking and America is adopting fiscal austerity measures your portfolio should be hedged against deflation by owning; long dollar funds, utilities, municipal bonds, and going short risk assets like precious metals, base metals and energy. Purchasing in the money Put options on consumer discretionary and broad-market indexes should also be a prudent strategy. This trade is especially important to master because most retirement accounts that offer tax-deferred investing do not allow you to short stocks or own put options on individual shares.

I cannot provide specific stock and ETF advice in this forum for individuals without doing my due diligence on each and every one of you reading this book. However, I've given you enough adequate information for you to approach your advisor for individual equity selections. If your investment adviser isn't familiar with specific ideas that can hedge your portfolio according to this new dynamic, find one that is!

Of course, the eventual collapse of the U.S. dollar and debt markets would not bode well for assets based in the greenback. In fact, by definition, those assets would become destroyed. But the point here is that, for now, you simply cannot make long-term investment decisions about hedging against inflation or deflation and then set your portfolio on autopilot. Holding inflation hedges when the dollar is soaring and the U.S. money supply is contracting is a bad idea. Likewise, holding a deflation hedged portfolio when the dollar is crashing and the money supply is booming is also detrimental to your investment health.

Whereas I believe with a very high degree of confidence that the inexorable direction for the U.S. economy is toward inflation, there is no guarantee that we won't at some point just explicitly default on our debt rather than try to monetize it forever. As we approach the eventual debt and dollar collapse, the economy will experience wild swings between inflation and deflation. Your portfolio manager should be aware of this new investment dynamic and be prepared to move accordingly.

What to Own When U.S. Debt and the Dollar Collapse

Unfortunately, there is one consistent factor that is occurring while the United States continues to wax and wane between deflationary and inflationary cycles. That is the persistent accumulation of government debt both in nominal terms and as a share of gross domestic product (GDP). While the Fed is busy turning the inflation switch on and off, our federal government also toggles the switch between austerity and Keynesian deficit spending. There are times, like the debate over what to do about the fiscal cliff and debt ceiling, where government goes through a perfunctory pretense to care about deficits and debt. And then there are times where certain economists and politicians (you know who you are) urge the government to aggressively ramp up borrowing and spending—oops, sorry, I meant "investing"—money now to create more demand and consumption. The problem is that the seasons of deflation and austerity are infinitely shorter and milder than those of inflation and fiscal irresponsibility.

Both the Congressional Budget Office and the Office of Management and Budget put out projections on the deficit over the next decade. They come from different perspectives, but the general agreement is that our deficits will pile up about an additional $10 trillion of debt over the next 10 years.[1]

We now have reached the unenviable position of having more outstanding debt than our gross domestic product. What makes this condition even worse is that a great portion of our GDP is built on sand. We've all grown weary of hearing the statistic that the consumer is 70 percent of GDP. That means most of our economy is built on consumption, and our consumption is predicated on our ability to keep borrowing money.

Once our borrowing stops (remember what happened to the economy when consumers could no longer extract the phantom equity from their homes), GDP plummets. The saddest part is that the debt still remains. Therefore, once the credit card is removed, the debt-to-GDP ratio will explode to the upside.

So what will the debt situation really be in the next decade? Nobody knows for sure—least of all the government—but rest unassured, it will be devastating. For a good example of how bad a forecaster our government actually is about predicting our deficits, take a look back to what they said in July 2008. Even though we were already well into the real estate debacle, the White House projected a deficit of "just" $482 billion for the next fiscal year (2009). I put the word *just* in quotes because at the time it would have been the highest annual deficit ever recorded. However, the always-optimistic government was "just" a bit off. The actual amount of red ink for fiscal 2009 was $1.412 trillion! Any guesstimate of our debt accumulation over the next decade is just that—a guess. However, one can safely assume that the $10 trillion number is an optimistic one—even in the highly unlikely scenario that a grand bargain on entitlement reform gets done.

Once the economy starts to crumble due to rising interest rates, you can be sure of two things: debt service payments and deficits will soar, and our debt-to-GDP ratio will skyrocket, as the denominator washes away.

Around the years 2015–2016, our interest payments on the national debt will eat up about 30 to 50 percent of all federal revenue collected. Years of booming money supply growth rates, negative real interest rates and a massive accumulation of outstanding debt will cause an extreme level of anxiety about inflation and our country's ability to pay back our debt with money that is not rapidly losing its purchasing power. A catalyst will then exist to send interest rates significantly higher.

Remember, the bond bubble will not burst because robust economic growth suddenly returns for some unknown reason after five years of being absent. Bond yields will rise because there is going to be a lack of faith in our currency and rising concern about our credit risk.

Yields should then start to significantly rise in nominal terms, but should still stay negative in real terms. Inflation should finally start to soar due to the fact that the Fed has been printing dollars to purchase government debt for years on end. Congress may even change the Fed's charter and allow them to bypass banks and purchase government debt directly from the Treasury. I know that sounds farfetched, but nobody would have believed in 2007 that the Fed would be allowed to buy mortgage-backed securities, take interest rates rate to zero percent, and expand their balance sheet to $3 trillion and counting.

Our publicly traded debt now stands at $11.6 trillion. It was $5.1 at the start of the Great Recession in December 2007, and it should be near $15 trillion in the next few years. The amount of interest paid on all Federal debt during 2012 was about $220 billion.[2] If interest rates return to normal levels in the next three years that figure will be much closer to $1 trillion. I make the assumption that interest rates could and should even go much higher given the size of the Fed's balance sheet (that is growing quickly) and the unprecedented level of government debt—which is also increasing at breakneck speed.

But even if we just spend $1 trillion dollars in one year merely to service our debt, it should be enough to panic our bond holders in the same manner it did over in Europe. Inexorably rising bond yields will cause the Fed to act just as the European Central Bank is currently doing. That is, to pledge an unlimited amount of money printing to keep bond yields from rising.

There are many who claim that the United States should never have to be concerned about our surging national debt and bond market bubble because the Fed can always control interest rates. They believe any central bank with a fiat currency can always prevent interest rates from rising. Therefore, they guarantee that American will always service her debt with relative ease.

But the truth is that central banks are not ultimately in control of interest rates; it is the free market that has the last word on the cost of money. It is true that the Fed can be highly influential across the yield curve. However, in the long run, markets are the final arbiter to where interest rates are set.

While the Fed is capable of fooling investors and markets for a brief period of time, eventually rising rates of inflation must be reflected by a higher cost for borrowing money.

It is indeed a fact that our central bank can print an endless amount of money to purchase U.S. debt if they so desire. But anyone who has the mental faculties of an ameba with severe head trauma should be able to realize that they can't permanently control the private market for debt. As I mentioned in Chapter 5, the Fed can print money to infinity and always place a bid for U.S. Treasuries, but how high will mortgage rates increase? What about the corporate bond market and municipal debt? Will the Fed buy all that debt, too? And what will our foreign creditors think about such a strategy? What do you think would happen to GDP and the U.S. dollar during such a massive increase in money printing and inflation? Once you take the argument to its logical conclusion, it is plain to see how futile, ignorant and dangerous their position really is.

For all the reasons I describe in this book, it is prudent to prepare your portfolio for what is the significant probability of a huge bear market in the U.S. dollar and Treasury market in about three years. The start of our epic bear market will be easy to recognize. You'll know the time has arrived when bond prices, stocks and the U.S. dollar all plummet in value at the same time.

Your investments must be able to protect your wealth while interest rates are rising, the dollar is falling sharply, inflation is soaring and the economy is crumbling.

Going long most stocks will be a good way to lose a great portion of your capital and purchasing power. The only two exceptions will be the precious metals and energy sectors of the market. Precious metals and oil have a long history of responding favorably during times when the U.S. dollar is falling. As I mentioned earlier, precious metal and energy ETFs will work fine, but you should also own junior precious metal shares and energy Exploration & Production equities as well. Investors must also become familiar with how to profit from falling prices on certain market sectors and asset classes. Of course, the clear winner when U.S. bond prices collapse will be to go short Treasuries. The average investor can easily do this by purchasing one of several ETFs that rise in value as bond yields increase. All fixed-income funds will experience great tribulation when the bond bubble finally bursts. Shorting corporate and municipal bond funds or owning investments that profit when those yields rise will be very good move. Rising interest rates will crush the nascent and phony recover in real estate. The government-induced recovery in home prices will suffer greatly once the unemployment rate starts to rise and mortgage rates start to soar. Shorting the homebuilding ETF or buying in-the-money puts on individual equities should fare quite well. Also, shorting and/or owning puts on consumer discretionary funds should be a good idea because inflation will destroy the middle class's ability to buy things other than basic necessities.

Finally, any discussion of a bond and currency market debacle would not be complete without briefly mentioning the Japanese economy. In some ways, Japanese Government Bonds (JGBs) are in a worse condition than those of the United States. The leader of Japan's LDP party, Shinzo Abe, called for the Bank of Japan (BOJ) to raise its year-over-year inflation goal to 2 to 3 percent and to engage in unlimited money printing until deflation is fully vanquished. He said, if elected, he would forge an alliance with the BOJ to launch an all-out war on deflation and to attack the yen's value. He blames a strong currency as the primary impediment to Japan's economic recovery. Mr. Abe also called for the BOJ's policy rate to be cut below zero. With a debt-to-GDP ratio far north of 200 percent and a central bank that is moving toward monetizing more and more of that debt, the Japanese bond market will suffer a similar fate of the United States. Going short JGBs is easy to acquire due to an ETF that profits as yields in Japan finally start to rise.

Isn't that amazing! Central banks and governments created the debt bubble in the first place and now they will also be the ones who will prick it by adopting inflation targets. Once their inflation goals are reached, real yields will become so negative that bond holders will get destroyed and have no choice but to sell.

In summary, there are many things you can do to not only protect your portfolio but perhaps even increase your wealth when the collapse finally arrives. It is my fervent prayer that the collapse of the U.S. debt market will also be mollified to a great degree by the prudent decisions we need to undertake now in our government and by our central bank. That is why I wrote this book.

The preservation of our dollar as the world's reserve currency should be at the top of any politician's list. The notion on the part of the investing world that holding U.S. Treasuries is as good as gold must be restored. The cathartic effect of recessions and depressions must also be allowed to occur.

This book was written not only as a warning to those who live and invest in this great country but also, and primarily so, to allow those who read it an opportunity to anticipate and then react to the potential dramatic decline of living standards soon to be evident in America. In the end, we may not be able to significantly alter the pernicious course already set for this country. However, we now possess the relevant facts and knowledge to take the necessary steps to help our nation and ourselves. Whatever happens going forward, we will have no one to blame but ourselves. The choices are clear, but the decisions are difficult. Doing nothing is a decision—and a bad one at that. But, thank God, we still have the freedom to choose.

Notes

1. www.cbo.gov/publication/43288 and www.whitehouse.gov/sites/default/files/omb/budget/fy2013/assets/13msr.pdf. Accessed January 2013.
2. www.usnews.com/news/articles/2012/11/19/how-the-nations-interest-spending-stacks-up. Accessed January 2013.

About the Author

Michael Pento is the president and founder of Pento Portfolio Strategies (PPS). PPS is a registered investment advisory firm that provides money management services and research for individual and institutional clients.

Michael is a well-established specialist in markets and economics and a regular guest on CNBC, CNN, Bloomberg, FOX, and many other international media outlets. His market analysis can also be read in most major financial publications, including the *Wall Street Journal*. He also acts as a financial columnist for *Forbes*, Contributor to thestreet.com, and is a blogger at the Huffington Post.

Prior to starting PPS, Michael served as a senior economist and vice president of the managed products division of Euro Pacific Capital. There, he also led an external sales division that marketed their managed products to outside broker-dealers and registered investment advisers.

Additionally, Michael has worked at an investment advisory firm, where he helped create exchange-traded funds and unit investment trusts that were sold throughout Wall Street. Earlier in his career, he spent two years on the floor of the New York Stock Exchange. He has carried series 7, 63, 65, 55, and life and health insurance licenses. Michael Pento graduated from Rowan University in 1991.

Index